The Holocaust, the Church, and the Law of Unintended Consequences

How Christian Anti-Judaism
Spawned Nazi Anti-Semitism

A Judge's Verdict

Anthony J. Sciolino

iUniverse, Inc.
Bloomington

The Holocaust, the Church, and the Law
of Unintended Consequences
How Christian Anti-Judaism Spawned Nazi Anti-Semitism

The cover photo "Priests giving the Hitler salute at the fifth Catholic youth rally (Jugendtreffen)
in Berlin-Neukolln stadium in August 1933" provided by Bidarchiv Preussicher Kulturbesitz.

The New Revised Standard Version Bible (NRSV) With Apocrypha,
Thomas Nelson Publishers, Nashville, Tennessee, 1990

iUniverse books may be ordered through booksellers or by contacting:

iUniverse
1663 Liberty Drive
Bloomington, IN 47403
www.iuniverse.com
1-800-Authors (1-800-288-4677)

ISBN: 978-1-4759-6286-4 (sc)
ISBN: 978-1-4759-6288-8 (hc)
ISBN: 978-1-4759-6287-1 (e)

Library of Congress Control Number: 2012921851

Printed in the United States of America

iUniverse rev. date: 12/20/2012

This book is dedicated to the memory of the 1.5 million children murdered during the Holocaust, denied the chance to become the "persons" God intended them to be. It is also dedicated to the memory of the countless children of the six million victims of the Holocaust, denied the chance to be born.

The Church can only approach the Shoah ... in a spirit of repentance for the evil that so many of its baptized members perpetrated and so many others failed to stop ... The saving deeds and lives of Catholics that we remember [who acted righteously] ... represent crucially important moral lights in a period of darkness. Our celebration of the brightness of that light and the preciousness of that witness is at once intensified and muted by the poignant awareness that they were, when all is said and done, relatively few among us, and no one can say how many, because some surely perished with those they tried to save.

—William Henry Keeler,
Cardinal Archbishop Emeritus of Baltimore

God of our fathers, You chose Abraham and his descendants to bring your Name to the Nations: we are deeply saddened by the behavior of those who in the course of history have caused these children of yours to suffer and asking your forgiveness we wish to commit ourselves to genuine brotherhood with the people of the Covenant.

—Pope John Paul II

Until we [Christians] embrace the depth of the problem and identify what it is in the Christian faith itself that not only gave anti-Semitism its birth but also regularly sustains it, we will continue to violate the very people who gave us the Jesus we claim to serve.

—John Shelby Spong,
former Episcopal bishop of Newark

I looked out of the open window, over a large area of Amsterdam, over all the roofs and on to the horizon, which was such a pale blue that it was hard to see the dividing line. As long as this exists, I thought, and I may live to see it, this sunshine, these cloudless skies, while this lasts I cannot be unhappy.

—Anne Frank

Contents

Foreword

THE SILENCE AND COMPLICITY OF the Christian hierarchy, both Catholic and Protestant, during the Shoah, and the complicity of millions of Christian bystanders and perpetrators, is a vexing issue. As Judge Anthony J. Sciolino writes in this remarkably comprehensive and well-documented book, "Clearly, something went terribly wrong for Christianity during the Holocaust, for what was practiced by most of the faithful was certainly not what Jesus preached." It is a painful fact that the perpetrators of Nazi crimes, and those who acquiesced to Nazi policies, were overwhelmingly Christian, at least in a nominal sense.

By the outbreak of World War II, the majority of Europeans were still baptized, taxpaying members of an established Christian church. They were raised in homes, schools, and churches where the Christian Bible was read and taught, where commemorations of the birth and death of Jesus marked the high points of the year, where Christian prayers and hymns were familiar parts of daily life. Indeed, as Judge Sciolino points out, the legacy of the Nazi era belongs to the heritage of all Christians. Jews struggle with the Holocaust and ask, "Where was God?" Christians must do the same but ask, specifically, where were the Christians and the Church?

How did Christians get to the point of excluding Jews from the Gospel of Love?

Judge Sciolino provides a cogent and powerful analysis of Christian doctrine and Church history to help answer the question of what went wrong. It is both a personal journey for him as a faithful Catholic who began as early as 1959 to confront the realities and implications of the Shoah, as well as a scholarly endeavor informed by objectivity and reasoned judgment befitting his profession. We are all the beneficiaries of this honest and suggestive work, whether we are Christians or Jews. There is much for us to learn.

Judge Sciolino demonstrates that Nazism's racial anti-Semitism was rooted in Christian anti-Judaism. From at least the third century, Christianity's "teaching of contempt" concerning Jews set the encounter between Jews and Christians on a tragic course. These were two related religions that shared many sacred texts and ideas. Christianity emerged out of Judaism originally as a Jewish sect. It laid claim to the Hebrew Bible and to the covenant with God. But the fact that the majority of Jews did not become Christians was a source of concern and hostility to early Christian leaders and was a theological threat to the very legitimacy of Christianity.

Too many Christians faced that challenge through the centuries, as Judge Sciolino points out, by adopting stereotypes that came to have a tenacious hold on the Christian imagination. Jews, most Christians believed, had not only rejected and persecuted Jesus the Messiah, but were responsible for his death. Because of this they were an accursed people who were incapable of receiving the "truth." They were seen as evil and "of the devil." They were also, in Christian societies, dispersed, miserable, and powerless. And so the Jews, demoralized, marginalized, and persecuted, were neutralized as a threat to Christianity and, perversely, became its living proof.

Judge Sciolino delineates this history with skill and erudition. The book ends with a discussion of the religious introspection and accounting within the Catholic Church since Vatican Council II—a process that has led to remarkable statements on the Holocaust, Jews, Judaism, and forgiveness. These trends, which Judge Sciolino exemplifies in his own religious journey, have been helpful in terms of healing and reconciliation. But he is calling for more. He is asking, maybe pleading, for a post-Auschwitz, post–Vatican Council II Christianity to be "resurrected" in a moral and religious atmosphere in which anti-Judaism will be unthinkable. The book was written in that spirit and hope. We ignore its message to our peril.

Michael N. Dobkowski
Professor, Department of Religious Studies
Hobart and William Smith Colleges

Preface

I was born in Rochester, New York, on February 6, 1945, the fifth and youngest child of Italian immigrant parents. I was raised in a loving extended family in a home within walking distance of three Roman Catholic churches—St. Andrew, St. Phillip Neri, and Annunciation. My mother's widowed and childless uncle, Zio Luigi, who lived with us until he died at age 101, served as my caregiver while my folks worked outside the home. A gifted storyteller who spoke mostly Italian, Zio Luigi would entertain me for hours with captivating stories from the Bible. Although my home was located in a multiethnic city neighborhood, to the best of my recollection, there were no Jewish families in the neighborhood.

My introduction to the Holocaust came in 1959. I was an eighth grader at Benjamin Franklin Junior-Senior High School when I read *The Diary of Anne Frank*. A Jewish girl in Occupied Holland, Anne was just thirteen when she began writing a diary in 1942, twenty-two days before going into hiding with her mother, father, and sister in Amsterdam. The family remained in hiding for twenty-five months until they were betrayed in August 1944 and deported to Bergen-Belsen concentration camp, where Anne died of typhus in March 1945. Even as a young man, I was troubled and filled with sorrow by Anne's story, perhaps, in part, because she began writing her diary at the very age that I was reading it. Over the decades since, I have had many experiences that deepened my understanding of the Holocaust and increased my sorrow over it. In junior high, for the first time there were Jewish classmates in my circle of friends. What struck me is that they were just like me or anyone else, not at all like the pejorative labels spoken about

Jews in crude jokes. And some of those early friendships have lasted to the present day.

My next encounter with the Holocaust came in 1964. I was nineteen and a freshman at Columbia College in New York City when I saw *The Deputy,* Rolf Hochhuth's controversial play accusing Pope Pius XII of failure to take action or speak out against the Holocaust. Hochhuth alleged that Pius's "silence" was criminal, inhuman, and cowardly. The typical official Catholic reaction at the time was that the play was an atrocious calumny against the memory of a good and courageous world leader occupying the Chair of Peter during one of the great crises of humanity. Cardinal Francis Spellman of the Archdiocese of New York condemned the play as "an outrageous desecration of the honor of a great and good man, and an affront to those who know his record as a humanitarian who love him and revere his memory." As a noncritical thinking, pre-Vatican Council II "pay, pray and obey" Catholic who believed the pope could do no wrong, I was scandalized by *The Deputy* and rejected Hochhuth's accusation as preposterous. Meanwhile, my college professors were challenging me to question my belief systems, to open my mind to differing points of view, to be wary of absolutist claims, and to eschew noncritical thinking.

In 1965 I saw *The Pawnbroker,* directed by Sidney Lumet, the first American movie to depict the impact of the Holocaust from the viewpoint of a survivor. I was deeply moved by actor Rod Steiger's powerful portrayal of Sol Nazerman, a German-Jewish university professor who was dragged along with his family to a concentration camp. His two children die (one while riding in a cattle car) as does his wife, after being raped by Nazi officers. In the movie, Nazerman, who lives alone in an anonymous Bronx high-rise apartment, owns a pawnshop in East Harlem. Numbed by his concentration camp experiences, Nazerman is disillusioned, bitter, and alienated, viewing people around him as "rejects and scum." He interacts cynically with the many desperate characters who pass through his shop to pawn their goods. Jesus Ortiz, the young Puerto Rican shop assistant, idolizes his boss, but Nazerman rejects the young man's friendship and the kindly overtures of a neighborhood social worker. After Nazerman angrily declares that Ortiz means nothing to him, the young man, in spite, arranges for the pawnshop to be robbed. During the robbery, Nazerman refuses to hand over his money and Ortiz takes a bullet intended for Nazerman and then dies in his boss's arms. The critically acclaimed movie struck a number of responsive chords in me.

After graduating from college in 1967, I married my high school sweetheart Gloria Skalny and began attending Cornell Law School, where I learned how to analyze complex cases and fact patterns according to legal principles, how to formulate conclusions based on facts, and how to advocate persuasively for a proposition or cause. Later, as a Monroe County Family Court judge from 1986 to 2006, I honed my skills at fact-finding, dispassionately weighing evidence through the lens of my life experiences, applying legal principles and rendering what I considered to be just decisions in thousands of difficult and sometimes controversial cases. My favorite biblical passage is Micah 6:8: "What does the Lord require of you but to do justice, and to love kindness, and to walk humbly with your God." Serving as a judge for twenty years afforded me a unique opportunity and challenge to put those words into action.

In 1993, at the suggestion of my pastor at Church of the Transfiguration in Pittsford, New York, Father Gerald Appelby—an exemplary priest and consummate homilist—I began to consider entering the deacon formation program of the Roman Catholic Diocese of Rochester. After a good deal of reflection and prayer, at age fifty-four, I decided to enter the program. Four years later, in 1998, I earned a master of theology degree from St. Bernard's Institute of Theology and Ministry and was ordained a deacon. My graduate level courses included Theology of Church and Church History. Some of what I learned troubled me, quite frankly, especially the Church's attitude toward and treatment of Jews through the centuries.

In 2004, accompanied by two Jewish friends, Jeffrey and Rachel Wicks, I saw Mel Gibson's movie *The Passion of the Christ*, which some critics claimed was anti-Semitic. After viewing the film detailing Jesus's final hours and crucifixion, filled with excessively long and graphic violence and grossly exaggerated depictions of stereotypical Jews, embarrassed that my friends viewed it with me, I concluded the critics were right. In contrast, however, when Father Augustine Di Noia, a spokesman for the Congregation for the Doctrine of the Faith, oldest of the nine congregations of the Vatican Curia and successor of the

Holy Inquisition, was asked about the film's faithfulness to the New Testament account, he replied, "Mel Gibson's film is not a documentary, but a work of artistic imagination … Gibson's film is entirely faithful to the New Testament."

During our forty-five years of marriage, Gloria and I have often traveled to places connected in some way to the Holocaust. For example, following my graduation from law school in 1970 we traveled to the Netherlands, where we toured the Anne Frank House Museum in Amsterdam; then, in Germany, we saw the Dachau concentration camp outside Munich. On a trip in 1983 that included Poland, we toured the killing camp of Majdanek on the outskirts of Lublin. Gloria is of Polish descent, and on that trip we also visited the rural village of Rudnik Na San, site of her grandmother's family home, a rustic structure with a wood-burning stove and no indoor plumbing. We stayed there overnight, sleeping in a bed with a straw mattress. The next day, one of Gloria's cousins told us that for a few days during Poland's Occupation, a Nazi soldier slept in that very bed. Upon his departure, perhaps heading toward the Eastern front and the siege of Stalingrad, the soldier left behind a painting, saying he would return to retrieve it. He never did, and the painting hung on a wall in the living room.

While on a trip to Rome in 2006, in addition to Vatican City, we toured Rome's historic Jewish Ghetto, established by order of Pope Paul IV in the sixteenth century. According to my research, on October 16, 1943, following Mussolini's fall from power, the Nazis rounded up over one thousand Italian Jews and amassed them in a piazza within the ghetto. Ironically, the piazza, within walking distance to the papal apartments in St. Peter's Square, is named *Santa Maria del Pianto* (Mother of Sorrows) after the church located there. Many of the Jews rounded up that day were leaving evening Yom Kippur services in Rome's historic synagogue adjoining the piazza. The convoy of trucks transporting them to the railway terminal took a route along the Tiber that passed St. Peter's Square. Shortly after arriving at the terminal, the captives were deported to the Auschwitz-Birkenau death camp where 811 of them were gassed on arrival. Only sixteen survived. As Gloria and I strolled along the shops and restaurants lining the piazza, I noticed a plaque on a building dedicated to the infants rounded up while in their mothers' arms. It read: *E Non Cominciarono Neppure A Vivere* ("They never even had a chance to live"). And in 2008, we visited, for the first time, the US Holocaust Memorial Museum in Washington, DC.

The Holocaust, a.k.a. *Shoah* ("catastrophe"), was the systematic, state-organized persecution and murder of six million Jews, including 1.5 million children, by Nazi Germany and its European collaborators. Also targeted were five million members of other groups—homosexuals, Sinti and Roma (Gypsies), Poles and other Slavic people, Soviet POWs, Jehovah's Witnesses, Freemasons, people with mental and physical disabilities, communists, socialists, and other political and religious dissidents. With poison gas, bullets, noose, knives, combustion engine exhaust, clubs, fists, disease, starvation, death marches, and overwork, the perpetrators slaughtered two-thirds of Europe's Jews and one-third of world Jewry. According to its visitors' guide, the US Holocaust Museum's mission is threefold—to advance and disseminate knowledge, to preserve the memory of those who suffered, and "to encourage … visitors to reflect upon the moral and spiritual questions raised by … the Holocaust." For many years, I have been troubled by one of those moral and spiritual questions: How could one of the worst catastrophes in human history have started in one of the most Christian countries of Christian Europe, birthplace of Martin Luther and the Protestant Reformation?

Several weeks after I retired from the bench in 2007, Rabbi Laurence C. Kotok, senior rabbi at Temple B'rith Kodesh in Rochester, invited me to participate with a number of others in planning and team-teaching an interdisciplinary, multisession adult study course eventually entitled, "The 2000 Year Road to the Holocaust—An Interfaith Project of the Greater Rochester Community."[1] Looking for projects that would keep me busy in retirement and wanting to learn still more about the Holocaust, I accepted the invitation without hesitation. Eager to use my college, law school, and judicial skills to research a topic that had fascinated and disconcerted me for many years, I began my inquiry. In identifying and weighing the historical evidence, I was determined to keep an open mind, while simultaneously hoping that my conclusions would exonerate Pius XII in particular, and Christianity in general, from complicity in the Holocaust. The first of the fifteen sessions began in October 2008, at Temple B'rith Kodesh. Four-hundred-plus students

---

1 See www.holocaustroad.org.

took the course, which was presented three times between 2008 and 2011.

In April 2009, Gloria and I traveled to the Holy Land on a trip sponsored by Temple B'rith Kodesh and led by Rabbi Kotok. We were two of only three Catholics on the tour along with thirty-two Jews. In Jerusalem we visited the *Yad Vashem* Holocaust Museum and Memorial and observed an exhibit that included a photo of Pius XII next to a placard on which was written a brief history of his controversial actions during the twelve years of the Third Reich. I learned later that the Holy See formally protested the historical accuracy of the caption and that on his visit to Jerusalem in May 2009, Pope Benedict XVI refused to enter the main building of the Yad Vashem complex where the caption and photo are located.

In May 2010, I went on a Student Leadership Mission to Germany and Poland entitled "The March: Bearing Witness to Hope," sponsored by Nazareth College and Hobart and William Smith Colleges. It was a most informative and emotional experience. We visited and learned about primary sites associated with the Holocaust, including, in Berlin, Bebelplatz, where the Nazis staged book burnings of Jewish authors and, outside Berlin, the villa on Lake Wannsee where participants at the Wannsee Conference formulated the Final Solution, Hitler's plan to exterminate European Jewry. In Poland, the group toured many sites, among them the Warsaw Ghetto, the Auschwitz-Birkenau, Majdanek, and Treblinka death camps, the Plaszow concentration camp (one of the filming site's of *Schindler's List*, director Stephen Spielberg's seven-academy-award-winning movie), and the village of Tykochen in northeast Poland. Our Israeli guide informed us that in June 1941, the German army marched into many such towns and villages in Eastern Europe caught up in what has been termed "Holocaust by Bullets." On August 25, 1941, all of Tykochen's Jewish residents—men, women, and children—were ordered to assemble in the market square. From there, fourteen hundred were transported in trucks to large pits dug in the forest outside the village and executed. Our group visited and prayed at the execution site.

In September 2010, Gloria and I traveled to Eastern Europe where in Slovakia, near Prague, we toured the Theresienstadt concentration camp in the town of Terezin. My friend, Henry Silberstern, a survivor who was part of the Bearing Witness to Hope March earlier that year and is on the faculty of the "Two Thousand Year Road to the Holocaust," was interned as a child in both Theresienstadt and Auschwitz-Birkenau. While in Budapest, Gloria and I went to the Shoes on the Danube Promenade, a memorial on the bank of the Danube River that honors Hungarian Jews killed in 1944 by local fascist militiamen. Late in the war, victims were marched to the site, ordered to take off their shoes, and shot in the back of the head at water's edge, so their bodies would fall into the river and be carried away. The evocative memorial represents the shoes left behind on the bank.

Using judicial skills to identify and weigh the evidence of my research, viewing the evidence through the lens of my life experiences, these are among my findings of fact and conclusions (of law):

- The Holocaust was a unique, clearly defined historical event, but its causes—including anti-Semitism, racism, fear, envy, greed, sadism, hatred, ignorance, intolerance, careerism, territorial expansionism, nationalism/patriotism, the fog of war, failure of conscience, lack of moral guidance, bigotry, and evil—are still present.
- The Holocaust happened in Christian Europe, the heart of Western civilization, little more than sixty-seven years ago. But even today, genocide, ethnic cleansing, and other state-sanctioned crimes against humanity take place worldwide.
- For close to two thousand years the Roman Catholic Church harbored a powerful anti-Jewish bias that became, albeit inadvertently, a powerful force for evil.
- In every human heart exists the capacity to do both good and evil.
- Scripture has been misinterpreted and/or misused to justify slavery, religious intolerance, subjugation of women and homosexuals, unjust wars, torture and burning of heretics, and the killing of infidels—all in the name of God.
- Blind obedience to authority often leads to calamitous results.
- Clergy were part of the Nazi race attestation bureaucracy used to identify and target Jews.

- Clergy acted as cheerleaders for the German war effort, even when the war was clearly being lost.
- Most Christians of the period were guilty in varying degrees for what happened.
- There were many righteous Christians, however, who risked their lives to protect and comfort their persecuted brothers and sisters.
- Pius XII should be given credit for what he did to mitigate the extent of the crime but also held accountable for what he failed to do.

History is the study of human behavior and the human spirit, even when both have been profoundly corrupted. The Holocaust is an extreme example of what can happen when prejudice and intolerance run amok, when some people dehumanize and target other people. Therefore, it is imperative that we study the Holocaust to understand how and why such horrific depravity took place, so that we can prevent it from taking place again. This book is my understanding of and judgment on the Holocaust—the product of an inquiry that began over fifty years ago when an adolescent boy read about an adolescent girl who kept a diary. This book is my verdict in a difficult and controversial case.

November 5, 2012
Pittsford, New York

Acknowledgments

As a first-time author navigating the arcane waters of writing and publishing a book, I owe a debt of gratitude to many people, including my editor and alter ego, Mark Hare, and Victoria Barnett of the US Holocaust Memorial Museum. I am indebted to Raymond S. Iman and Dama Zefers Jung, two inspirational high school social studies teachers who whet my appetite for the study of history.

I am also indebted to my fellow instructors of the adult education course, "The 2000 Year Road to the Holocaust—An Interfaith Project of the Greater Rochester Community:" Barbara G. Appelbaum, Bonnie Abrams, Professor Charlie Clarke, Professor Michael Dobkowski, Deacon Thomas Driscoll, Warren H. Heilbronner Esq., Steven Hess, Rabbi Laurence Kotok, Helen Levinson, Marion Ein Lewin, Hon. Michael J. Miller, Rosemarie Molser (of blessed memory), Hon. Karen Morris, Professor Susan E. Nowak SSJ, Dr. Ronald Sham, Henry Silberstern, Rev. Theodore J. Weeden Sr., and Dr. Morris Wortman—all of whom taught me a great deal about the Holocaust.

I am grateful to those who reviewed and commented on the numerous revisions and drafts of what eventually became this book: Dr. Louis Baskin, Ira Born, Daniel Brent, Jeanne Levin Carlivati, Deacon George Dardess, Christopher Lindley, Hinda Miller, Professor Devendra Mishra, Dr. Morton Oberstein, Camille Perlo, Wayne M. Perlo, Karen Rinefierd, Dr. Morris Wortman, and James (Jimmy) Yost.

I am particularly grateful to my sainted mother, Rose Sciolino, who first modeled for me empathy and unconditional love; and to my father, Joseph Sciolino, who, a target of discrimination and prejudice in the workplace, taught me, among other things, about tolerance. And I am most grateful to my friend of fifty-four years and wife of forty-five, Gloria Skalny Sciolino, the wind beneath my wings.

CHAPTER I

Christianity's Original Sin: Anti-Judaism

MOST CATHOLICS ARE AWARE OF the countless saints, martyrs, popes, bishops, priests, deacons, religious, and laity who, throughout church history, have lived ethical, even heroic lives—pursuing justice, feeding the poor, clothing the naked, educating the ignorant, liberating captives—as Jesus taught in his Gospel of Love.[2] Clearly, this legion of righteous people has been a tremendous force for good in the world. But what most Catholics, and non-Catholics, are unaware of, because it is not generally known outside academic circles, is that at the same time, the Roman Catholic Church, hereinafter "Church," and later, Protestant churches, harbored a powerful anti-Jewish bias—a bias that became, albeit inadvertently, a powerful force for evil in the world.[3]

Grounded in scripture and the writings of the Church Fathers, this nineteen-hundred-plus-year bias, termed "anti-Judaism," was a deeply ingrained theological position of the Church, permeating two of its core doctrines:

- Supercessionism: (1) God rejected the Jews, unilaterally revoked God's covenants with them, and thereafter favored

2   See, for example: Deuteronomy 16:20; Isaiah 61:1–4; Matthew 25:35–46; Luke 4:16–21, 6:35–38, 10:27; and John 15:12–14.

3   "The line separating good and evil passes through every human heart … and even in the best hearts there remains an unuprooted small corner of evil" (Aleksandr Solzhenitsyn).

Christians as the new chosen people; and (2) Christianity fulfilled and superseded Judaism, rendering it insignificant in salvation history.

- Collective responsibility (collective guilt): All Jews, from the first century forward, are responsible/guilty for the death of Jesus, the Jewish messiah and Son of God.

That anti-Judaism became a powerful force for evil in the world is an example of what social scientists term the law of unintended consequences.[4] Christian culpability for the Holocaust is a quintessential example of an unintended consequence. Father Michael McGarry, CSP, a Paulist priest and rector of Tantur Ecumenical Institute in Jerusalem, articulates this most disconcerting reality:

> We Christians need to remember that studying the Shoah is not simply reading about what happened to the Jews, but what some Christians—some still worshiping, others long drop-outs from the Church—did to the Jews. The Shoah is part of Christian history. It is part of our history if we are Christian. This is frightening, this is sickening, this is, for many, unbelievable. But the first thing we Christians need to recognize is that we study the Shoah because it is part of our history, as well as part of Jewish history. Not only do we study what happened to them but what happened to us Christians.

Tragically, the image of Jews as deicides, God-killers, and their obstinate refusal to convert to Christianity fueled a long tradition of intolerance, hatred, and violence against them. In 66 CE, for example, the newly Christianized residents of Alexandria, Egypt, massacred the city's Jewish population. When in 70 CE, the Roman occupiers of Judea under Emperor Titus starved and slaughtered at least six hundred thousand Jews in Jerusalem, destroying the city and the (second) Temple, early Christian theologians proclaimed that Jews brought the massacre

---

4   "Unintended consequences" (sometimes unanticipated consequences or unforeseen consequences) is defined as "outcomes that are not the intended results of purposeful action."

upon themselves.[5] According to Rosemary R. Ruether,[6] anti-Judaism was fundamental to early Christianity's self-understanding as the true Israel, and of its Lord as the Jewish messiah. She maintains that within two decades of Jesus's death, anti-Judaism had become "the left hand of Christology." James Carroll, distinguished-scholar-in-residence at Suffolk University, a former priest and author of *Constantine's Sword: The Church and the Jews,* terms anti-Judaism the Church's "primordial sin."

It is an indisputable fact of history that, for close to two millennia, Jews have been humiliated, victimized, denigrated, discriminated against, banished from countries, and forced to live in ghettos. They have been marginalized, demonized, stigmatized as "other," portrayed as offspring of the devil,[7] wrongly blamed for causing human and natural catastrophes, accused of libels like the ritual murder of Christian children,[8] tortured, and killed—by Christians! Regrettably, Nazi propaganda in the twentieth century effectively exploited this shameful tradition to pave the way for the Holocaust.

The dark side of church history[9] chronicles how the Bible has been misused to justify intolerance and persecution of racial, ethnic, or other

5   This is an early example of "blaming the victim," a phrase coined by William Ryan in his 1971 book, *Blaming the Victim,* in which he describes victim blaming as an ideology used to justify racism and social injustice against African Americans in the United States.

6   Rosemary Radford Ruether is the Carpenter emerita professor of feminist theology at Pacific School of Religion, as well as the Georgia Harkness emerita professor of applied theology at Garrett Evangelical Theological Seminary. Distinguished scholar, teacher, and activist in the Church, she is a groundbreaking figure in Christian feminist theology.

7   "No one need be surprised if among our people the personification of the 'devil,' as the symbol of all evil, assumes the living shape of 'the Jew'" (Hitler, *Mein Kampf*).

8   Ritual murder is killing a Christian child in a religious ritual; blood libel is using the child's blood in the same or a different ritual.

9   Christopher Hitchens, an avowed atheist, in his book *God Is Not Great: How Religion Poisons Everything,* wrote that organized religion is "the main source of hatred in the world" because it is "violent, irrational, intolerant, allied to racism, tribalism, and bigotry, invested in ignorance and hostile to free inquiry, contemptuous of women and coercive toward children," and accordingly it "ought to have a great deal on its conscience."

minorities, including native peoples, blacks, women, homosexuals, and adherents of other religions,[10] prompting French philosopher Blaise Pascal[11] to opine: "Men never do evil so completely and cheerfully as when they do it from religious conviction." Scripture has been invoked to justify slavery, subjugate women, to bless unjust wars, torture heretics, burn witches, and kill infidels—all in the name of God. "Anti-Semitism,"[12] writes Episcopal Bishop John Shelby Spong, "is a terrifying prejudice that is rooted so deeply in the church's life that it has distorted our entire message." Widespread failure of conscience was clearly one of the major causes of the Holocaust. Formation of conscience (i.e., teaching how to differentiate between right and wrong) is a primary function of religion. Tragically, anti-Judaism prevented most Christian clergy, Catholic and Protestant alike, from performing this most important function regarding the persecution of Jews. The Church failed to prevent the Holocaust because Jews were never included within the circle of Catholic concern.

After the French Revolution in 1789, liberal Enlightenment ideas encapsulated in the slogan *liberté, égalité, fraternité* began to gain currency. Despite church opposition, Jews finally began to achieve citizenship status in European countries, something denied to them for centuries, including in the Papal States. Gradually thereafter, Jews also began to be assimilated into European society[13] in varying degrees, particularly in Western Europe. Liberalism, however, did not eliminate Christian animus toward Jews. "Judaeophobia," a sociological pathology termed "the world's oldest prejudice," which predates Christianity, continued unabated into the twentieth century, especially in Eastern Europe, where it was particularly ingrained and where the mass killing of the Holocaust took place.

---

10   Shakespeare has one of his main characters in *The Merchant of Venice* say: "The devil can cite scripture for his purpose." Ironically, Antonio, the Christian merchant, speaks the line referring to Shylock, the Jew.

11   Blaise Pascal's writings were placed on the Church's Index of Prohibited Books.

12   The term "anti-Semitism" was first coined by German writer, journalist, and anti-Semite Wilhelm Marr in 1879. The word "Semite" actually describes all Arabs, but as used in this term applies only to Jews.

13   French philosopher Voltaire in the eighteenth century claimed that Jews were "stubborn, greedy, perverse and particular, kept to themselves" and could not be assimilated into enlightened society, no matter what they did.

In the Beginning

When Jesus began his public ministry in the Roman province of Judea circa 28 CE, the "Jesus movement" became one of several competing Jewish religious/political movements of the time, including the Sadducees, Pharisees, Essenes, Zealots, and followers of John the Baptist.[14] Jesus defined his mission not against Judaism, but against the imperium of Rome, specifically against its substitution of Caesar for God.[15] Most scripture scholars agree that Jesus and his followers considered themselves a reform movement within Judaism, not the vanguard of a new religion. According to Bart D. Ehrman, professor of religious studies at the University of North Carolina at Chapel Hill, a former pastor of the Princeton Baptist Church but now an avowed agnostic, Jesus was an "apocalypticist," who expected the world to end within the lifetime of his followers.[16] This premise, therefore, contradicts the scriptural claim that Jesus established a church on "the rock of Peter" to continue his mission on earth after his death.[17]

Jesus was born, lived, and died a Jew. His apostles and original followers were all Jews who, according to Bishop John Shelby Strong,[18] did not separate from the synagogue until the year 58 CE. Consistent with Jewish rabbinic tradition, Jesus, a rabbi himself, taught love of God and neighbor,[19] Torah observance,[20] the need for repentance,[21]

---

14   The Sadducees were an aristocratic, priestly group who collaborated with the Roman authorities to maintain the status quo; the Pharisees were devoted to the traditions of Mosaic law and sought religious purity among God's chosen people; the Essenes withdrew from society into quasimonastic conclaves in the Qumran region of Judea (followers of St. John the Baptist were probably Essenes), and the Zealots agitated for political freedom for Judea from Roman rule.

15   Jesus taught his followers to "render to Caesar what belongs to Caesar and to God what belongs to God" (Matthew 22:21).

16   See Bart D. Ehrman, *Jesus: Apocalyptic Prophet of the New Millennium*, 64.

17   "And I tell you, you are Peter, and on this rock I will build my church, and the gates of Hell will not prevail against it" (Matthew 16:16–19).

18   "The division between Christianity and Judaism," says Spong, "is a very late division … The Christian inability to place its story into a Jewish context is the primary source … of the way the Christian story has been distorted with literalism."

19   Matthew 22:35–40.

20   "I came to fulfill the law and the prophets, not to abolish it" (Matthew 5:17–20).

21   Mark 1:14–15.

liberation of the oppressed,[22] and, most importantly, the pursuit of justice, especially for social outcasts.[23] He championed the oppressed, not the oppressor. The Gospels show him practicing concern for everyone without exception, reaching out to "sinners," enemies, prostitutes, lepers, epileptics, even those denounced as traitors for collecting Roman taxes. He urged his followers to love their enemies and not to judge others. Admittance into God's kingdom was open to all—rich, poor, men, women, Jew, Gentile, slave, Greek. The only requirement was to practice deeds of loving kindness toward others such as feeding the hungry, clothing the naked, and visiting the sick and imprisoned.

Although a pacifist who rejected violence, Jesus suffered a violent death, nailed to a cross like a common criminal. It was Roman, not Jewish, power that crucified him in order to prevent public disorder and political upheaval in Judea. The Roman occupiers of Judea feared that a segment of Jesus's followers (the Zealots), who viewed him as a political messiah, would try to overthrow Roman rule, restore the Davidic dynasty, and make Jesus "king" of the Jews.[24] Concern for public disorder and upheaval also explains why the Romans destroyed Jerusalem and the (second) Temple forty years later.

The tendency to exonerate the Romans and fix blame on the Jews for Jesus's death intensified as early Christian missionary activity expanded into the ancient Mediterranean world. To make converting non-Jews (i.e., Gentiles) easier and less threatening to the ruling authority, Roman involvement in the crucifixion was diminished as Jewish culpability increased. This is illustrated in the Gospel of Peter, widely read by some second-century Christians, although not included in the New Testament canon. The author of the Gospel of Peter wrote: "The Jews, the elders, and the priests realized (after the crucifixion) how much evil they had done to themselves and began beating their breasts, saying, 'Woe to us because of our sins; the judgment and the end of Jerusalem are near.'"

22   Luke 2:16–21.

23   "What you do for the least of my brethren, you do unto me" (Matthew 25:40).

24   Some scripture scholars contend that the assertion, as related in the passion narratives of the four Gospels, that during Jesus's trial, Pontius Pilate, whose political career depended on maintaining public order in Judea, freed Barabbas, an insurrectionist Zealot, at the insistence of the Jewish crowd, instead of freeing Jesus, a pacifist, strains credulity.

This last phrase—"the judgment and the end of Jerusalem are near"—echoes the charge made by early Christian theologians that the destruction of Jerusalem and the (second) Temple signified God's judgment on the Jewish people for their rejecting Jesus as messiah and killing him.[25]

Conflict erupted soon after Jesus's death, not only within and between early Christian groups, but also between Christian groups and various Jewish groups, some of which is recorded in the New Testament. References to persecution of Jewish Christians and Pauline Christians (followers of the apostle Paul) by Jewish groups are also included. Reverend Dr. Theodore J. Weeden Sr., a fellow of the Jesus Seminar,[26] characterizes the "squabbling" that occurred among disparate religious groups during this contentious period of early church history as intrafamilial, or a "family feud." The feud, however, would eventually turn deadly.

Martyrdom

Since the earliest days of the Church, hundreds of thousands of Christians have been martyred for their faith, beginning with St. Stephen, the first deacon, who was stoned to death circa 34 CE.[27] For three centuries, Christians, because they refused to worship Roman gods or to pay homage to the emperor as divine, endured intermittent periods of persecution by the Roman authorities, particularly under the reign of Emperor Diocletian (284–316). In the Roman Empire, refusing to worship the emperor or the empire's gods was tantamount to refusing to swear an oath of allegiance to the governing authority.[28] Some early Christians actually sought out and welcomed martyrdom. The martyrs' willing embrace of death was perceived as a heroic victory over persecution, which, as it did in Judaism, became an aspect of Christian self-identity. Persecution was viewed by early Christians

25   Scripture scholars point out, however, that the deicide charge can be considered antithetical to the doctrine that Jesus died for the sins of humanity to bring about humanity's redemption/salvation—in which case his crucifixion served a salvific purpose.

26   See http://holocaustroad.org/2010-11readings/Session2—Weeden—expanded8-16-08.pdf.

27   Acts 6:1–8, 7:54 to 8:2.

28   In Nazi Germany, civil servants, including clergy members, the military, the judiciary, and police personnel were required to swear an oath of absolute allegiance to Hitler and to offer the *Seig Heil* salute. Jehovah Witnesses were persecuted by the Third Reich because, among other reasons, they refused to swear such an oath, maintaining that only God deserved absolute allegiance.

and later historians as a crucial influence on the growth and development of the early Church and its evolving theology. Regarding martyrdom, second-century Church Father Tertullian, wrote: "The blood of martyrs is the seed of the Church," implying that a martyr's witness motivates nonbelievers to convert to Christianity and earns the martyr entry into heaven. An unintended consequence of martyrdom, however, is that all too often a person willing to die for his/her religion may also be willing to kill for it, as occurred among the Crusaders and Conquistadors, and is occurring today among Muslim extremists, most notably in New York City on 9/11.

Sadly, during the Holocaust there were relatively few Christian martyrs,[29] but millions of Jewish ones.

Misinterpretation/Misuse of Scripture

The New Testament is a collection of twenty-seven books[30] written at different times by various writers, who were early Jewish disciples of Jesus of Nazareth. Jesus and his disciples were lower class, illiterate, Aramaic speaking peasants from Galilee. Illiteracy was widespread throughout the Roman Empire, the condition of about 90 percent of the population. Original biblical texts were written in the first and second centuries, most likely in Koine Greek, the common language of the Eastern Mediterranean from the conquests of Alexander the Great (335–23 BCE) until the evolution of Byzantine Greek (circa 600 CE). All writings that would eventually be incorporated into the New Testament canon were probably written no later than 150 CE. Every word in the New Testament about Jesus was orally transmitted for forty to seventy years before anybody wrote it down. There are tens of thousands of manuscripts of the New Testament, in part or in whole, dating from the second century to the late fifteenth century, when the printing press was invented; all these manuscripts were copied—over and over again—by hand.

29   A Christian martyr of Nazi Germany whose witness was truly remarkable is Franz Jägerstätter, a conscientious objector who refused to serve in Hitler's unjust war. Before execution for "undermining military morale," Jägerstätter was criticized for failing in his duty as a German citizen, especially by fellow Catholics who dutifully served in the military. See *In Solitary Witness: The Life and Death of Franz Jägerstätter*, by Gordon C. Zahn.

30   Bart Ehrman identifies forty-seven writings, which he terms "Lost Scriptures," that were not included in the New Testament canon: seventeen noncanonical gospels, five noncanonical acts of the apostles, thirteen noncanonical epistles and related writings, seven noncanonical apocalypses and revelatory treatises, and five canonical lists. See *Lost Scriptures: Books That Did Not Make It into the New Testament*.

According to Bart D. Ehrman, there are no known original texts of the writings, or even first copies of the originals. In fact, he says, there are no known copies of the copies of the originals, or copies of the copies of the copies of the originals. What do exist are copies made later—much later. In most instances, these copies were made many centuries later. And, these copies all differ from one another in many thousands of places and are filled with discrepancies large and small.

Ehrman contends that the New Testament is riddled with contradictory views. All the Gospels were written anonymously, and none of the writers claimed to be an eyewitness. Ehrman writes: "Many of these authors, no doubt, felt they were inspired by God to write what they did, but they had their own perspectives, their own beliefs, their own views, their own needs, their own desires, their own understandings, their own theologies and these perspectives, beliefs, views, needs, desires, understandings, and theologies informed everything they wrote."

Based on his extensive study of scripture, Ehrman draws a number of provocative conclusions, including:

- The King James Bible was based on inferior manuscripts that in many cases do not accurately represent the meaning of the original texts.
- The favorite story of Jesus forgiving the woman caught in adultery[31] does not belong in the Bible.
- Scribal errors were so common in antiquity that the author of the book of Revelation threatened damnation to anyone who "adds to" or "takes away" words from the text.
- The authors of the New Testament have diverging views of who Jesus was and how salvation works.
- The New Testament contains books that were forged in the names of the apostles by Christian writers who lived decades later.
- Jesus, Paul, Matthew, and John all represented fundamentally different religions.
- Paul did all his writing between the years 51 and 64, before any Gospels were written down; only seven of the thirteen letters attributed to him were actually written by him.

---

31   John 8:3–11.

- Established Christian doctrines—such as the suffering messiah, the divinity of Jesus, and the Trinity—were the inventions of still later theologians.[32]

The Jesus Seminar is a group of about 150 scholars and laymen founded in 1985 by Robert Funk under the auspices of the Westar Institute. John Dominic Crossan,[33] professor emeritus of religious studies at DePaul University in Chicago, a former Catholic priest and noted Jesus scholar, is a prominent member of the seminar, which uses votes with colored beads to decide the membership's collective view of the historicity of the deeds and sayings of Jesus. The seminar has produced new translations of the New Testament and Apocrypha[34] to use as textual sources and has published its results in three reports: *The Five Gospels* (1993), *The Acts of Jesus* (1998), and *The Gospel of Jesus* (1999).

The seminar's reconstruction of the historical Jesus portrays him as an itinerant Hellenist Jewish sage and faith healer who preached a gospel of love and liberation from injustice, using provocative parables and aphorisms. An iconoclast, Jesus broke with established Jewish theological dogmas and social conventions both in his teachings and behaviors, often by turning commonsense ideas upside down, confounding the expectations of his audience. The seminar treats the canonical Gospels both as historical sources that represent Jesus's actual words and deeds, but also as collaborations/interpretations of the early Christian faith communities and of the Gospel authors. Unconcerned with canonical boundaries or conventional wisdom, fellows of the seminar assert, for example, that the noncanonical Gospel of Thomas may have more authentic material than the Gospel of John. Breaking with mainstream scripture scholars, they maintain that Jesus was less concerned about the

---

32   See Bart D. Ehrman, *Misquoting Jesus: The Story Behind Who Changed the Bible and Why*, and *Jesus, Interrupted: Revealing the Hidden Contradictions in the Bible (and Why We Don't Know About Them)*.

33   See John Dominic Crossan, *Who Killed Jesus? Exposing the Roots of Anti-Semitism in the Gospel Story of the Death of Jesus*.

34   Books included in the Septuagint (Greek version) and Vulgate (Latin version) of the Bible, but excluded from the Jewish and Protestant canons of the Hebrew Bible/Old Testament.

apocalypse or the world to come and more concerned about repairing the broken world in the here and now.

With the preceding as background, it is important to understand that in the New Testament numerous passages are misinterpreted and/ or misused to justify the persecution of Jews. The favorite text of anti-Semites is found in the Gospel of Matthew, written circa 70 CE. In this narrative, during the trial scene before Pontius Pilate, the Roman governor of Judea, the Jewish crowd is portrayed as responding to Pilate's protestation of Jesus's innocence by proclaiming, "His [Jesus's] blood be on us and on our children."[35] Based on the "collective guilt" implied in these words, Christians have maligned and mistreated Jews for close to two millennia. No other biblical verse has been responsible for so much violence and bloodshed, with the possible exception of "Let every man be subject to the powers placed over him."[36]

In his First Letter to the Thessalonians (circa 52 CE), the oldest known Christian document, Paul, a Jew himself, declares: "For you, brothers and sisters, become imitators of the churches of God in Christ Jesus that are in Judea, for you suffered the same things from your own compatriots as they did from the Jews, who killed both the Lord Jesus and the prophets, and drove us out; they displease God and oppose everyone by hindering us from speaking to the Gentiles so that they may be saved."[37]

In Paul's Letter to the Romans (circa 56 CE), the author, quoting from Isaiah, refers to Jews as those to whom God has given "a spirit of stupor, eyes that would not see and ears that would not hear down to this very day."[38] The Gospel of John (circa 90–100 CE) quotes Jesus as saying: "You (the Jews) are of your father the devil and you choose to do your father's desires. He was a murderer from the beginning, and has nothing to do with the truth because there is no truth in him. When he lies, he speaks according to his own nature, for he is a liar and the father of lies. But because I tell you the truth you do not believe me."[39]

---

35   Matthew 27:25.

36   Romans 13:1.

37   1 Thessalonians 2:14–16.

38   Romans 11:7–8.

39   John 8:44–45.

Whenever the phrase "the Jews" appears in John's Gospel, it is with a pejorative undertone. For example, in scenes where Jesus speaks to a gathering of people, the gathering is referred as "the Jews," although Jesus and his disciples were themselves Jews. To cite another example, when the author of John describes the first post-Easter apparition of the risen Jesus, he wrote that the disciples were hiding behind locked doors, "for fear of the Jews."[40] In Matthew's Gospel, a detachment of temple guards is placed around Jesus's tomb, because the chief priests and Pharisees told Pilate that "this imposter" has predicted that "after three days, 'I will arise again.'"[41]

The not-so-subtle message of the four Gospels and other books of the New Testament is that Jews are evildoers who purposefully murdered the Lord. Most scripture scholars agree that this is a misinterpretation of the biblical texts, which resulted from reading the words without regard to their Jewish context.[42]

In the second century, because marking a cross on the forehead or chest was regarded by Christians as a talisman against evil powers, the Church Fathers had to defend against the charge made by non-Christians that Christians were worshipers of the cross. Additionally, it was common practice for Christians to swear oaths by the power of the cross. During the Crusades (1095–1291), Crusaders marched off to free the Holy Land from infidels with crosses on their tunics, banners, and shields. The cross would eventually become the primary symbol of Christianity after Emperor Constantine's conversion to Christianity in the fourth century; and the crucifix (cross with corpus affixed) would first appear in the fifth century. Jews would probably have fared far better in church history if Christianity's symbol had been based on Jesus's resurrection to new life, rather than on his suffering and death—emphasizing Easter Sunday's hope, rather than Good Friday's travail.

---

40   John 20:19.

41   Matthew 27:62ff.

42   A modern approach to biblical interpretation (opposed by the Holy See until the midtwentieth century), known as "historical/contextual criticism" advocates reading the words of scripture in historical context. Biblical scholars using this approach conclude that passages used over the centuries to vilify Jews are read "out of context." In biblical criticism, "*Sitz im Leben*" is a German phrase roughly translating to "setting in life." In other words, there can be no authentic meaning of an ancient text without understanding the context within which it was written.

The Church Fathers

Because of misinterpretation and/or misuse of biblical texts,[43] anti-Jewish bias permeated the writings and sermons of the earliest theologians, the Church Fathers—Polycarp, Justin Martyr, St. Jerome, and Tertullian, to name a few. The doctrine of supercessionism,[44] for example, was originally espoused by Justin Martyr and Irenaeus of Lyon in the second century. A primary motivation of these early church leaders/theologians was fear that newly baptized, formerly Jewish, Christians would revert to Judaism or that Gentile converts would find Judaic practices preferable to Christian ones. To combat this so-called Judaizing of Christianity, the Church Fathers often wrote and preached against Judaism in inflammatory language. When read today, their words[45] are still stark and chilling. Jews, for example, were referred to as evil, vermin, unclean, and *unfit to live*—words widely used in Nazi propaganda.[46]

No one railed against Judaism more vehemently (and effectively) than St. John Chrysostom (Greek, "golden-mouthed") (347–407), archbishop of Constantinople and Doctor of the Church, who initiated and perfected the *Adversus Judaeo* (anti-Judaic) sermon genre. Known for his eloquence in preaching and public speaking, he proclaimed: "The Synagogue is a brothel, a hiding place for unclean beasts ... Jews are the most worthless of all men (who) are lecherous, greedy and rapacious ... perfidious murderers of Christ and for killing God there is no expiation possible, no indulgence or pardon. Christians may never cease vengeance ... Jews must live in servitude forever ... God always hated Jews. It is incumbent upon all Christians to hate Jews." St. John

---

43   Jesus and his disciples, as noted previously, spoke Aramaic. Original biblical texts were written in Koine Greek (the Septuagint), then retranslated into Latin (the Vulgate). Copies of texts were made by many copyists by hand, which explains why textual errors, and edits were common.

44   NB, Islam, like Christianity, is a supercessionist religion.

45   Words, obviously, have consequences, intended and unintended, especially when they lead to action, which can be good or evil.

46   Hitler, in *Mein Kampf,* advocated elimination of Jews from Germany and Europe to prevent defilement of Aryan blood and the corruption of society. He referred to them, *inter alia,* as "vermin, parasites, maggots, polluters and destroyers of Aryan humanity." Moreover, a provision of the Nuremberg Laws of 1935 authorized forced sterilization of *lebensunwertes leben* ("life unworthy of life"). In 1939, the Third Reich authorized a euthanasia program, Aktion T-4, to eliminate life unworthy of life. Aktion T-4 was a precursor of the Final Solution.

Chrysostom provided a hint of what shaped his rhetoric when he wrote: "Don't you realize if the Jewish rites are holy and venerable, our way of life must be false?"

The Church Fathers faced this dilemma—without Judaism, Christianity had no independent meaning. Judaism, therefore, had to be preserved for Christian self-identification, but in a weakened state so as not to undermine the "one true faith." Judaism and Jews had to be marginalized because the existence of an independently thriving Jewish community, which persisted in denying the validity of Christianity by its refusal to convert, would undermine the Church's evangelization efforts. To undermine Judaism's credibility, they employed a process, termed "value-inversion" (i.e., they turned Jewish values upside down, a process first employed in response to the crucifixion itself). Ancient people, Jews and Gentiles alike, regarded crucifixion, a widely employed Roman execution method, as a demeaning mode of death. Early theologians, however, transformed the "scandal of the cross" into an act of metaphysical and eschatological (end-times) importance. A seemingly meaningless execution in the political life of the Roman Empire and Judean politics became, for believers, the most meaningful act in human history. Jesus's death (and resurrection) brought eternal life not only to him, but to all who believed in him.

In the second century Marcion, bishop of Sinope (85–160 CE), proclaimed that the God of the Jews was demonic. Marcion even went so far as to propose that the Old Testament be excluded from the Christian canon. He and his followers sought to edit all references to Jews out of the New Testament in order to sever Christianity from its Jewish roots. Despite the Church's rejection of Marcion's views, excommunicating[47]

---

47   In addition to heretics like Marcion, Jan Hus, John Wycliffe, Girolamo Savonarola, Giordano Bruno, and Martin Luther, popes excommunicated prominent Catholic secular rulers, including Holy Roman Emperor Henry IV (1076); King Henry II (1174), King Henry VIII (1533), and Queen Elizabeth I (1570) of England; Napoleon Bonaparte (Napoleon I) of France (1809); King Victor Immanuel II of newly unified Italy (1870); and President Fidel Castro of Cuba (1962). It is noteworthy, however, that Pope Pius XII did not excommunicate Adolf Hitler, Joseph Goebbels, Heinrich Himmler, or any prominent Catholic Nazi.

and condemning him as a heretic, his brand of anti-Judaism continued to resurface in history, including in Nazi Germany.[48]

Deicide and Collective Guilt

Also in the second century, 167 CE, Melito, bishop of Sardis, made the first recorded charge of deicide. "The blood of Jesus," wrote Origen (185–254), "falls not only on the Jews of that time, but on all generations of Jews up to the end of the world" (the doctrine of collective guilt). St. Eusebius of Caesarea (263–339) taught that Jews forfeited both the promises due them under biblical covenants and their special status as God's "chosen people." St. Cyprian wrote in 248 that the Jews "have fallen under the heavy wrath of God because they departed from the Lord and followed idols." In 367 St. Hilary of Poitiers referred to Jews "as a perverse people who God has cursed forever."

In 380, St. Gregory of Nyssa referred to them as "Murderers of the Lord, assassins of the prophets, rebels and detesters of God … companions of the devil, a race of vipers, informers, calumniators, darkeners of the mind, pharisaic leaven, Sanhedrin of demons, accursed, detested … enemies of all that is beautiful."

Synagogue Burning

In 388, a Christian mob, purportedly incited by their bishop, looted and burned the synagogue in Callinicum, a town in modern-day Iran. St. Ambrose, bishop of Milan and Doctor of the Church, defended the righteousness of the mob's action. He reprimanded Emperor Theodosius the Great for ordering the local bishop to pay restitution, even though expropriation was illegal under Roman law. Ambrose allegedly offered to burn the synagogue in Milan himself. Theodosius later changed his position on synagogue burning, approving the practice if it served a "religious purpose." During *Kristallnacht* ("Night of Broken Glass"), November

---

48   For example, the *Deutsche Christen* were a group of fanatical Nazi Protestants that became a schismatic faction of German Protestantism. Their symbol was a traditional Christian cross with a *swastika* in the middle and the group's German initials "D" and "C." Supportive of Nazi race ideology, their movement advocated deemphasizing the Old Testament in Protestant theology and removing parts deemed "too Jewish." Some adherents sought to eliminate the Old Testament from the Bible altogether. Nazi storm troopers, in particular, favored getting married in *Deutsche Christen* churches.

9–10, 1938, starting point of the Holocaust, hundreds of synagogues were burned throughout Nazi Germany and Occupied Austria.

Rule of Christendom

The teachings of St. Augustine (354–430), a doctor of the Church, on the other hand, provided the theological basis for securing legal recognition and protection for Jews within the Roman Empire. It was this recognition, in part, that enabled Jews to survive under the "Rule of Christendom." For Augustine, Jews witnessed to the truth of Christianity and, therefore, had to be sheltered from harm. Accordingly, various popes, such as St. Pope Gregory I (590–604) and Pope Gregory X (1271–76), attempted to protect Jews, including from forcible conversion to Christianity. (Pope Leo VII in 937, for example, encouraged the newly appointed archbishop of Mainz to expel from his archdiocese any Jew who refused to convert.) Tragically, the Rule of Christendom has been routinely ignored throughout history, most egregiously during the Holocaust, when six million, men, women, and children lost their lives. And some of Augustine's own teachings were used to justify the persecution. For example, Augustine wrote that Jews were possessors of the "mark of Cain," whom God required to wander the earth in "perpetual servitude" until they voluntarily converted to Christianity. Referring to Jews as "slave librarians" who exist "for the salvation of the nation but not for their own (salvation)," Augustine also wrote: "the Church admits and avows the Jewish people to be cursed, because after killing Christ they continue in impiety and unbelief."

Chapter 2

A Supercessionist Church

FOUNDED IN THE FIRST CENTURY, the Church is the oldest continuously functioning institution in the world and, for most of its history, one of the world's most powerful. The popes, heads of the Church, are, according to believers, successors of St. Peter the Apostle, the "rock" upon whom the Church was founded[49] and to whom Jesus gave the "keys of the kingdom."[50] This divine conferral of authority made popes, in effect, gatekeepers of heaven and judges of who would enter (heaven) and receive eternal life. Excommunication from the Church, therefore, was a most severe sanction indeed, especially during the Middle Ages when ignorance, illiteracy, and superstition prevailed among the populace. The Protestant Reformation and, later, the Age of Reason, the advent of modern science and the French Revolution, however, would weaken the papacy's claim to absolute authority over the spiritual realm.

The Church steered Western civilization through watershed events like the fall of the Roman Empire, the Dark Ages, the Middle Ages, the Protestant Reformation, the Enlightenment/Age of Reason, the dawn of modern science, the rise of nationalism, and the Age of Revolution. It made deep contributions to philosophical and religious thought through the works of Sts. Ambrose, Jerome, Augustine, Thomas Aquinas, and

---

49   "If Jesus never uttered the words at all, '… you art Peter and upon this rock I will build my church,' the Roman Catholic Church, far from being founded on a rock, rests on very shaky foundations indeed" (John Julius Norwich, *Absolute Monarchs*, 4).

50   Matthew 16:16–19.

others. It helped shape secular institutions, civil law, literature, music, art, and architecture, and influenced rulers of empires, kingdoms, principalities, dukedoms, and nation states. The papacy is the oldest continuing absolute monarchy in the world, ruling over the Papal States in central Italy for eleven centuries. To countless millions of Catholics, the pope is the vicar of Christ, God's deputy on earth, the infallible interpreter of divine revelation and scripture. But to nonbelievers, among them, Martin Luther, John Calvin, Thomas Cranmer, John Knox, and Cotton Mather, he was the Antichrist.

Heaven's Gatekeepers

For close to two millennia, popes have had an enormous impact on the world stage[51] in religious, geopolitical, legal, social, artistic, and cultural matters. Because for so many centuries popes participated as advocates or critics in every important moment of history, papal history has mirrored the history of Western civilization. Many hundreds of millions of Catholics throughout the world have looked to the pope for guidance on moral issues.[52] Additionally, many non-Catholic Christians and non-Christians alike have respected the pope as the world's preeminent spiritual leader. However, not all of the 265 popes who have reigned to date have lived up to the high ethical standard expected of the vicar of Christ.

Admittedly, some popes have led exemplary lives, like Blessed Pope John XXIII, who convened Vatican Council II and in five short years, starting in 1958, opened up the Church to the twentieth century, bringing about much-needed reform and renewal. But other popes have led less exemplary lives, seemingly more interested in worldly than spiritual matters, like the notorious Rodrigo Borgia who became Pope

---

51   When Josef Stalin (1878–1953), the brutal dictator of Soviet Russia, was advised that Pope Pius XII opposed his policies, Stalin derisively replied: "How many divisions has the pope?" A half-century later, in November 1989, when without a bullet being fired, the Berlin Wall came down, Eastern Europe came out from behind the Iron Curtain, and the Soviet empire fell, Stalin's successor, Mikhail Gorbachev, said: "Everything that happened in Eastern Europe in these last few years would have been impossible without John Paul II." Stalin failed to realize that spiritual leaders can, indeed, influence historical events, even without commanding armed forces—by the power of moral suasion.

52   Critics of Eugenio Pacelli, the future Pius XII, who was Pius XI's secretary of state and the wartime pope, fault Pius XII for failing to provide moral guidance to the faithful, both before and during the Holocaust.

Alexander VI (1492–1503). Alexander VI is infamous for being the most corrupt and most secular of the Renaissance popes. Some popes have lived saintly lives; others, on the other hand, have been scoundrels. Some have been wicked, incompetent, narrow-minded, power hungry, lecherous, and/or profligate; others have been holy, visionary, learned, inspirational, and prophetic. Moreover, from 217 to 1447, there were more than thirty antipopes; two were excommunicated for heresy, namely, Liberius (352–66) and Honorious (625–38). The history of the papacy illustrates the sinful aspect of human nature and amply demonstrates that even God's deputies on earth can lose their way.

Dante Alighieri, for example, contended that the medieval papacy's overriding sins were greed and venality. In the first part of his epic poem, *Divina Commedia* (*The Divine Comedy*), written between 1308 and 1328, Dante envisioned two groups in hell—the misers and the avaricious—running toward each other along opposite sides of a circle. After they run and crash into each other, they turn and run back along the circle, only to crash again on the other side of it. This back-and-forth running and crashing continues through eternity. Prominent in the scene are the shaven heads of clergymen: "Here Popes and prelates butt their tonsured pates: Mastered by avarice that nothing sates."[53]

For many centuries church and state were twin pillars of divinely ordained society; both closely aligned, each promoting and reinforcing the other's authority. This mutually cooperative arrangement began in 312 CE, when Emperor Constantine (306–37) converted to Christianity, and was solidified in 380 when Emperor Theodosius the Great (379–95) declared Nicene Trinitarian Christianity[54] to be the only officially recognized religion in the Roman Empire. Church and state at that time were so closely joined at the hip that Constantine not only called

53   Dante Alighieri, *Inferno*, 7.46–48.

54   Orthodox Christianity was defined by the First Council of Nicea, a council of Christian bishops meeting in Nicea (present-day Iznik in Turkey), convened in 325 by Emperor Constantine. This first ecumenical council was the first effort to attain consensus in the Church among proponents of varying versions of Christianity, through an assembly representing all of Christendom. Among the First Council's main accomplishments were: (1) settlement of the Christological issue regarding the relationship of Jesus the Son to God the Father (i.e., two-thirds of the Trinity), (2) settlement of Jesus's nature (i.e., both human and divine), (3) construction of the first part of the Nicene Creed, (4) settling how to determine the date to celebrate Easter each year, and (5) promulgation of early canon law.

the First Council of Nicea (325) into session but also made its decrees law of the Roman Empire. Other competing versions of Christianity, heresies like Gnosticism, Docetism, Manicheanism, Monophysitism, Nestorianism, Pelagianism, and Arianism, were rejected and repressed. From that time forward a partnership between secular authority and the church hierarchy persisted into the mid-twentieth century, when even as Vatican Council II was being organized, Cardinal Alfredo Ottaviani, prefect of the Supreme Congregation of the Holy Office, adamantly held to the position that in Catholic countries the state had an obligation to profess and favor the Catholic faith and to limit the practice of other faiths.

Constantine's Sword

Before Emperor Constantine's reign, the cross lacked religious and symbolic significance. According to theology of St. Paul, the crucifixion was essential to humanity's salvation, earned by Christ's death. Being "crucified with Christ"[55] became an essential aspect of accepting the faith. But even for Paul, the cross did not compete, for example, with the waters of baptism as the faith community's metaphoric representation of dying with Christ. As Paul put it, "All of us who have been baptized into Christ Jesus were baptized into his death."[56] Accordingly, water was central to Christian symbolism; wood (of the cross) was not. Prior to the fourth century on the walls of Rome's catacombs, in addition to water, Christianity was depicted by palm branches, the dove, the peacock, the bird of paradise, or the monogram of Jesus, the most common of which became "HIS" or "IHC," denoting the first three letters of the Greek name of Jesus, *iota-eta-sigma*, or ΙΗΣ. The sacred fish too was a favorite symbol, not only because of various Gospel scenes that featured fish, but also because the Greek word for fish, *ichthys*, could be viewed as an acrostic of "Jesus Christ, Son of God, Savior." It is noteworthy, therefore, that before Constantine, the cross was *not* a symbol of Christianity.

The place of the cross in Christian imagination changed, however, with Constantine's conversion to Christianity following the Battle of the Milvian Bridge, which took place by and over the Tiber River in northern Rome in 312. According to the Christian historian Eusebius, on the day before the momentous battle that would decide who would lead

---

55   Romans 6:6.

56   Romans 6:3; Galatians 3:27.

the empire, at about noon, Constantine saw above the Milvian Bridge "the trophy of a cross of light in the heavens above the sun, bearing the inscription, *in hoc signo vinces* ('in this sign you will conquer.')" The next day, Constantine's soldiers carried into battle a new standard in the shape of a cross; the battle was won; Constantine gained complete control over the Roman Empire; he became convinced of the truth of Christianity, and the rest, as they say, is history. Describing the effect on Christianity of Constantine's victory, James Carroll writes:

> Constantine put the Roman execution device, now rendered with a spear, at the center not only of the story of his conversion to Christianity, but of the Christian story itself. When the death of Jesus—rendered literally, in all its violence, as opposed to metaphorically or theologically—replaced the life of Jesus and the new life of Resurrection at the heart of the Christian imagination, the balance shifted decisively against the Jews.[57]

It is noteworthy that before 312, Christians were a persecuted minority within the Roman Empire. Following Constantine's conversion and Theodosius the Great's reign, however, Christianity, which had been a countercultural force in the ancient world, became a cultural force. Emperors, kings, and princes, thereafter, used it (and some critics of the Church contend corrupted it) as a means for maintaining political control over empires, kingdoms, and principalities. The Church, in turn, used secular authority (i.e., "Constantine's Sword") to protect its institutional interests, to enforce its doctrinal orthodoxy, and to evangelize by force.[58] Any deviance from orthodox Christian teaching became a crime tantamount to treason, punishable by death. During the Middle Ages (from the fourth to the fifteenth centuries), especially when feudalism flourished between the ninth and fifteenth centuries, this mutually beneficial relationship worked particularly well. Church and state cooperated closely, reinforcing each other's authority. Docility and compliance were maintained among the people. Disobedience and rebellion were repressed. The Church was at the pinnacle of its power. And popes reigned supreme.

---

57   James Carroll, *Constantine's Sword*, 175.

58   Islam also is a religion that evangelized by force.

Pontifex Maximus

Innocent III (1198–1216) was one of the most powerful popes in church history. His pontificate is considered to have been the summit of the medieval papacy. As pope, Innocent claimed authority over not only the whole Church but over the whole world as well. "Princes have power on earth, priests over the soul," he wrote, and, "As much as the soul is worthier than the body, so much worthier is the priesthood than the monarchy."[59] Innocent thought of himself as Melchizedek, the biblical priest-king. Although not the first pope to use the title vicar of Christ, he was among the most emphatic in its use. In a letter to the patriarch of Constantinople, for example, he wrote: "The Lord left to Peter the governance not of the Church only but of the whole world."

When England's King John refused to recognize Innocent's appointee for archbishop of Canterbury in 1208, Innocent placed the kingdom under interdict (i.e., English priests were not permitted to perform marriages, baptize, absolve sins, or bury the dead in consecrated ground). King John retaliated by expelling most of England's bishops, but that only made matters worse because Innocent responded by excommunicating King John, declaring the English throne vacant, and inviting the French king to invade John's kingdom. By 1213 John finally, albeit reluctantly, recognized that Innocent was, indeed, his superior. When another quarrel erupted between them, however, Innocent declared the Magna Carta,[60] signed by King John in 1215, null and void, because it violated the divinely ordained order of hierarchy, and John had entered into it without Innocent's prior consent. The medieval papacy's claim to absolute authority over the spiritual and secular realm will lead to numerous unintended and calamitous consequences through history.

---

59   James Carroll, *Constantine's Sword*, 175.

60   The Magna Carta, which established the principle that monarchs are not above the law, is one of the documents that influenced drafters of the US Constitution and the French *Declaration of the Rights of Man and of the Citizen*.

Papal Absolutism

Based on its doctrine of the divine right of kings,[61] the Church demanded obedience from the faithful to the authority of secular rulers who, in turn, demanded obedience from their subjects to church authority. For eleven centuries, from 754 until 1871 when *Il Risorgimento* ("The Resurgence") culminated in unifying the Italian peninsula into the Kingdom of Italy with a republican form of government, popes reigned as absolute monarchs[62] of the Papal States,[63] blurring the distinction between and often conflicting

---

61   The divine right of kings was a political and religious doctrine of royal and political legitimacy. It asserted that a monarch was subject to no earthly authority, deriving his/her right to rule directly from the will of God. The king, therefore, was not subject to the will of his people, the aristocracy, or any other estate of the realm, including (in the view of some, especially in Protestant countries) the Church. Only God could judge an unjust king. Any attempt to depose the king or to restrict his/her powers was contrary to the will of God and constituted sacrilege. Accordingly, regicide was an egregious and unpardonable blasphemy.

62   The papal tiara was a crown worn by popes from the eighth to the twentieth century, last used by Pope Paul VI.

63   The Papal States comprised territories under the direct sovereign rule of the papacy, and, at its zenith of power, covered most of the regions of Romagna, Marche, Umbria, and Lazio in central Italy. This governing authority was commonly called the temporal power of the papacy, as opposed to its ecclesiastical primacy. According to tradition, the territory was given to the pope and his successors in 754, by first King of the Franks of the Carolingian dynasty Pepin the Short, son of Charles Martel and father of Charlemagne. The last and now only papal state, Vatican City, was formally established as a separate state by the Lateran Treaty of 1929. Another purported gift of territory to the papacy, however, was proven to be fraudulent.

The "Donation of Constantine" (*Donatio Constantini*) was a forged Roman imperial decree by which Emperor Constantine supposedly transferred authority over Rome and the western part of the Roman Empire to the papacy. The Donation of Constantine purported to grant Pope Sylvester I (314–35) and his successors dominion over lands in Judea, Greece, Asia, Thrace, and Africa, as well as the city of Rome and other parts of Italy, and the entire Western Roman Empire; Constantine retained imperial authority in the Eastern Roman Empire from his new imperial capital of Constantinople. The text claimed that Donation of Constantine was St. Emperor Constantine's gift to Pope Sylvester for instructing him in the Christian faith, baptizing him, and miraculously curing him of leprosy. During the Middle Ages, Donation of Constantine was often cited in support of the Church's claim to absolute spiritual and temporal authority over Western Christendom. Italian priest and humanist Lorenzo Valla is credited with being the first to expose the forgery in 1439, although Donation's authenticity had been doubted since at least the twelfth century, when the *False Decretals of Isidore* came to light.

with their dual roles as spiritual and secular rulers. Critics of Pope Pius XII charge that before and during the Holocaust he played the role of politician when the world desperately needed a prophet.

In his papal bull of 1302, *Unam Sanctam* ("One Holy Church"), Pope Boniface VIII (1294–1303),[64] pushing papal spiritual supremacy to its historical extreme, proclaimed that it "is absolutely necessary for salvation that every human creature be subject to the Roman pontiff." Most significantly, the bull proclaimed *extra ecclesiam nulla salus* ("outside the Church there is neither salvation," nor the remission of sins). This absolutist claim that outside the Church there is no salvation (modified somewhat by the Vatican Council II) is one of the Church's most controversial doctrines, which, together with the dogma of papal infallibility, continues to divide Christians to the present day and alienate non-Christians.

"Let every man be subject to the powers placed over him"[65] is the scriptural basis for a Christian's duty to obey authority, both religious and secular. Unfortunately, this scripture passage has been misused throughout history to justify unquestioning/blind obedience to evil authority, including obedience to tyrants like Adolf Hitler. Blind obedience to authority was among the causes of the Holocaust. Nazi war criminals, all of whom were ostensibly Christian, commonly defended themselves with the excuse, "I was only following orders."

For centuries popes and other secular rulers regularly engaged in power struggles and political intrigues. Lord Acton, a nineteenth-century English Catholic nobleman, charged that the Renaissance papacy's primary sin was "power and politics."

---

64   Today, Boniface VIII is probably best remembered for his feuds with Dante Alighieri, who placed him in the Eighth Circle of Hell in *Divina Commedia*—among the simonists (i.e., buyers and sellers of church offices).

65   Romans 13:1.

Absolutist Doctrines

In his seminal work, *The City of God*, St. Augustine[66] wrote: "the Church now on earth is both the kingdom of Christ and kingdom of heaven." He also taught that error has no rights. These dicta reinforced other dicta such as the Church is the "spotless bride of Christ,"[67] and the Church is the "only means to salvation," which, in turn, reinforced the evolving mind-set among theologians that church doctrine was divinely ordained, inerrant, and, therefore, not to be questioned. These and other absolutist doctrines would have a number of unintended consequences in centuries to come.

According to the Rule of Christendom, Jews were to be protected from harm, not only because they witnessed to the truth of Christianity, but also because, as related in the book of Revelation, they had an important role to play in triggering the "end-times" (Jesus's "Second Coming"): Their conversion to Christianity (and the nonexistence of Judaism as a living religion) would usher in the "end-times." As noted previously, however, because all Jews, past, present and future, were responsible for the death of the Messiah, they had to be marginalized on the fringes of society as outcasts, but they could escape their fate by renouncing Judaism and converting to Christianity. Unfortunately, however, in practice, even if they converted, the genuineness of their conversion was often considered suspect,[68] another unintended consequence.

During the patristic age (fourth to tenth centuries) theological attacks on Jews were carried out by means of anti-Jewish creeds (teaching prayers) and in the liturgy itself. Until Vatican Council II ended the

---

66   St. Augustine is also noteworthy for originating the Christian just war theory (*Bellum iustum*), which holds that a violent conflict ought to meet philosophical, religious, and political criteria. World War II, an unprovoked war, started by Nazi Germany to accomplish, among other things, territorial conquest of sovereign nations, subjugation of captured populations, and genocide, was clearly an unjust war. Most German bishops and priests, nonetheless, supported the war in various ways, including rallying the faithful to the cause.

67   Ephesians 5:25.

68   The Nazis, pursuant to racial profiling criteria established in the Nuremburg Laws of 1935, refused to recognize converted Jews as Christians, treating them instead as nonconverted Jews, and, eventually, as objects for annihilation. St. Edith Stein, a nun, for example, was executed at Auschwitz. German priests became part of the Nazi race attestation bureaucracy in 1933 when they provided to the Reich authorities information from baptismal and marriage registries.

practice in 1965,[69] the congregation responded to the Good Friday Gospel reading from Matthew in the Latin Rite (Tridentine) Mass with language ascribed to the Jewish crowd at Jesus's trial: "His blood be upon us and upon our children."[70] It was not uncommon for anti-Jewish violence to break out following Good Friday liturgies.[71] From the pulpit, in sermons throughout the liturgical year, not only during Holy Week, preachers routinely derogated Jews, urging that they be shunned by Christians.

Additionally, this prayer for the conversion of Jews was recited in Catholic liturgies until 1955. It read:

> Let us pray also for the perfidious Jews: that Almighty God may remove the veil from their hearts[72] so that they too may acknowledge Jesus Christ our Lord. Almighty and eternal God, who does not exclude from your mercy even Jewish perfidiousness: hear our prayers, which we offer for the blindness of that people; that acknowledging the light of your Truth, which is Christ, they may be delivered from their darkness. Through the same Lord Jesus Christ, who lives and reigns with you in the unity of the Holy Spirit, God, forever and ever. Amen.

Church Councils and Synods of Bishops

Like the writings and sermons of the Church Fathers, decrees of church councils and synods of bishops were laced with anti-Judaism. In 306 the Council of Elvira, for example, decreed that Christians and Jews were forbidden to engage in sexual intercourse, intermarry, or even eat together. The First Council of Nicea in 325 decreed that Easter and Passover would, henceforth, be celebrated on different days, stating: "let us have nothing in common with this odious people …" In 337 the marriage of a Jewish man to a Christian woman (miscegenation) became punishable by death.

---

69   It is noteworthy, however, that in 2007, Pope Benedict XVI removed Vatican Council II's restriction on celebrating the Tridentine/Latin Rite Mass with its offensive language to Jews.

70   Matthew 27:25.

71   Passion plays, like the famous Oberammergau passion play in Germany, performed every ten years, often vilified Jews in their portrayal of the passion of Jesus. These plays too incited violence against Jews.

72   2 Corinthians 3:13–16.

In 339 converting to Judaism became a criminal offense. The Third Synod of Orleans decreed in 538 that Jews were not permitted to show themselves on the streets during Holy Week. Christians were forbidden to patronize Jewish doctors by the Trulanic Synod of 692. The Synod of Toledo in 681 ordered the burning of the Talmud and other Jewish books.

It should be noted that in Berlin, 1,252 years later, on May 10, 1933, only three months after Hitler became chancellor of Germany, the Nazis staged a book burning of Jewish authors and of non-Jews suspected of writing in a "Jewish spirit." Similar events took place in other cities throughout Germany and elsewhere during the Third Reich.

The Third Lateran Council of 1179 decreed that Jews could not be plaintiffs or witnesses against Christians in court cases and forbade them to disinherit their descendants who had converted to Christianity. In 1270, St. Thomas Aquinas, a doctor of the Church, wrote that Jews sin more in their unbelief than do pagans because they have abandoned the way of justice "after knowing it in some way." In 1434 the Council of Basel decreed that Jews could not obtain university degrees. The council of Oxford, in 1222, prohibited the construction of new synagogues. Forty-five years later, in 1267, the Synod of Breslau instituted compulsory ghettos for Jews. The Synod of Often in 1279 forbade Christians from selling or renting real estate to Jews. And in 1310, the Synod of Mainz declared that Jewish converts who reverted to the practice of Judaism were guilty of heresy.

Secular rulers, with church approval, barred Jews from owning real estate, holding public office or civil service positions, attending public schools or universities, hiring Christian servants, and practicing various professions. Because doctrine forbade Christians to practice usury, Jews became bankers and jewelers, which created an opportunity for them to become the dominant financiers of Europe, an unintended consequence. Even kings and popes borrowed money from Jewish bankers. Involvement in banking, however, bound them to the biblical story of Judas Iscariot[73] who, according to Christian tradition, betrayed Jesus for thirty pieces of silver. The Judas story fed the stereotypical prejudice that Jews were venal "money-grubbers" who cheated Christians.

---

73   Bart D. Ehrman, in his book *The Lost Gospel of Judas Iscariot*, on the other hand, contends that Judas Iscariot was the only disciple who actually understood Jesus's mission and that Judas's "betrayal" is essential in salvation history (i.e., it was necessary to bring about humanity's redemption).

A sad truth of history is that many of the anti-Jewish laws promulgated by the Third Reich and its collaborationist regimes had direct antecedents in church laws and practices. Raul Hilberg[74] has compiled an outline entitled "Canonical and Nazi Anti-Jewish Measures," in which he identified fifteen canon laws with direct parallels to Nazi race laws. One of them is the Fourth Lateran Council's decree of 1213 requiring Jews to wear distinctive markings on their clothing; another is the Synod of Breslau's decree of 1267 mandating that they live in ghettos.

Jews were forced to wear the Star of David on their outer clothing in Nazi Germany and in other Nazi-occupied or collaborationist countries and forced to live in ghettos in Eastern Europe, particularly in Poland, where most of the killing camps were located. In 1516, the closed Jewish Quarter in Venice was dubbed *Geto Nuovo* ("New Foundry") because the area in which it was located contained a foundry. "Geto" would later become the basis for the word "ghetto."

The Holy Inquisition

The medieval Church condemned religious diversity and independent thinking.[75] A fundamentalist/literalist approach to biblical interpretation prevailed into the twentieth century. Most Catholics during the Middle Ages and subsequent centuries were uneducated and illiterate, particularly before Gutenberg invented the printing press in 1440, but those who were educated and literate were, nonetheless, discouraged from reading scripture for fear they would misunderstand its meaning. Interpretation of scripture, therefore, was the exclusive province of the Church.[76] Beginning in the thirteenth century, orthodoxy among the faithful was preserved by rooting out and suppressing heresy, which, as already noted, included Judaizing (reverting to the practice of Judaism), primarily through the Holy Inquisition, *Inquisitio Haereticae Pravitatis* ("inquiry on heretical

74 Raul Hilberg, an Austrian-born American political scientist and historian, was widely considered to be the world's preeminent scholar of the Holocaust. His three-volume work *The Destruction of the European Jews*, is regarded as a seminal study of the Final Solution.

75 Condemnation of religious diversity and independent thinking remained official church teaching until reversed and repudiated by Vatican Council II in 1965.

76 Pope Innocent III (1198–1216) declared that anybody caught reading the Bible would be stoned to death by soldiers of the church militia.

perversity"). Established in 1231 by Pope Gregory IX (1227–41), the Inquisition continued in one form or other for almost seven hundred years, with its last execution occurring in 1826. The first Inquisition is referred to as the Medieval Inquisition. Burning at the stake, termed *auto-da-fé*, or "act of faith," was the preferred method of execution, in part because of its supposed endorsement in scripture, especially in this verse from the Gospel of John: "Whoever does not abide in me is thrown away like a branch and withers; such branches are gathered, thrown into the fire and burned."[77]

The *auto-da-fé* involved a solemn Mass, prayer, a public procession of the convicted, and reading of the sentence. The ritual took place in public squares and lasted several hours with ecclesiastical and civil authorities in attendance. Execution was carried out by the civil authority. The trial occurred before an ecclesiastical court with the accused often not knowing what witnesses would be called to testify for the prosecution. There was no right to cross-examine adverse witnesses, no right to defense counsel, and no right to call defense witnesses. Accused heretics were often tortured until they "confessed" their guilt. Methods of torture included starvation, forced consumption of large quantities of water or other fluids,[78] and the heaping of burning coals on parts of the body.

Strappado was a particularly brutal form of torture initiated by the Medieval Inquisition. In one version, the torturers tied the hands of the accused behind his back and looped the rope over a brace in the ceiling of the chamber or attached it to a pulley. Then they raised the subject, hanging him by his arms, which could pull the shoulders out of their sockets. Sometimes, the torturers added a series of drops, jerking the subject up and down. Other times, they added weights to the ankles and feet to make the hanging even more painful.

The rack was another widely used form of torture in which the accused's hands and feet were tied or chained to rollers at one or both ends of a wooden or metal frame. The torturer then turned the rollers with a handle, which pulled the chains or ropes in increments and stretched the accused's joints, often dislocating them. If the torturer continued turning the rollers, the accused's arms and legs could be torn off. Not surprisingly, often simply seeing someone else being tortured on

---

77   John 15:6.

78   Cf. modern-day water boarding.

the rack was enough to make an observer confess to anything the torturer suggested. Terming the Inquisition, "God's Jury,"[79] Cullen Murphy, author of *God's Jury: The Inquisition and the Making of the Modern World*, contends that the Inquisition pioneered surveillance, censorship, and "scientific" interrogation methods that became tools of secular persecution. The Gestapo, for example, used some of these methods during the Nazi reign of terror, another unintended consequence.

Pope Sixtus IV launched the notorious Spanish Inquisition in 1478 during the reign of King Ferdinand and Queen Isabella. Established at their request, the Spanish Inquisition was directed primarily at *conversos*, Jewish converts to Christianity, a.k.a. *Marranos* (derived from a Spanish word for "swine"), whose conversions were suspect. It also focused on Muslim converts to Christianity suspected of reverting to Islamic practices. Between 1480 and 1520, up to four thousand Marranos were tortured and condemned to death as heretics and/or as Judaizers. The first inquisitor general in Spain, Tomas de Torquemada, a Dominican monk, whose name became synonymous with the Inquisition, had two thousand or more people executed within a few years of assuming office. In 1492, the Spanish Inquisition's recommendation led to the expulsion of Jews from Spain, notwithstanding that Jews had lived on the Iberian Peninsula since, at least, the days of the Roman Empire. Under terms of the Spanish monarchy's Edict of Expulsion, however, any Jew who converted to Christianity could return to Spain.

The Church eventually repudiated the violence of the Inquisition, but it continued to hold to the ideas that justified it—such as the necessity of policing of orthodoxy and silencing critics.

The Crusades

The Crusades[80] (1095–1291) were a series of religious expeditionary wars blessed by the papacy to restore Christian access to holy places in and around Jerusalem. The First Crusade was called in 1095 by Pope Urban II,

79   See Cullen Murphy, *God's Jury: The Inquisition and the Making of the Modern World*, 86–94.

80   The origin of the word "crusade" may be traced to the cross made of cloth and worn as a badge on the outer garment of crusaders. Since the Middle Ages the meaning of crusade had been extended to include all wars undertaken in pursuance of a vow, and directed against infidels (i.e., Muslims, pagans, heretics, or those under the ban of excommunication).

who promised "eternal reward in heaven" to anyone who led a contingent of believers to the Holy Land to kill infidels and free the holy places from defilement. With crosses displayed on their tunics, banners, and shields, Crusaders, accompanied by priests, attempted to evangelize along the way and in the process murdered over ten thousand Jews in France and Germany.[81] The Crusaders' zeal to convert others to the faith began with good intentions,[82] but quickly degenerated into a bloodbath. Unfortunately, consistent with their motto, "one infidel is as good as another," some crusaders killed Jews and Muslims indiscriminately. Crusaders generally gave infidels the choice—convert or die. To those who made the wrong choice, crusaders spoke the words, *Deus vult* ("God wills it") as they thrust a sword into the infidel's midsection. Some Jews committed suicide or killed their children rather than submit to forced conversion. Subsequent crusades led to the killing of more Jews and Muslims. In 1204, Crusaders sacked Constantinople, the center of Eastern Christendom, including the historic Cathedral of Saint Sophia, seat of the Orthodox Patriarch of Constantinople. The violence and destruction wreaked during the Crusades, ostensibly called for a noble purpose, was an unintended consequence.[83] Ironically, both Crusaders and Saracens killed each other with moral certitude that their deaths would earn them immediate entry into paradise, albeit different paradises.

It should be noted that in January 1937, German bishops called for a modern-day crusade against Bolshevism. In a New Year pastoral letter read from pulpits throughout Germany, the bishops identified Bolshevism as an existential threat to all of Europe. Invoking religion and patriotism, linking civic and moral duty, they anointed Hitler to

---

81   Crusaders massacred so many men, women, and children in and around Jerusalem that a Christian chronicler, Fulcher of Chartres, described an area as "ankle-deep in blood." While burning Jews alive, some crusaders reputedly sang, "Christ, We Adore Thee."

82   "The road to hell is paved with good intentions" (St. Bernard of Clairvaux).

83   In October 2011, Pope Benedict XVI expressed "great shame" for violence committed in the name of Christianity, including centuries of evangelization by the sword. He apologized, in particular, for the use of force to spread the faith in the Old World, citing Crusades in the eleventh, twelfth, and thirteenth centuries. He made no mention, however, of the Spanish Conquistadors who, in the fourteenth, fifteenth, sixteenth, and seventeenth centuries, did the same thing in the New World. Hernán Pizarro, for example, is the Spanish conquistador responsible for destruction of the Aztec Empire in Mexico and the Inca Empire in Peru and Ecuador in the sixteenth century.

lead the crusade and exhorted the faithful to cooperate with and support him "by all means possible," while Germany was marching inexorably toward an unprovoked and unjust war.

Other Manifestations of Anti-Judaism

In 1171, in the town of Blois, southwest of Paris, Jews were accused of ritual murder and blood libel. Several adult Jews of the city were arrested and most were executed after refusing to convert. Over thirty were killed; a number of Jewish children were forcibly baptized. Beginning in the thirteenth century, as noted previously, Jews were among the tens of thousands of people burned at the stake for heresy by the Holy Inquisition.[84] In 1235, thirty-four Jews were burned to death in Fulda, Germany, on a blood libel charge. Several Jews in Röttingen, Germany, were killed in 1298, charged with profaning the host.

As it permeated the writings and rhetoric of the Church Fathers, anti-Judaism also permeated the writings and rhetoric of popes, a practice that continued into the twentieth century. One example, Innocent III, in 1205 wrote: "The Jews, by their own guilt, are consigned to perpetual servitude because they crucified the Lord … As slaves rejected by God, in whose death they wickedly conspire, they shall by the effect of this very action, recognize themselves as the slaves of those whom Christ's death set free …"

Dominican monk Bernard Gui, who was appointed papal inquisitor in 1307 by Pope Clement V to deal with heretical Cathars around Toulouse, ordered copies of the Talmud and other Jewish books burned publically, as the Nazis would do in May 1933, within months of coming to power. Over a period of fifteen years, Gui pronounced approximately 630 people guilty of heresy. Like inquisitors before and after him, Gui performed his role with moral certitude in the rectitude of his cause.

In 1411, Vincente Ferrer, also a Dominican monk, reignited anti-Jewish hysteria in Spain by, among other things, characterizing Jews as "cohorts of the Devil and the Antichrist … clever, warped and doomed."

---

84   Joan of Arc, nicknamed "The Maid of Orléans," a national heroine of France, was burned at the stake for heresy in 1431. In 1920, 489 years later, she was rehabilitated of heresy and canonized a saint.

During the Middle Ages into the nineteenth century, ritual degradation of Jews during Lenten carnival celebrations was commonplace. In the sixteenth century, Pope Gregory XIII (1572–85) initiated the practice of compelling Jews to attend special Masses where they were forced to listen to conversionary sermons delivered by particularly gifted preachers. Additionally, while the pope was en route to the basilica of St. John Lateran, Rome's chief rabbi would ritualistically present him a copy of the Torah; the pope then turned the book upside down and returned it to the rabbi with thirty silver coins. The pope would then proclaim that, although he respected the Law of Moses, he disapproved of the hard hearts of Jews. Though officially contrary to canon law, Jews were for centuries forcibly converted to Christianity.

Jews were expelled en masse from Catholic countries in Europe, including England in 1290, France in 1306, Hungary in 1349, Spain in 1492, and Portugal in 1497. French and Spanish Jews were required to forfeit ownership of most of their property.[85] During the Middle Ages, baseless and vile myths about Jews circulated freely throughout Europe. Jews were crudely stereotyped, ostracized, vilified, and demonized. As noted previously, they were forced to live in ghettos, including one erected in Venice in 1517, which figured prominently in William Shakespeare's play, *Merchant of Venice*, and another in Rome erected by decree of Pope Paul IV in 1556. Sadly, a review of European history amply demonstrates that for many hundreds of years, prior to the twentieth century, civil authorities denied Jews their civil and human rights,[86] with church approval.

Charges of ritual murder, blood libel, and host desecration resulted in the Chmielnitzki Massacres of 1648–56, when Catholic Ukrainians (Cossacks) under the leadership of Bohdan Chmielnitzki slaughtered more than one hundred thousand Jews in cities and towns across Poland

---

85   Before resorting to the Final Solution, drafted at the Wannsee Conference in January 1942, Hitler's regime attempted to expel Jews from the Third Reich by forced emigration. Jews permitted to emigrate, however, were required to forfeit the bulk of their property to the Reich.

86   The Nuremburg Laws of 1935 stripped German Jews of their civil and human rights. Similar anti-Jewish laws were passed in fascist Italy, Vichy France, fascist Croatia, fascist Slovakia, fascist Romania, and other Nazi-allied or Occupied European countries.

in the largest mass murder of Jews until the Holocaust. Between 1871 and 1906, especially following the assassination of Czar Alexander II in 1881, for which Jews were wrongly blamed, close to two hundred pogroms broke out in 160 cities and towns of Russia.

Catholic Defenders of Jews

It is important to emphasize that not all Catholics embraced anti-Judaism, at least in its more extreme forms. There were clergy and laity who rejected it. In 1247 Pope Innocent IV, for example, wrote in defense of Jews:

> They are wrongly accused of partaking of the heart of a murdered child at the Passover ... Whenever a corpse is found somewhere, it is to the Jews that the murder is wickedly imputed. They are persecuted on the pretext of such fables ... they are deprived of trial and of regular judgment; in mockery of all justice, they are stripped of their belongings, starved, imprisoned and tortured.

Another who opposed anti-Judaism was St. Bernard of Clairvaux (1090–1153), a doctor of the Church and founder of the Cistercian order. Pope Calixtus II (1119–24) condemned attacks on Jews during the Crusades, opposed forced baptism, and forbade the destruction of synagogues and Jewish cemeteries. During the fourteenth century, when Jews were blamed for causing the Black Death (bubonic plague) that wiped out a third of Europe's population, Pope Gregory X (1271–76) came to their defense. In 1247, Pope Innocent IV promulgated the first of several papal bulls refuting the "ritual murder" libel.[87] Pope Gregory X, in 1272 similarly condemned the libel, as did Pope Martin V in 1422 and Pope Paul III in 1540. In 1348, Pope Clement VI issued a papal bull refuting the charge that Jews caused the plague, saying that the charge had "no plausibility." Pope Boniface IX (1389–1403) expanded the papacy's protection of Jews, including recognizing Roman Jews as full citizens of the Papal State of Rome in 1402. Pope Martin V, in his "Edict of Protection of 1422," warned Franciscan friars under the leadership of Abbot Giovanni da Capistrano, the infamous "scourge of the Jews," to stop inciting Italians against Jews.

---

87   Accusations of ritual murder continued into the twentieth century.

Alexander VI (1492–1503), the notorious Borgia pope who fathered, by three women, eight children, including notorious siblings Cesare (named a cardinal) and Lucretia, nonetheless, was one of the most pro-Jewish popes in history. Alexander created the first chair in Hebrew at the University of Rome, frequently entertained Rome's chief rabbi at the Vatican, and provided a safe haven for Marranos fleeing the Spanish and Portuguese Inquisitions. Pope Leo X (1513–21) repealed the obligation that Jews wear distinctive articles of clothing.

Pope Paul III (1534–49) also encouraged Marranos to settle in Italy. His successor, Pope Julius III (1549–55), continued the open door policy. Pope Clement XIV (1730–40) endorsed the rights of Jews to travel freely and manage shops outside the Rome ghetto, to practice medicine, to work as artisans, and to open small silk and hat factories. Pope Leo XIII (1878–1903) spoke in defense of Captain Alfred Dreyfus, the Jewish military officer falsely accused of treason in 1894 France. Despite the beneficence of some popes, religious leaders, and lay Catholics, anti-Judaism stubbornly persisted within the Church until it was officially reversed and repudiated by Vatican Council II in the document *Nostra Aetate* ("In our Age"), the Declaration on the Relation of the Church with Non-Christian Religions, promulgated on October 28, 1965.

Index Librorum Prohibitorum

The *Index Librorum Prohibitorum* ("List of Prohibited Books") was the Church's six-century attempt to maintain orthodoxy by censuring publications read by Catholics.[88] A first version (the Pauline Index) was promulgated by Pope Paul IV in 1559 and contained a number of forbidden books. The index included authors and intellectuals such as Johannes Kepler, Voltaire, Denis Diderot, Jean-Jacques Rousseau, Immanuel Kant, David Hume, Rene Descartes, Francis Bacon, John Milton, John Locke, Galileo Galilei, Blaise Pascal, Victor Hugo, and Hugo Grotius—just about

---

88   The Index of Prohibited Books was finally abolished by Pope Paul VI in 1966 for being contrary to Vatican Council II's teaching on freedom of inquiry and speech. See, *Gaudium et Spes* ("Joy and Hope"), the Pastoral Constitution of the Church in the Modern World, No. 62: "Let it be recognized that all the faithful, clerical and lay, possess a lawful freedom of inquiry and thought, and the freedom to express their minds humbly and courageously about those matters in which they enjoy competence."

all of whose works are now on college required reading lists worldwide.[89] The avowed aim of the index was to protect the faith and morals of the faithful by preventing them from reading works containing theological error. Various editions of the index also contained rules relating to the reading, selling, and preemptive censorship of books, including translations of the Bible into common tongues.

Canon law to the present day recommends that works on scripture, theology, canon law, church history, and, especially, any writings concerning religion or morals, be submitted to the judgment of the local Ordinary (religious authority). The local Ordinary consults someone considered competent to give a judgment, and, if that person gives the *nihil obstat* ("nothing forbids") the local Ordinary grants the *imprimatur* ("let it be printed"). Members of religious institutes require the *imprimi potest* ("it can be printed") of their major superior to publish books on matters of religion or morals.

Anti-Jewish Myths and Libels

Various myths generated and popularized during the Middle Ages incited violence against Jews, including: blood libel/ritual murder, host desecration, and Black Death.

Blood Libel/Ritual Murder: In 1144, an unfounded rumor circulated in England that Jews had kidnapped a Christian child, tied him to a cross, stabbed his head to simulate Jesus's crown of thorns, killed him, drained his body of blood, and mixed the blood into Passover matzos (unleavened bread). The rumor, purportedly, was started by a converted Jew named Theobald who had become a monk. He reported that certain Jews gathered each year in Narbonne, France, where it was decided in which city a Christian child would be sacrificed.

The boy involved in the Theobald hoax became known as St. William of Norwich. Pilgrimages were made to his tomb and miracles were said to have resulted from prayers to him. The myth demonstrates a lack of understanding of Judaic belief because, aside from the Torah prohibition against killing innocent people, the Torah specifically

---

89   James Carroll recalls that as a young seminarian in the 1960s, he once had to surrender a copy of Jean-Paul Sartre's *The Age of Reason* because, the rector declared, it was "on the index." Carroll goes on to say, 'What really seemed amazing was that books on the Index were available in paperback.'" Quoted from Murphy's *God's Jury*, 115.

forbids the drinking, eating, or touching of any form of blood. This particular rumor, nonetheless, persisted for centuries. Pope Innocent IV (1243–54) ordered an investigation in 1247 that found the myth to be an invention used to justify Jewish persecution. At least four other popes subsequently vindicated the accused from culpability, but blood libel/ritual murder accusations, trials and executions continued.[90] There have been at least 150 recorded alleged cases of blood libel/ritual murder, including in the United States,[91] most of which led to violence against Jews.

Additionally, in April 1840, newspapers throughout Europe reported a story from Damascus, Syria, about the disappearance of an elderly Italian Capuchin monk, Father Tommaso da Calangiano della Sardegna. Fellow monks spread a rumor that Father Tommaso had last been seen heading for the city's Jewish quarter. Twelve Jewish leaders were arrested. Four died from mistreatment; most of the rest, all of whom were tortured, "confessed" their involvement in the monk's ritual murder. Jasper Chasseaud, an American diplomat in Beirut, wrote: "A most barbarous secret for a long time suspected in the Jewish nation ... at last came to light in the city of Damascus that of serving themselves of Christian blood in their unleavened bread ... a secret which these 1840 years must have made many unfortunate victims."

Host Desecration: Catholics believe that during the rite of the Mass, bread (the host) is transformed into the body of Jesus, and wine into his blood (transubstantiation). The host and wine are then consumed by the priest and believers in attendance. A variation of the blood libel myth involving the host surfaced in Europe early in the eleventh century. Instead of accusing Jews of killing an innocent child, they were accused of desecrating the host, sometimes by stabbing pins into, or stepping on it. Other times, they were accused of stabbing the host with a knife or nailing it to a cross in symbolic replay of the crucifixion.

---

90   Pope Pius IX in the nineteenth century and St. Pope Pius X in the twentieth century, however, lent credence to the blood libel myth.

91   In 1928, a four-year-old girl went missing just before Yom Kippur in the upstate New York community of Massena. A town resident suggested it could be a blood libel kidnapping. Although the little girl turned up unharmed, after having wandered into the woods, there was speculation that she was released only because the plot was discovered. Accordingly, the mayor organized a boycott of Massena's Jewish-owned businesses, as the Nazis would do in Germany in April 1933.

Black Death: The Black Death was one of the most devastating pandemics in human history, peaking in Europe between 1348 and 1350, estimated to have killed 30 to 60 percent of Europe's population, reducing world population from an estimated 450 million to between 350 and 375 million in the fourteenth century. The aftermath of the plague created a series of religious, social, and economic upheavals, which had profound effects on the course of European history. It took 150 years for Europe's population to recover. The plague resurfaced at various times, killing more people, until it finally retreated from Europe in the nineteenth century. Jews were blamed for causing outbreaks of the plague by poisoning water wells, which in fact, were contaminated by rat-carried fleas. As a result, hundreds of Jewish communities were destroyed in pogroms. That Jews also died from the epidemics made no difference whatsoever as the suspected culprits were tortured until they confessed their guilt. During the Black Plague, ethnic Germans slaughtered thousands of Jews, who throughout history have been falsely scapegoated for natural and human catastrophes. The Nazis, for example, scapegoated the Jews for the Russian Revolution; Bolshevism; Germany's defeat in WWI; the humiliating terms of the Versailles Treaty; the chaotic social, economic, and political conditions of postwar Weimar Germany; and for WWII itself, among other things.

CHAPTER 3

The Papacy under Siege

DURING THE MIDDLE AGES AND thereafter, the Church taught that Roman Catholicism was the one true faith and only means to salvation; other religions were false and, as error had no rights, subject to repression. The papacy exercised absolute authority over Western Christendom. The Protestant Reformation, however, ruptured the unity of Western Christendom and created havoc within the Church. It began in 1517 when Martin Luther (1483–1546), a German monk and professor of theology at the Wittenberg University, posted his ninety-five theses on the door of Wittenberg castle church. Luther sought to reform what he perceived as false doctrines and ecclesiastic abuses, especially, the sale of indulgences, nepotism, and simony (selling and buying of clerical offices). Additionally, he and other reformers, such as John Calvin, John Knox, John Wycliffe, and Huldrych Zwingli, were appalled by the lavish and dissolute lifestyles of popes and other high clerics. What started as a simple act of protest sparked a movement that challenged not only the papacy's absolute power, in particular, but also the absolute power of secular rulers, in general. The Protestant Reformation struck a monumental blow for freedom of conscience and freedom of thought that shook the medieval world order to its foundations and paved the way for the Enlightenment/Age of Reason.

Martin Luther

In 1516, Johann Tetzel, a Dominican monk and papal commissioner for indulgences,[92] was sent to Germany by Pope Leo X (1513–21) to sell indulgences to raise money to rebuild St. Peter's Basilica in Rome. Catholic doctrine held that faith in Jesus alone could not gain salvation in heaven (i.e., "justify" mankind; justification rather depended on faith active in charity and good works, *fides caritate formata*). Additionally, the benefits of good works could be obtained by donating money to the Church, which was a papal dictum based on the doctrine that the pope, as gatekeeper of heaven, determined the criteria for entry.

Strongly disputing the claim that freedom from punishment for sin could be purchased, Luther asserted that the pope had no right "to sell" salvation—one of his Ninety-Five Theses. Concomitantly, he asserted that (1) the Bible contained all the knowledge necessary for salvation and holiness; (2) all the baptized were part of the holy priesthood, not just the ordained; (3) Matthew 16:18 ("You are Peter and upon this rock I will build my church …") did not confer on popes the exclusive right to interpret scripture; and, accordingly, (4) popes and church councils were not infallible. Salvation, for Luther, could not be earned by good works, but could only be received as a free gift of God's grace through faith in Jesus Christ. For refusal to retract his heretical ideas, as commanded of Pope Leo X in 1520 and by Holy Roman Emperor Charles V at the Diet of Worms in 1521, Luther was excommunicated by the pope and condemned as an outlaw by the emperor.

Luther is reputed to have said at his trial in the Diet of Worms: "Here I stand, I can do no other. God bless me, Amen!" The Diet of Worms was a general assembly of the estates of the Holy Roman Empire

---

92 An indulgence was full or partial remission of temporal punishment in purgatory for sins already forgiven, granted after a sinner had confessed and received absolution. Indulgences drew on the Treasury of Merit accumulated by Christ's superabundantly meritorious sacrifice on the cross and the virtues and penances of saints. They were granted for specific good works, like donating money to the Church, and for prayers. In contemporary Catholic theology, purgatory, like heaven and hell, are considered to be states of being of the spirit or soul, rather than actual places. Limbo (from the Latin word *limbus*, edge or boundary, as "edge" of hell) was a speculative idea about the afterlife for those who died in Original Sin without being assigned to the Hell of the Damned. Limbo was not an official doctrine of the Church. Medieval theologians described the underworld ("hell," "Hades," *infernum*) as divided into four distinct parts: Hell of the Damned (which some called Gehenna), Purgatory, Limbo of the Fathers or Patriarchs, and Limbo of the Infants.

that took place in Worms, a town on the Rhine. Luther escaped being burned at the stake only because Frederick III, the elector of Saxony, intervened and placed him in protective custody in Wartburg Castle at Eisenach. While there, Luther translated the New Testament from Greek into German, making it more accessible to ordinary people, and continued to issue doctrinal and polemical writings, including his controversial *On the Jews and Their Lies*, written in 1543.

Although initially sympathetic toward Jews, later in life Luther became virulently anti-Jewish. Angered by their refusal to convert to Christianity, in *On the Jews and Their Lies*, he depicts Jews as Christ killers and criminals bent on ruling the world.[93] He contended, *inter alia*, the Jews were a "base, whoring people, no people of God, and their boast of lineage, circumcision, and law must be accounted as filth." They were full of the "devil's feces … which they wallow in like swine …" The synagogue was a "defiled bride … an incorrigible whore and an evil slut." He advocated that their synagogues and schools be set on fire, their prayer books destroyed, rabbis forbidden to preach, their homes razed, and their property confiscated. "My advice … is first, that their synagogues be burned down and that all who are able toss sulfur and pitch; it would be good if someone could also throw in some hellfire." They should be shown no mercy or kindness, afforded no legal protection, and these "poisonous envenomed worms" should be drafted into forced labor or expelled "like mad dogs" from the land for all time. Luther also, albeit unintentionally, sanctioned their killing, by writing: "We are at fault in not slaying them." Luther's incendiary rhetoric concerning Jews was in the tradition of the Church Fathers.

The city of Nuremberg presented a first edition of *On the Jews and Their Lies* to Julius Streicher, editor of the Nazi newspaper *Der Sturmer*, on his birthday in 1937. Streicher described it as the most radically anti-Semitic tract ever published. The tract was publicly exhibited in a glass case at Nuremberg rallies and quoted in a fifty-four-page explanation of Aryan Law by Dr. E. H. Schulz and Dr. R. Frercks. In December 1941, seven Protestant regional church confederations issued a statement agreeing with the Nazi policy of forcing Jews to wear the Star of David, "since after his bitter experience Luther had already suggested preventive

---

93   The conspiracy to rule the world theme reappears in the twentieth century forgery and hoax *The Protocols of the Elders of Zion*, a cornerstone of Nazi racist propaganda.

measures against the Jews and their expulsion from German territory." Hitler was particularly fond of quoting from *On the Jews and Their Lies.*

Counter Reformation

The Counter Reformation began with the Council of Trent (1543–65) and ended at the close of the Thirty Years' War in 1648. Convened by Pope Paul III (1534–49) to deal with the Protestant crisis, the Council of Trent, among other things, condemned Protestant reformers as heretics and defined various church teachings in the areas of Original Sin, Justification, Tradition, the Sacraments, the Eucharist, and the veneration of saints. Luther and other reformers were excommunicated; some, like Jan Hus, were burned at the stake. And their books were burned. To counter Protestant claims of "justification by faith alone" and *sola scriptura* ("scripture alone"),[94] Trent reiterated that papal interpretation of scripture was inerrant and that anyone who disputed papal interpretation was a heretic, and reiterated that scripture and Tradition were equally authoritative. Trent, however, failed to correct some problematic church practices like the sale of church offices and indulgences for fear of acknowledging and, therefore, legitimizing the reformers' claims. It should be noted that throughout its long history absolutist doctrines (e.g., papal inerrancy, the image of church as a spotless bride of Christ, and the Church as the embodiment of God's kingdom on earth) coupled with its reluctance to cause or admit scandal, have made it difficult for the Church to acknowledge error and change course. The Church's reluctance to cause or admit scandal figures into its controversial response to the recent worldwide child sex abuse scandal by pedophile priests.[95]

In an attempt to blunt the rise of Protestantism and spearhead the Counter-Reformation, Pope Paul III in 1542 established the Roman Inquisition, which expanded the range of targets to include rationalists and

---

94   For Catholics, on the other hand, understanding scripture is mediated by the universal teaching authority of the Church (the *Magisterium)*, which has primacy over the Word.

95   The worldwide scandal began when, in January 2002, the *Boston Globe* published a front-page story entitled, "Church Allowed Abuse by Priests for Years." It was an account of how Boston's archbishop, Cardinal Bernard Law, and his predecessors had protected pedophile priests, enabling them to continue what was widely characterized as their predatory crime spree against children. An abused child had finally told his story to his mother, explaining the delay in his report by saying, "We couldn't tell you because Father said it was a confessional" (*Boston Globe*, January 6, 2002, A1).

scientists. After the Protestant Reformation, a siege mentality gripped the papacy, as it increasingly viewed itself under attack on all sides by evil forces. This mentality intensified during the French Revolution and would lead, in the nineteenth century, to Pius IX's declaration of war on Modernism. Rather than acknowledge and reform the admittedly problematic practices denounced by Martin Luther and others, the Church chose to stay the course, variously described by historians as "hunkering down" or "circling the wagons."

St. Robert Bellarmine

St. Robert Bellarmine (1542–1621), Jesuit priest, cardinal, and Doctor of the Church, canonized a saint in 1930, was one of the most influential figures of the Counter Reformation. As a papal inquisitor, he represented the Roman Inquisition in the controversy surrounding Galileo Galilei and Giordano Bruno, both proponents of the Copernican view that the earth revolves around the sun, which collided with the Church's worldview that the sun revolves around the earth. Both men were tried for heresy.[96] Their trials, however, were less about science and more about obedience to church authority.

A Perfect Society

Building on doctrines that describe the Church on earth as both the kingdom of Christ and kingdom of heaven, and that liken the Church to a spotless bride of Christ, Cardinal Bellarmine added, "the Church is

---

96   The Roman Inquisition compelled an aged Galileo to recant in 1633 under threat of torture. Earlier, in 1600, in another trial, with Cardinal Bellarmine sitting on a panel of judges, the Inquisition found Giordano Bruno, monk, philosopher, and scientist, guilty of heresy and because, unlike Galileo, Bruno refused to recant, he was burned at the stake. The execution site was in the Piazza del Compo dei Fiori in Rome, where a statue of the hooded monk now marks the spot of the execution.

In 1992, after twelve years of deliberations, the Church finally admitted that Galileo had been right in supporting the Copernican theory but, at the same time, noted that Galileo had also erred in his arrogance in thinking that his theory would be accepted without physical evidence. No such admission of error, however, has been made in Giordano Bruno's case, whose writings were placed on the Index of Prohibited Books and remained there until the Index was abolished in 1966.

On the four-hundredth anniversary of Bruno's death in 2000, Cardinal Angelo Sodano declared Bruno's death a "sad episode" but, despite his regret, he defended Bruno's prosecutors, maintaining that the Inquisitors were "motivated by the desire to serve the truth and promote the common good, also doing their utmost to save his life" by trying to convince him to recant and subsequently by appealing the capital punishment with the secular authorities of Rome.

a 'perfect society,'"[97] all of which continued to undergird the Church's dogmatic and static worldview. These and other absolutist doctrines were used to justify its continued condemnation of dissent and freedom of thought and its refusal to change problematic practices. Blessed John Henry Newman (1801–90), an Anglican priest who converted to Catholicism, wrote: "To live is to change; and to live long is to have changed often."

In 1964, Vatican Council II in *Lumen Gentium* ("Light of the Nations"), the Dogmatic Constitution on the Church, modified the perfect society doctrine. It decreed: "The Church ... will receive its perfection only in the glory of heaven, when the time for the renewal of all things will have come."[98]

Pope Paul IV

Giovanni Pietro Carafa was elected pope by the College of Cardinals in May 1555, taking the name Paul IV (1555–59). Although hailed as a reformer, he soon reverted to the old medieval papal style: authoritarian, triumphalistic, absolutist, and intolerant. Hostile to all efforts at reconciliation with the Lutherans, and as head of the reactivated Inquisition, he exercised his authority with unusually brutal severity. His involvement in a war against Spain ended in defeat. He denounced the Peace of Augsburg (1555), which recognized the coexistence of Catholics and Protestants in Germany, and upon the death of Queen Mary I of England in 1558 he insisted on the restitution of all church properties and demanded that Queen Elizabeth I submit all of her claims to him. Not surprisingly, the fortunes of Protestantism in England were bolstered considerably by the pope's imperious and outrageous behavior.

Paul IV opposed reconvening the Council of Trent, believing he could wage war against Protestantism more effectively on his own. Accordingly, he increased the authority of the Roman Inquisition and regularly attended its sessions. So extreme was his sense of orthodoxy that he had Cardinal Giovanni Morone, suspected of being a secret Protestant, imprisoned for heresy in Castel Sant'Angelo, a towering cylindrical building that functioned as mausoleum of Emperor Hadrian

97   "The Spanish State recognizes in the Catholic Church the character of the 'perfect society' ..." So begins Article 2 of fascist Generalissimo Francisco Franco's concordat with the Holy See signed in 1953, echoing St. Robert Bellarmine's dictum, which would be reiterated in Pope Pius IX's encyclical "Syllabus of Errors" (Article 19).

98   Acts 3:21.

and as a papal fortress. In 1557 he instituted the Index of Forbidden Books, severely restricting the reading and writing of books that existed until abolished by order of another pope named Paul, Paul VI, in the twentieth century. Because Paul IV suspected Jews of aiding Protestants, he restricted them to a nearby neighborhood that became Rome's ghetto, and in the Papal States they were required to wear distinctive clothing (yellow hats for men, and veils or shawls for women).

Paul IV strongly affirmed the supercessionist dogma, *extra ecclesiam nulla salus* (outside the Church there is no salvation). Among his first official acts was to order that Michelangelo paint the nudes in his masterpiece, *The Last Judgment,* in the Sistine Chapel more modestly, which Michelangelo refused to do. The nudes were, nonetheless, draped with veils and loincloths and for the master artist's defiance, Paul IV ordered that Michelangelo's pension be terminated. As was customary with Renaissance popes, Paul IV worked to benefit his family as well as the papacy. As Cardinal-nephew, Carlo Carafa became his uncle's chief adviser and the prime mover in their plans to ally with the French to expel the Spanish from Italy. Carlo's older brother Giovanni was made commander of the papal forces and Duke of Paliano after the pro-Spanish Colonna family was deprived of control over the town of Paliano in 1556. Another nephew, Antonio, was given command of the papal guard and made Marquis of Montebello. The conduct of his relatives became so notorious even by lax contemporary standards, however, that after a calamitous war with Phillip II of Spain and numerous scandals, the pope in 1559 publicly disgraced his nephews and banished them from Rome.

The Roman ghetto Paul IV established consisted of four square blocks in the Sant'Angelo district of Rome within walking distance of St. Peter's Basilica. At the time it had only one gate, which was locked at night. The gates of the ghetto (other gates were added over time) would be torn down in 1871 when Italy was unified into the Republic of Italy, but Jews would continue to reside in the neighborhood voluntarily into the twentieth century—where on October 16, 1943, 1,007 of them, descendants of those living there when Paul IV was alive, would be forcibly rounded up, locked in cattle cars, deported to Auschwitz-Birkenau and gassed to death.[99]

Besides ordering Jews to live in the ghetto and to wear distinctive clothing, Paul IV also ordered them not to engage in most trades, only certain ones like glass, jewelry, and ceramic making. Additionally, he forbade them to employ Catholic servants and increased their taxes. All these restrictions were abolished when Italy was unified under Giuseppe Garibaldi and Camillo Cavour at the successful conclusion of *Il Risorgimento* in 1871 but reinstated in fascist Italy under Benito Mussolini pursuant to Manifesto della Raza in 1938, patterned after the Nuremburg Laws of 1935.

The Institutional Model of Church

Cardinal Avery Robert Dulles, author of *Models of Church,* characterized the Council of Trent, or Tridentine model of church, as institutional (or hierarchical/pyramidal). This model defined the Church until Vatican Council II redefined it as "People of God." "Institutional model" might be defined in a contemporary religious encyclopedia as follows:

> Institutional model of church, aspects of: 1. *Clericalism*—views clergy, especially the higher clergy, as the source of all power and initiative; tends to reduce the laity to a condition of passivity, demanding docility and obedience, and to make the lay apostolate a mere appendage of the hierarchical apostolate; 2. *Juridicism*—views church authority in same way as state authority; tends to exaggerate the role of human authority and thus turns the gospel into a new law, characterized by excessive concern with legalistic formalities, to the neglect of the spirit and of service; 3. *Triumphalism*—dramatizes the Church as an army set in array against Satan and the powers of evil. This model seeks to save

---

99   Cardinal Edward Idris Cassidy, president emeritus of the Pontifical Council for Promoting Christian Unity with the Vatican, headed the Commission of the Holy See for Religious Relations with the Jews. Addressing groups of Jewish and Catholic scholars on the subject of the Vatican declaration, "We Remember: A Reflection on the Shoah," in May 1998, he forthrightly acknowledged the connection between the Church-enforced ghettos of Europe and the death camps of the Nazi era. While speaking privately to James Carroll in March 1999, Cardinal Cassidy referred to Church-enforced ghettos as the "antechamber of Nazi death camps." See Carroll, *Constantine's Sword*, 381.

souls by converting them to Catholicism, sees the Church as "God's kingdom on earth," a "perfect society," a "spotless bride of Christ" etc. It tends to become rigid, doctrinaire and conformist, absolutist, authoritarian and supremacist. This model of church fostered a "circle the wagons" or "siege mentality" that developed after the Council of Trent, the Enlightenment, and French Revolution, and eventually formed its quasi pathological fear of modernism and communism in the nineteenth and twentieth centuries. This model characterized the Church until it was changed by Vatican Council II (1962–65).

The Enlightenment/Age of Reason[100] and the revolutions sparked in the eighteenth and nineteenth centuries further challenged Church power and influence, which had already been seriously challenged by the Protestant Reformation in the sixteenth century. Enlightenment thinkers, casting off superstition and fear that characterized much of the medieval world, employed reason to explore the world around them. Their effort to discover natural laws governing the universe led them to make scientific, political, and social advances. Enlightenment thinkers examined the rational basis of all belief systems, including religion, and in the process, they came to reject absolute authority,[101]

---

100   The Age of Enlightenment (a.k.a. Enlightenment or Age of Reason) was a cultural movement of intellectuals in eighteenth-century Europe, which sought to reform society and advance knowledge. It promoted science and intellectual interchange and opposed superstition, intolerance, and abuses in the aligned church and state. Originating in the late seventeenth and early eighteenth centuries, it was sparked by philosophers such as Baruch Spinoza (1632–77), John Locke (1632–1704), and Pierre Bayle (1647–1706), by physicist Isaac Newton (1643–1727), and by historian Voltaire (1694–1778). The wide distribution of the printing press, invented in 1440, made possible the rapid dispersion of knowledge and ideas that precipitated the Enlightenment. Ruling princes often endorsed and patronized Enlightenment thinkers and even attempted to apply their ideas of government in what was known as enlightened despotism. The Enlightenment flourished until the French Revolution, after which the emphasis on reason gave way to emphasis on emotion ushered in by the Romanticism movement.

101   A contemporary view of absolute authority is expressed by philosopher, cognitive scientist, historian, and activist Noam Chomsky, who wrote:
"I think it only makes sense to seek out and identify structures of authority, hierarchy, and domination in every aspect of life, and to challenge them; unless a justification for them can be given, they are illegitimate, and should be dismantled, to increase the scope of human freedom."

both church and state authority. Immanuel Kant[102] expressed the motto of the era as *Aude Sapere* ("Dare to think!").

The modern nation state system evolved from the concept of national sovereignty established by the Peace of Westphalia in 1648. Before then, sovereignty, as noted previously, was assumed to be embodied in absolute monarchs who ruled by divine right. The American Declaration of Independence and the French Declaration of the Rights of Man and of the Citizen rejected sovereignty by autocratic monarchs as the source of national authority and legitimacy in favor of sovereignty of, by, and for the people endowed with God-given rights. Enlightenment thinkers substituted reason for faith as the means to establish an authoritative system of aesthetics, ethics, government, and religion. In their view "enlightened" religion empowered individuals to obtain objective truth, unmediated by the Church. The Age of Faith was eclipsed by the Age of Reason. Scientists like Galileo and Isaac Newton proposed theories of the universe that conflicted with the Church's cosmology based on scripture and tradition, and thereby further challenged its absolute authority over the spiritual and secular realms.

In the sixteenth century, the Protestant Reformation dealt the first serious blow to the Church's unity and authority. By the eighteenth century, social, economic, religious, and cultural forces unleashed by the Enlightenment dealt a second serious blow. With the outbreak of the French Revolution in 1789, the crisis for the Church became a catastrophe.

The French Revolution

The French Revolution (1789–99) was a period of political and social upheaval when the Kingdom of France, an absolute monarchy ruled by divine right, was violently overthrown. King Louis XVI and Queen Marie Antoinette (of Austria) were both executed on the guillotine. French society was radically transformed as traditional feudal, aristocratic, and religious privilege crumbled under assault from liberal political groups and the masses in the street. Medieval ideas about hierarchy, class status, and authority yielded to new Enlightenment principles of citizenship, equality, and the inalienable rights of man. A person's position in society, from the serf at the bottom to the aristocrat at the top, would no longer

---

102   All of Kant's writings were placed on the Index of Prohibited Books.

be determined by the accident of birth. Enlightenment principles rejected concepts like the divine right of kings, divinely ordained society, and the absolute authority of the Church and state.

After the Revolution, the French national government was transformed into a republic, based on equal rights for citizens, freedom of religion, freedom of thought and expression, and separation of church and state.[103] These changes seriously impacted the Church, the biggest landowner (in possession of approximately 10 percent of the total). Its extensive real property holdings were confiscated; its state tax subsidy abolished; and its privileged place within French society rejected. Furthermore, many high clerics, as members of the hated aristocracy, together with certain priests and nuns, were among those executed on the guillotine. And for the first time in European history, Jews were granted equal rights of citizenship.

The Catholic Bourbon monarchy's close ties to the French Church were severed in the wake of widespread anticlericalism. Radical ideas based on reason, encapsulated in the slogan *liberté, égalité, fraternité*, tore at the fabric of church authority. Similar to Martin Luther's reaction to the Peasants' Revolt in 1524 Germany, French church leaders were appalled at the social disorder and mob rule that prevailed. Granting equal rights of citizenship to Jews violated doctrine that called for them to be marginalized as punishment for deicide and their continued obstinacy in refusing to convert. Because Jews benefited from the revolutionary changes sweeping over France and the rest of Europe,[104] they were blamed for causing them—continuing a long tradition of scapegoating Jews for catastrophic events they had little or nothing to do with.

Napoleon Bonaparte (1769–1821), who became emperor of the nascent French Empire as Napoleon I, shaped European politics during the early nineteenth century, as his Napoleonic Wars embroiled every major European power. After a string of victories, France achieved dominance in continental Europe. Napoleon's military occupation of

---

103   The Church condemned religious tolerance and separation of church and state until those doctrines were officially reversed and rejected by Vatican Council II in 1965.

104   The Netherlands granted citizenship rights to Jews in 1796; Denmark in 1814; Greece in 1830; Belgium in 1831; Hungary in 1867; Italy in 1869; England and Germany in 1871.

Italy (1796–1814) temporarily ended eleven centuries of the papacy's rule of the Papal States. Two successive popes, Pius VI (1775–99) and Pius VII (1799–1823), were driven into exile; the Roman Inquisition was abolished, and some religious orders were suppressed. The gates of Rome's ghetto were torn down. As happened in France after the French Revolution, Jews in Italy were granted rights of citizenship. Napoleon's regime, however, collapsed in 1814 at the Battle of Waterloo, and when French occupation of Rome ended, papal authority was restored. Pope Pius VII, returning from exile, thereupon excommunicated Napoleon and abolished all Napoleonic reforms in the Papal States.

The Age of Revolution[105] and the rise of nationalism threatened the Church to its core. In an effort to protect the Church from outside evil forces, popes entered into concordats (treaties) with secular rulers, a practice which continued into the twentieth century when the Holy See negotiated concordats with fascist regimes in Europe, including Mussolini's Italy (1929), Hitler's Germany (1933),[106] and Franco's Spain (1953).

Anti-Jewish Myths Perpetuated

In 1825, a book written by Ferdinand Jabalot, procurator general of the Dominican order, was published and widely distributed throughout Europe. It restated traditional libels against Jews (e.g., they were deicides crazed with the lust for lucre and a desire to bring about the ruin of Christians). So intense was their hatred of Christianity, Jabalot wrote, that no evil was

---

105   The Age of Revolution is a term used to denote the period from approximately 1775 to 1848 in which a number of significant revolutionary movements occurred on both sides of the Atlantic in Europe and the Americas. The period is noted for changes of national governments from autocracies to constitutionalist states and republics. The Age of Revolution included the American Revolution, the French Revolution, the Haitian Revolution, the slave revolts and independence movements of Latin America countries. During this period the power of imperialist European states was weakened, as they lost control of major assets in the New World. The loss of the American Colonies brought about a change in direction for the British Empire, with Asia and the Pacific becoming new targets for outward expansion.

106   James Carroll, author of *Constantine's Sword*, terms the Reich Concordat, the Holy See's treaty with Nazi Germany, a "foundation stone of the Shoah." Negotiated on behalf of the Holy See by then Secretary of State Cardinal Eugenio Pacelli, the future Pope Pius XII, it was the first treaty to be concluded with Hitler, which Pius's critics contend legitimized the new regime and vitiated Catholic political opposition to Nazism.

too great for them: "They wash their hands in Christian blood, set fire to churches, trample the consecrated Host ... kidnap children and drain them of their blood, violate virgins." Jews are ever busy "cheating, and hoodwinking Christians," which was no surprise, since the Talmud called on Jews to cheat Christians at every opportunity. Christians unfortunate enough to fall into their clutches, are likely to emerge "not only without their shirt, but without their skin." Pope Leo XII (1823–29) subsequently appointed Father Jabalot head of the Dominican order worldwide.

Forced Baptism
According to church practice, a Jewish child baptized with or without parental knowledge and consent could not be returned to the custody of nonconverted parents. Jews entering the House of Catechumens, a residence for converts located in Rome and other Papal States, therefore, were required to have their children baptized. Between 1814 and 1818, according to David I. Kertzer,[107] the papal police, under orders of Pope Pius VII (1800–23), entered Rome's ghetto on twenty-two different occasions, always at night, to seize Jews and take them to the local House of the Catechumens. In that brief period, seventeen married women, three women engaged to be married, and twenty-seven children were removed by force. Mothers had a simple choice: accept baptism and keep your children or leave without them.

Pope Pius IX
Giovanni Ferretti became pontiff in 1846, taking the name Pius IX (a.k.a. *Pio Nono*). His pontificate (1846–78) was filled with military, political, and cultural turmoil, as Italian nationalists sought to unify Italy into a modern nation state. Pius IX strenuously opposed the unification movement, *Il Risorgimento* ("Resurgence"), because, among other things, its success would sound the death knell for the Papal States. He believed, like popes before him, that temporal sovereignty of the Holy See (the so-called Patrimony of St. Peter) was indispensable to the Church's spiritual authority. The

---

107   David I. Kertzer is Paul Dupee Jr. university professor of social science, professor of anthropology (1992–present), professor of history (1992–2001), and professor of Italian studies (2001–present) at Brown University. He was provost of Brown from July 1, 2006, to June 30, 2011. In 2005 he was elected a member of the American Academy of Arts and Sciences. His book *The Kidnapping of Edgardo Mortara*, was a finalist for the National Book Award in Nonfiction in 1997. His 2001 book, *The Popes against the Jews: The Vatican's Role in the Rise of Modern Anti-Semitism*, has been published in nine languages.

Papal States were regarded as an obstacle to Italian unification because they stretched across most of central Italy, cutting off the south from the north. Risorgimento was the ideological and literary movement that roused Italian nationalism and led to a series of political events that eventually freed Italian city-states and principalities from foreign domination. Rather than adapt the Church to the liberal trends unleashed by the Age of Revolution, Pius IX, also like his predecessors, chose to resist them. He declared war on Modernism—a war waged by the Church until 1965, when Vatican Council II finally declared a truce.

For Pius IX, modernity signified everything that was evil in society, including, among other things, freedom of religion/ religious tolerance; freedom of speech, of thought, and of press; and separation of church and state. In his attempt to stem the tide of history, he made Jews symbols of modernity because they were among its leaders and beneficiaries. They were, in short, an existential threat to the Church and divinely ordained society. In November 1848, Pius IX's secretary of state was assassinated. Fearing chaos and popular revolt, Pius IX became the third pope in fifty years to flee Rome into exile. The following month Giuseppe Garibaldi's republican army entered Rome. A unified Italian Republic was declared. As happened when Napoleon's army occupied Rome earlier in the nineteenth century, Jews were freed from the ghetto and granted rights of citizenship. Jewish emancipation, however, once again proved to be short-lived, because in 1850 temporal authority of the Papal States was restored, this time, ironically, by French troops, pursuant to a concordat between the Holy See and Emperor Napoleon III. Returning from exile, contending that the Church was a perfect society, Pius IX denounced the Italian revolutionary movement and reestablished his antinationalist, paternalistic regime, thereby alienating most educated Catholics and his own counselor, Monsignor Giovanni Corboli-Bussi, who described it as "reactionary and maladroit." A united Italy and end of the papacy's rule of the Papal States, Pius declared, was blasphemy.

The Communist Manifesto

While Pius IX was in exile in 1848, Karl Marx and Friedrich Engels published the *Communist Manifesto,* which quickly became a nightmare for the papacy. *Manifesto* advocated a classless and stateless society, abolition of private property, free love, and the abolition of inheritance. Worst of all, it advocated the abolition of religion, describing it as the "illusory happiness of the people" and as the "opiate of the people"—obvious shots across the bow of absolutist church authority. That Karl Marx was a Jew, predictably fueled animosity against Jews. The papacy's nightmare became reality some seventy years later when the Russian Revolution (1917–18) resulted in the overthrow of the Czarist absolute monarchy, execution of the royal family, expropriation and confiscation of church property, and elimination of churches (Roman Catholic and Russian Orthodox) in Russia. Religion in Russia was abolished and replaced with materialistic atheism. Like Judaism, Bolshevism in the twentieth century would become an existential threat to the Church and European society, a situation which Hitler would exploit in his writings and rhetoric by railing against Judeo-Bolshevism.

The Kidnapping of Edgardo Mortara

Bologna, 1858: A police squad, acting on orders of the Inquisitor, invaded the home of a Jewish merchant, Momolo Mortara, wrenched his crying six-year-old son, Edgardo, from his arms, and rushed him off in a carriage bound for Rome. Edgardo's mother was so distraught that she collapsed in grief and had to be taken to a neighbor's house. With this terrifying scene, David I. Kertzer, begins his book *The Kidnapping of Edgardo Mortara*, and launches into his investigation of the dramatic abduction, showing how this previously little-known incident contributed to the eventual collapse of the Church's temporal power in Italy. As Edgardo's parents desperately searched for a way to get their son returned to them, Kertzer relates, they learned why he, out of their eight children, was taken away. Years earlier, the family's Catholic servant girl, fearful that the infant Edgardo might die of an illness, had secretly baptized him. Edgardo recovered, but when the story of the baptism reached the Roman Inquisitor, it resulted in an order for Edgardo to be seized and sent to a special monastery where Jews were converted into Catholics.

The Inquisitor's justification for taking the child was based on Church practice (not doctrine): No Christian child could be raised by Jewish parents. The case of Edgardo Mortara became an international cause célèbre. Although such kidnappings were not uncommon in Jewish communities across Europe, this time the political climate had changed dramatically. Public opinion began to turn against the Vatican as news of the family's plight spread to Britain, where the influential Rothschild family got involved; to France, where it mobilized Napoleon III; and even to the United States. Refusing to return the child to his family,[108] Pius denied even the Mortaras' repeated pleas to see their son. The pope considered Edgardo as his son and eventually adopted him. Later Edgardo was ordained a priest.

According to John Cornwell, author of *Hitler's Pope*, the notion of Jewish obstinacy was a crucial element in the case of Edgardo Mortara. He wrote:

> When the parents of the kidnapped Edgardo pleaded in person with the Pope for the return of their son, Pio Nono told them that they could have their son back at once if only they converted to Catholicism which, of course, they would do instantly if they opened their hearts to Christian revelation. But they would not, and did not. The Mortaras, in the view of Pio Nono, had brought all their suffering upon their own heads as a result of their obduracy.[109]

Despite an international outcry and strong diplomatic pressure from Emperor Napoleon III of France (whose troops were defending Rome against the Italian republican army) and Emperor Franz Joseph of Austria, Pius IX refused to change his position. No less than twenty critical editorials were published in the *New York Times* alone. Pius' obstinate refusal to relent undermined whatever public support remained for continuation of the Papal States.

Syllabus of Errors

In December 1864, Pius IX published the encyclical *Quanta cura* ("How much care") with the famous *Syllabus Errorum* ("Syllabus of Errors") attached, a list of eighty errors that he, as pope, condemned, including religious freedom; separation of church and state; freedom of thought, expression, and press; Bible societies; rationalism; socialism; democracy;

---

108   In 1946, Pope Pius XII refused to permit the return to surviving relatives of "hidden" Jewish children of French nationality who were baptized during the Holocaust. In 2005, the Italian newspaper *Corriere della Sera* discovered a letter dated November 20, 1946, in which Pius XII ordered that Jewish children baptized during the Holocaust were not to be returned to their parents. Pius's defenders claim that the letter is either a forgery or a misinterpretation.

109   John Cornwell, *Hitler's Pope*, 27.

communism; and the end of church control of public schools. One of the errors read:

> That in the present day, it is no longer necessary that the Catholic Church be held as the only religion of the State, to the exclusion of all other modes of worship; whence it has been wisely provided by the law, in some countries nominally Catholic, that persons coming to reside therein shall enjoy the free exercise of their own worship … That the Roman Pontiff can, and ought to, reconcile himself to, and agree with, progress, liberalism and modern civilization.

Article 19 of the Syllabus of Errors declared that the Church was a perfect society and, therefore, had no need to change. Later, contending that the Church was besieged by demonic forces, a conspiracy of secret sects (i.e., Freemasons and Jews), Pius XI proclaimed: "It is from them (the Jews) that the synagogue of Satan, which gathers its troops against the Church of Christ, takes its strength."

Also in 1864, Maurice Joly published a satire attacking Napoleon III entitled, *Dialogue aux Enfers entre Montesquieu et Machiavel* ("Dialogue in Hell Between Montesquieu and Machiavelli"). Joly's work would become the basis for the literary hoax, *Protocols of the Elders of Zion*, to be published in the early twentieth century.

Papal Endorsement of the Blood Libel Myth

In 1867, Pius IX endorsed the blood libel myth when he decreed that the cult surrounding an allegedly martyred child, Lorenzino of Marastica, would be accorded official status. According to church accounts, on Good Friday 1485, when Lorenzino went out to play, Jews seized him, tore off his clothes, and crucified him on a nearby tree, draining his blood to make Passover matzos. In 1869, Henri Gougenot des Mousseaux published a book entitled *The Jew: Judaism and the Judaization of Christian Peoples*, arguing that Jews required the blood of Christian children for their Passover matzos. Pius IX praised the book and its author, awarding him the Cross of Commander of the Papal Order.

Also in 1867, Pius IX spearheaded the effort to have Peter Arbues, an Augustinian monk and a fifteenth century inquisitor famed for the forcible conversion of Jews, canonized to sainthood. In the canonization document of St. Peter Arbues, Pius IX wrote: "Divine wisdom has arranged that in these sad days, when Jews help the enemies of the Church with their books and money, this decree of sanctity has been brought to fulfillment."

Vatican Council I

The pending collapse of the Papal States exacerbated the papacy's siege mentality. In response to the revolutionary waves battering the Church, Pius IX convened Vatican Council I (1869–70), which, under his firm control, affirmed the Syllabus of Errors, and proclaimed as dogma[110] the doctrine of papal infallibility.[111] The pope, the Council decreed, has:

> full and supreme authority of jurisdiction over the whole Church, not only in matters that pertain to faith and morals, but also in matters that pertain to the discipline and government of the Church through the whole world. Further, this power is 'ordinary' (i.e. not to be delegated) and immediate (i.e. not exercised through any other party) ... over each and every Church (and) over each and every shepherd and faithful.
>
> [Infallibility] is divinely revealed dogma that the Roman Pontiff, when he speaks *ex cathedra* ("from the Chair"), that is, when acting in the office of shepherd and teacher of all Christians, he defines, by virtue of his supreme apostolic authority, a doctrine concerning faith or morals to be held by the universal Church, possesses through the divine assistance promised to him in the person of Blessed Peter, the infallibility with which the divine Redeemer willed his Church to be

---

110   Dogma is defined as "the established belief or doctrine held by a religion or ideology that is authoritative and not to be disputed, doubted, or diverged from." In Roman Catholicism, for example, "Jesus is the Lord" and the "Immaculate Conception of Mary" are dogmas.

    The Immaculate Conception of Mary doctrine, which maintains that the Blessed Virgin Mary was free of original sin from the moment of her conception, was proclaimed as dogma by Pius IX in 1854. This assertion is rejected by most other Christian faith traditions on the ground that there is no scriptural basis for the claim.

111   Lord Acton (1834–1902), in a letter to Bishop Mandell Creigton in 1887, penned his famous, "Power tends to corrupt, and absolute power corrupts absolutely," to express his opposition to papal infallibility.

endowed in defining the doctrine concerning faith or morals; and that such definitions of the Roman Pontiff are therefore irreformable of themselves, not because of the consent of the Church.

About Vatican Council I's declaration of papal infallibility, Father Richard P. McBrien wrote: "No definitions could have been further removed from the teaching of the Council of Constance (1414–18), from the theology and practice of the Eastern Churches, and from the practice of the universal Church, West and East alike, of the first Christian millennium ..."[112]

Publishing the Syllabus of Errors and declaring papal infallibility as dogma were intended to reinforce the doctrines of supercessionism, triumphalism, and ultramontainism,[113] both attempts to bolster and centralize authority within the Vatican. Ironically, the papacy's loss of political authority over the Papal States led to an increase of spiritual authority over Catholics worldwide, because, at a time of increasing democratization in Europe and elsewhere, the Church became more autocratic. Vatican influence over the lives of the faithful increased, as authority became more centered in Rome and the authority of bishops within their dioceses and in bishop conferences within regions was diminished. At the same time, Judaism continued to be a primary threat to Christianity, second only to atheistic communism. As noted previously, that Jews were among the wealthiest and most influential backers of modernity, which benefitted them in particular, made them especially dangerous to church and state, an attitude that stoked the fires of nascent anti-Semitism. Jacques Kornberg, professor emeritus of history, University of Toronto, and author of *The Vatican and Hitler*, asserted that ultramontanism "mobilized anti-Semitism for its campaign against liberalism."

In August 1870, Pius IX declared: Before Jesus, the Jews "had been children in the House of God." But all that changed, for "owing to their

112   Fr. Richard P. McBrien, *Lives of the Popes*, 347.

113   "Triumphalism," a corollary of supercessionism, is defined as the claim that a particular doctrine, culture, or social system is superior to and should triumph over all others. "Ultramontanism," which means "beyond the mountains" (i.e., looking to Rome for guidance), was a movement that sought to counter liberal tendencies within the Church and centralize authority within the Vatican.

obstinacy and their failure to believe, they became dogs." Speaking to a group of pilgrims, only a few months after Italian Jews were freed from Rome's ghetto and made citizens of unified Italy, Pius lamented the result, saying: "We have today in Rome unfortunately too many of these dogs, and we hear them barking in all the streets, and going around molesting people everywhere."

Papal Infallibility

Papal infallibility, as noted previously, is the dictum that by action of the Holy Spirit, the pope is preserved from error when he solemnly promulgates dogmatic teachings on faith or morals. By 1870 most Catholics already believed that a pope had power to define dogma without the concurrence of a church council, which Pius, in fact, did in 1854 when he declared the Immaculate Conception of Mary to be dogma, but no pontiff to that time had ever claimed the power explicitly. Some bishops, including Bernard McQuaid, bishop of Rochester, New York—who attended Vatican Council I but left before the vote on papal infallibility was taken—believed that making papal infallibility dogma would be a calamity. When the archbishop of Bologna suggested to Pius that church tradition argued against papal infallibility, Pius IX retorted, *"Tradizione! La Tradizione son Io!"* ("Tradition! I am tradition!"),[114] and thereupon reassigned the archbishop to a monastery.

According to John Julius Norwich, author of *Absolute Monarchs: A History of the Papacy*, for ultramontanists Pius IX was "absolute ruler, unquestioned leader, and infallible guide." No discussion was permitted once the pope had spoken; no suggestion tolerated that there might be two sides to any argument. Norwich contends, "Roman Catholicism was in danger of becoming akin to a police state, illiberal and bigoted." Furthermore, he recounts, Britain's representative to the Holy See, Odo Russell, reporting back to his superiors in London, wrote of the pope's "unbridled pretensions to absolute control over the souls and bodies of mankind" and his position "at the head of a vast ecclesiastical conspiracy against the principles which govern modern society." "Liberal Catholics,"

---

114   Cf. Louis XIV (1638–1715), a.k.a. "Sun King" (French: *le Roi-Soleil*), another absolute monarch, who ruled as king of France and Navarre. The longest reigning monarch in European history, reigning for over seventy-two years, Louis XIV said *"L'État, c'est moi"* ("I am the state").

Russell continued, "can no longer speak in her (the Church's) defense without being convicted of heresy."[115]

Pius IX's absolutist notion of papal power created serious problems both within and outside the Church. A schism, for example, developed in Holland and elsewhere (i.e., the Old Catholic Church, comprised of former Roman Catholics who rejected the dogma of papal infallibility), and a wave of anticlericalism erupted across Europe, exemplified by *Kulturkampf* in Germany. Austria repudiated its concordat with the Vatican, and religious confrontations broke out in Switzerland.

Unification of Italy

In August 1871, French troops occupying Rome withdrew to fight in the Franco-Prussian War. The next month, republican troops recaptured Rome, and it was declared the capital of unified Italy. In September 1871, the Republic of Italy was born, and the final curtain fell on eleven centuries of theocratic rule over much of Italian territory. Europe's last theocratic government collapsed, along with its governing model characterized by state-sanctioned discrimination against adherents of other religions, a church monopoly of education and social services, and the use of police power to enforce canon law and religious observance.

Following the unification of Italy, Pius IX, proclaiming himself to be a prisoner of the Vatican, refused to recognize the new Italian state and forbade Catholics, upon penalty of excommunication, to vote or otherwise participate in Italian civic life. Charging that "the ideals of Italian patriots are the work of the devil," he excommunicated King Victor Emmanuel II, Giuseppe Garibaldi, Camillo Benso (the count of Cavour), and anyone who supported the Italian nationalist movement.

---

115   John Julius Norwich, *Absolute Monarchs*, 410.

Kulturkampf

The dogma of papal infallibility caused considerable consternation in newly unified Germany[116] under the leadership of Otto von Bismarck, nicknamed the "Iron Chancellor." As a consequence, during *Kulturkampf* ("Culture Struggle"), from 1871 to 1878, Bismarck spearheaded a movement to enact anti-Catholic legislation. Despite losing temporal power over the Papal States, the papacy still retained considerable influence over the secular affairs of most European countries, especially those with large Catholic populations. Catholics made up about one-third of Germany's population, residing, for the most part, in the State of Bavaria, with Munich as its capital. Accordingly, Bismarck viewed Catholics in Germany as the enemy within, a potentially divisive force in the newly formed "Second Reich." Allegiance to the pope, Bismarck feared, would diminish German Catholic allegiance to the German state.[117] By imposing controls on church activities, Bismarck sought to neutralize Vatican influence in Germany. In particular, Bismarck feared the influence of the Catholic Center Party, a political party formed in 1870, which sixty-three years later would be disbanded as a condition of the Reich Concordat of 1933 between the Holy See and Nazi Germany. In the Reich Concordat, the Church agreed not to interfere in German state affairs, and Hitler agreed not to interfere in church affairs.[118] After several years of clashes between Bismarck and the Vatican, an uneasy truce developed—giving the German church more liberty in exchange for its greater acceptance of state authority.

---

116   For Jews, a benefit of the unification of Germany in 1871 was full citizenship in the Second Reich, which was stripped away during the Third Reich by the Nuremburg Laws of 1935. The German Empire (German: *Deutsches Kaiserreich*) is the common name given to the state officially named the *Deutsches Reich* (literally: "German Realm"), designating Germany from its unification and the proclamation of Wilhelm I as German emperor on January 18, 1871, to 1918, when it became a federal republic (the Weimar Republic) after Germany's defeat in World War I. The German Empire, consisting of twenty-seven constituent territories (most of them ruled by royal families), the largest being the Kingdom of Prussia, ended with the abdication of the Emperor Wilhelm II in 1918.

117   The same fear of undue papal influence over affairs of state was raised by Protestants in the United States when Al Smith, a Catholic, was a candidate for president in 1928, and again when John F. Kennedy was a candidate for president in 1960.

118   The Holy See's agreement not to interfere in German state affairs and its subsequent policy of neutrality during World War II were significant constraints on German Catholic opposition to the Nazis.

Kulturkampf began with a series of laws intended to curb abuse of the pulpit for political ends. Subsequent laws, among other things, mandated state control of religious education, conferred power on the state to dismiss pastors, and gave the state authority to confiscate church property and to withdraw government subsidies from priests who refused to cooperate with the regime. In 1872, priests and religious were banned from teaching posts in public schools, and Jesuit priests were ordered out of Germany. In May 1873 the Reichstag (parliament) enacted two laws, one granting the state authority to oversee the training and assignments of priests, and the other placing bishops under state control. Many clergy and religious resisted, and hundreds of them, including a few bishops, were jailed or exiled. Lay Catholics supported their clergy and in many towns, especially in Bavaria, where spontaneous rallies erupted when angry demonstrators gathered as police arrested priests.

In 1875, an angry Pius IX issued a papal bull declaring the latest legislation to be null and void "since they (the offending laws) are completely contrary to the God-given institution of the Church." He ordered German Catholics to "passively resist"[119] them. Further, he decreed that any priest or religious who cooperated in implementing the offensive laws would be excommunicated. As Pius IX intensified his opposition to *Kulturkampf*, becoming more and more of a political headache for Bismarck, the Iron Chancellor gradually moderated his antichurch policies. After Pius IX's death in February 1878, Bismarck quietly reconciled with Pius's successor, Leo XIII (1878–1903), lifting most of the offensive sanctions.

James Carroll, writing about the *Kulturkampf* confrontation between Pius IX and Bismarck, concluded:

> [That] Pius IX was able to get Bismarck to back down in his attempt to limit church authority in Germany, demonstrating the kind of resistance the Roman Catholic Church could mount, both locally and from the Vatican, when confronted with a ruthless, calculated and systematic attempt to destroy it. The Church's response to Bismarck, in that sense, sets a 'standard'

---

119 "Passive resistance" is a type of nonviolent "civil disobedience"—a tactic used effectively by Mahatma Gandhi in his struggle to free India from British colonial rule in the 1930s and '40s and by Dr. Martin Luther King Jr. during the American Civil Rights Movement in the 1960s.

against which its later behavior, in response to Hitler, must be measured.[120]

Pius IX's thirty-two-year pontificate, longest in papal history, marked the beginning of the "modern" papacy. It intensified the papacy's siege mentality, further concentrated church authority within the Vatican, ramped up church resistance to change, and continued anti-Judaism as a core doctrine. His reign was the most reactionary pontificate of the modern era.

Regarding the end of Pius IX's pontificate, Richard McBrien wrote:

When Pius IX died on February 7, 1878, he was an exceedingly unpopular pope with the people of Rome and with the educated classes generally, even though he had been an extraordinarily popular pope with the Catholic masses, especially outside of Italy both because of his warmly pious personality and also out of sympathy for all the troubles he had suffered with such serenity and courage. On July 13, 1881, there was a disruption of the procession accompanying his body from its original burial place in St. Peter's to *San Lorenzo fuori le Mura* (St. Lawrence's Outside the Walls). A mob tried unsuccessfully to seize the body and throw it into the Tiber River.[121]

Beatification of Pius IX

In September 2000, Pope John Paul II (1978–2005), despite public opposition, beatified Pius IX, the last step before canonization to sainthood. The announcement shocked many admirers of John Paul's historic fence-mending with Jews, including his prayer at Judaism's holiest site, the Western Wall in Jerusalem, on March 25, 2000. "It hit like a thunderbolt from heaven," said Elena Mortara, professor of American literature at the University of Rome and great-great-granddaughter of Edgardo Mortara's sister. "Pius IX's repression of Jews' civil rights," she added, "is in itself serious enough to stop this beatification."

---

120   James Carroll, *Constantine's Sword*, 487.

121   McBrien, *Lives of the Popes*, 347.

CHAPTER 4

Birth of Anti-Semitism

DURING THE LAST THIRD OF the nineteenth century, various thinkers began to reshape the perception of Jews based on race, resulting, in part, from technological progress and scientific advances in the fields of biology, psychology, anthropology, genetics, and evolution. This perception emerged within a broader racial worldview based on notions of inequality of races and the superiority of the white race over others. Beginning in the late eighteenth century, German philosophers, including Johann Fichte (1762–1814) and Georg Friedrich Hegel (1770–1831), espoused ideas of German superiority and nationalism that set the tone and direction of German anti-Semitism. By the third quarter of the nineteenth century, traditional blood accusations leveled against Jews merged with new pseudoscientific theories of Charles Darwin (Darwinism), Herbert Spencer (social Darwinism), and Frederic Nietzsche (will to power, death of God, master-slave mentality, herd instinct, ascendancy of a master race [*herrenrasse*], a superman [*ubermensch*], and existence of subhuman life forms [*untermenschen*]).

In 1878, Adolf Stoecker, a court chaplain, founded the anti-Semitic German Christian Social Party, which advocated that Jews be strongly encouraged to convert to Christianity. In 1880, petitions signed by some 250,000 German citizens demanded that Jews be banned from attending public schools and universities and from holding public office. In 1881, pogroms broke out across Russia following the assassination of Czar Alexander II, for which Jews were wrongfully blamed.

In 1879 and 1880, Heinrich von Treitschke, an influential German nationalist historian, published a series of articles that drew attention to what would become a fateful phrase: *Die Juden sind unser Ungluck* ("The Jews are our misfortune"). Eventually, that phrase would become the preferred slogan on banners at Nazi Party rallies. In 1881, Eugen Karl Duhring published *Die Jundenfrage als Rassen-Sitten, und Kulturfrage* (*The Jewish Question as a Racial, Moral, and Cultural Problem*). Between 1881 and 1884, pogroms swept across Poland, the Ukraine, and Russia.

German philosopher and poet Frederic Nietzsche greatly influenced Hitler's worldview (*weltanschauung*). So too did English biologist and sociologist Herbert Spencer, whose theory of social Darwinism adapted Darwin's theory of evolution and postulated that humans were not one race, but several different races biologically driven to struggle against one another for living space (*lebensraum*) to ensure survival of the fittest. Only races with superior qualities could win this struggle characterized by force and warfare. For anti-Semites, Jews were a lower and racially defective life form, albeit immensely powerful and dangerous. In 1883, Sir Francis Galton coined the term "eugenics" to encompass the notion of positive modification of natural selection through selective breeding of humans. On April 20, 1889, Adolf Hitler was born in Braunau am Inn, Austria.

Also fueling the rise of anti-Semitism was the nineteenth century German xenophobic *völkische* movement ("peoples' movement")—an expression of romantic German nationalism. The movement was made up of philosophers, scholars, and artists, including opera composer Richard Wagner, who viewed Jews as non-German and an obstacle to the fulfillment of Germany's rightful destiny. Nazi ideologues, influenced by the *völkische* movement, envisioned a new Germany firmly grounded in destiny, ultranationalism/patriotism and racial purity, which would catapult the *Vaterland* ("fatherland") to its deserved place on the world stage, reversing the national humiliation of Germany's defeat in World War I and the onerous terms of the Versailles Treaty. During the Third Reich, *Deutschland, Deutschland über alles* (literally, "Germany, Germany above all"), the first stanza of the national anthem, would assume ominous connotation, particularly when German troops without provocation marched into Poland on September 1, 1939, beginning the nation's second worldwide war of conquest. Citizens of this new Germany would be members of the Aryan master race, genetically healthy, socially useful, and politically reliable. And because Jews represented everything diametrically opposed to this vision of a new Germany, their elimination was essential.

The Catholic Press

As modern anti-Semitism began to take shape in the latter third of the nineteenth century, the Church was a major contributor. In Pope Pius IX's war on Modernism, no weapon was more effective than the Catholic press, which at the time consisted of hundreds of newspapers, journals, and other periodicals throughout Europe. To these publications, Pius gave the task of combating the forces of liberalism. And because Jews supported these forces, the Catholic press focused heavily on Jews, characterizing them, for example, as evil conspirators doing the devil's work, and warning of a rising Jewish peril.

The Edgardo Mortara forced baptism case demonstrated the power of the secular/popular press to shape public opinion against the Church. To counter this influence, Pius IX ordered the Catholic press to redouble its efforts to promote church positions. One influential Catholic periodical, regarded as the unofficial voice of the papacy, was the biweekly Jesuit newspaper, *La Civiltà Cattolica*, founded in 1850. In December 1880, *La Civiltà Cattolica* kicked off an anti-Jewish campaign with a series of thirty-six articles. Perpetuating traditional myths against Jews, the articles purported to explain why recent pogroms had occurred in Germany. In one article, the author wrote that it was because Jews were obligated to hate non-Jews that Christians despised them. European society, therefore, had to be protected, and so, governments would be well advised to introduce special laws for a "race" that was so exceptionally and profoundly perverse. These special laws, the author asserted, would actually benefit Jews, for only by restoring restrictions on them (removed by emancipation) would violence against them be prevented. Another article attempted to prove that ritual murder was an integral part of the ritual for Purim rather than the one for Passover, concluding: "It is in vain that Jews seek to slough off the weight of argument against them: the mystery has become known to all."

All thirty-six articles were written by a Jesuit priest, Father Giuseppe di Santo Stefano, one of the founders of *Civiltà Cattolica*. Certain themes were repeated continuously, for example, (1) Jews had always benefited from the kindness of the Church, especially the kindness of popes; (2) Jews had lived happily in ghettos and, therefore, Christians were able to live peaceably, protected from them; (3) forbidding Jews to own real property or to practice certain occupations in the Papal States actually benefited them because such restrictions not only prevented Jews from becoming wealthy, but also prevented them from being too despised; and (4) history had shown if this foreign Jewish "race" was left too free, it immediately became the persecutor, oppressor, tyrant, thief, and devastator of the countries where it lived. Accordingly, special laws were required to keep them in their appropriate place and to protect society from the hostility they harbor against all human society not belonging to their "race." Far from persecuting Jews, such restrictive legislation served to prevent Jews from persecuting Christians.[122]

Another founding editor of *La Civiltà Cattolica*, Father Giuseppe Oreglia, SJ, wrote in an article:

> The Jews, eternal insolent children, obstinate, dirty, thieves, liars, ignoramuses, pests and the scourge of those near and far … managed to lay their hands on … all public wealth … and virtually alone they took control not only of all the money … but of the law itself in those countries where they have been allowed to hold public offices … (yet they complain) at the first shout by anyone who dares raise his voice against this barbarian invasion by an enemy "race," hostile to Christianity and to society in general.

The most influential Catholic publication was the Vatican daily newspaper, *L'Osservatore Romano*. In 1892, with anti-Semitism gaining ascendancy throughout Europe, *L'Osservatore Romano* devoted a series of articles to the "Jewish question." One article argued that because recent pogroms in Russia had stirred up so much sympathy for Jews, it proved that the pogroms could only have been "engineered by the Jews themselves."[123] The author wrote: "We would not stray far from the truth if we said that the rather heavy-handed blow that the Muscovite

---

122   Kertzer, *The Popes against the Jews*, 136.

123   This is an example of "blaming the victim" for the victim's plight.

Empire has aimed at the children of Judah has played into the hands of Judaism, for it has engendered compassion for the Jews, against whom the Christian and civil world has, for good reason, begun to rebel." Similarly, the article's author contended that French, Russian, and Austrian anti-Semitic movements were actually the work of cosmopolitan Judaism.

In indicting Pius IX for using the Catholic press to shape public opinion against Jews, Kertzer, wrote:

> What, after all, were the major tenets of this modern anti-Semitic movement if not such warnings as these: Jews are trying to take over the world; Jews have already spread their voracious tentacles around the nerve centers of Austria, Germany, France, Hungary, Poland and Italy; Jews are rapacious and merciless, seeking at all costs to get their hands on all the world's gold, having no concern for the number of Christians they ruin; Jews are unpatriotic, a foreign body ever threatening the well-being of the people among whom they live; special laws are needed to protect society, restricting the Jews' rights and isolating them. Every single one of these elements of modern anti-Semitism was not only embraced by the Church but actively promulgated by official and unofficial Church organs.[124]

As other major institutions were coming to terms with liberal trends transforming Europe, the traditionalist Holy See, through the Catholic press and other means, was strenuously resisting them.

The Dreyfus Affair

In 1894, during a wave of anti-Semitism in France, Captain Alfred Dreyfus, the highest-ranking Jewish officer in the French army, was charged with passing military secrets to the German Embassy in Paris. Convicted of treason on false evidence, imprisoned on Devil's Island at hard labor, Dreyfus was eventually exonerated, but a segment of the French populace refused to believe him innocent. The campaign that led to his wrongful conviction was largely driven by French anti-Semites who denounced Dreyfus for his "perfidious Jewishness." The Order of Assumptionist Fathers spearheaded the campaign, making Dreyfus's conviction a special

---

124   Kertzer, *The Popes against the Jews*, 7.

mission of its daily newspaper, *La Croix*.[125] An article in *L'Osservatore Romano* defended the French mobs protesting the reversal of Dreyfus's conviction: "The Jewish race, the deicide people, wanderer throughout the world, brings with it everywhere the pestiferous breath of treason."

By the early twentieth century, most Catholic journalists were using the word anti-Semitism with approbation. For example, the Vienna correspondent for *La Civiltà Cattolica,* wrote in 1922: "In its original form, anti-Semitism is nothing but the absolutely necessary and natural reaction to the Jews' arrogance ... Catholic anti-Semitism—while never going beyond the limits of moral law—adopts all necessary means to emancipate the Christian people from the abuse they suffer from their sworn enemy."

In 1899, *Foundations of the Nineteenth Century,* a book by Houston Stewart Chamberlain, published in Germany, contended that human history was a battle between Jews and Aryans. Also in 1899, *Action Francaise* ("French Action"), an anti-Semitic group, was founded in France. In 1903 in Poland, the party platform of the nationalist and anti-Semitic *Narodowa Demokracja* ("National Democratic Party") was written, advocating pogroms and the forced emigration of Jews out of Poland. Between 1903 and 1906, a second wave of pogroms swept Poland and the Ukraine.

St. Pope Pius X

St. Pope Pius X (1903–14), born Giuseppe Melchiorre Sarto, prosecuted Pius IX's war against modernity with vigor. The first pope since Pope Pius V (1566–72) to be canonized a saint, he categorically rejected modernist interpretations of doctrine and condemned dissidents who urged that the Church adapt itself to modern times. Like his predecessors, he refused to recognize the legitimacy of the Republic of Italy but, fearing the rising influence of socialism[126] in

---

125 Owen Chadwick, author of *A History of the Popes: 1830–1914,* characterizes the *La Croix's* anti-Dreyfus campaign as: "The most powerful and extreme journalism ever conducted by an otherworldly religious order during the history of Christendom."

126 Socialism in the late nineteenth and early twentieth centuries was viewed as a powerful threat to conservative institutions because it opposed the existing social order in Europe and displayed overt hostility toward the Church. In Italy and elsewhere the influence of the socialist movement and its trade unions spread quickly, undermining previously unchallenged church functions like providing social welfare services to the poor. The threat only got worse when the Russian Revolution radicalized socialist forces throughout Europe.

Europe, he relaxed the ban on Catholic participation in Italian state elections. In 1907, Pius X issued *Pascendi Dominici gregis* ("Feeding the Lord's flock"), his encyclical against Modernism, in which he declared that: "Modernism constituted not a heresy, but the compendium and poison of all heresies." Building on the work of Pius IX, *Pascendi Dominici gregis* reinforced the dogmatic/authoritarian tone of church teaching, reiterated the absolute spiritual authority of the papacy, demanded unquestioning obedience from the faithful, and made clear that intellectual questions within the Church were not matters for scholarly discussion but matters of faith and morals[127] to be resolved by the pope. This continued church practice that encouraged docility and compliance from the faithful and discouraged independent thought and action. The role of the laity was derisively said to be to "Pay, Pray and Obey." Pius X was critical of countries with democratic forms of government because, among other reasons, they accepted pluralism. Instead, he favored countries with authoritative forms of government that respected the Church's traditional role in society and its conservative/unchanging worldview.

Anti-Modernist Oath

The Congregation of the Inquisition was formally abolished in 1908, but its functions, including the policing of orthodoxy, were rolled over into a new Congregation of the Holy Office. In 1910, the Holy Office, under Pius X's firm direction, issued a mandate requiring all priests to swear an oath denouncing Modernism. Known as the "Anti-Modernist Oath," it demanded unequivocal acceptance of all church teachings and acquiescence in the meaning and sense of all teachings decreed by the pope. John Cornwell, author of *Hitler's Pope*, termed the oath, "a form of thought control unrivalled even under fascist and communist regimes." Priests were required to take the oath (in Latin) until it was rescinded in July 1967, following Vatican Council II.

Pius X's aggressive stance against Modernism adversely affected Catholic biblical scholarship as newer, mostly Protestant, modes of

---

127   As noted previously, the dogma of papal infallibility declared that by action of the Holy Spirit, the pope is preserved from error when he solemnly promulgates teachings on faith or morals. Conscience assists the faithful to determine what constitutes ethical behavior (i.e., the difference between right and wrong). A primary cause of the Holocaust was the widespread failure of conscience which dulled Christian capacity to experience empathy for Jewish suffering. Clergy, for the most part, failed to assist the faithful in conscience formation on this issue. For this failure, popes, as chief shepherds of the flock and primary teachers on issues of morality, bear a measure of responsibility for the Holocaust.

study with modernistic or liberal tendencies were rejected as heretical. Some of those labeled Modernists were exponents of new forms of biblical interpretation that advocated understanding the Bible as a historical document, its truths conditioned by authors with particular points of view who wrote in the context of a particular time and place. Others suspected of Modernism focused on the sciences (e.g., the theory of evolution, geology, archeology, or paleontology). Still others focused on social issues connected to democracy, socialism, or nationalism, and speculated how the Church might respond and/or adapt.

Theologians suspected of pursuing lines of inquiry tainted with secularism, Modernism, or relativism were threatened with excommunication. Ironically, some of the theologians viewed with suspicion by the Holy See before 1960 became *periti* ("theological experts") of Vatican Council II.[128] The Church's fundamentalist/literalist approach to scripture continued into the mid-twentieth century. Modern biblical study methods,[129] reflecting approaches such as contextual/ historical criticism, were rejected until 1943 when Pope Pius XII issued his encyclical *Divino Afflante Spiritu* ("Inspired by the Divine Spirit") which eased the policy somewhat.[130] Pius X, in addition, authorized a network of clergy informants, known as the *Sodalitium Pianum* ("League of St. Pius V"), who reported to the Holy Office instances of deviation from doctrinal orthodoxy. Serious deviations from orthodoxy led to dismissal from faculty teaching positions in Catholic educational institutions and/or suspension from the priesthood—practices that continue to the present day. Pius's campaign against Modernism within the Church might be described as a nonviolent reign of terror.

128   Theologians viewed with suspicion included Fr. Karl Rahner SJ, Fr. M. J. Lagrange OP, Monsignor Louis Duchesne, Fr. M. D. Chenu, Fr. Yves M. J. Congar OP, Fr. John Courtney Murray SJ, Fr. Bernard Lonergan SJ, Fr. Hans Ur von Bathasar, Fr. Henri de Lubac SJ, and others. Some of their groundbreaking books were placed on the Index of Prohibited Books. A few of these theologians were later elevated to the rank of cardinal.

129   Other methods of biblical criticism include: textual, source, form, redaction, canonical, rhetorical, narrative, psychological, postmodern, and feminist.

130   Pius XII reversed his earlier position in *Divino Afflante Spiritu,* accepting some newer approaches to biblical study, when in September 1950, he issued his encyclical *Humani Generis* ("Of the Human Race"), which, according to John Julius Norwich, paralyzed contemporary Catholic scholarship and categorically condemned new or original Christian thinking (*Absolute Monarchs*, 450).

Pius's popularity in the United States plummeted in 1910 when he refused to receive former president Theodore Roosevelt at the Vatican, because Roosevelt was also scheduled to speak at a Methodist Church in Rome. In 1910, Pius condemned *Le Sillon,* a French ecumenical social movement that attempted to reconcile Catholicism with liberal political views. He also opposed trade unions that were not exclusively Catholic, but was tolerant of the right-wing, monarchist, and counterrevolutionary *Action Francaise.*[131]

Protocols of the Elders of Zion

The *Protocols of the Elders of Zion,*[132] first published in 1903 in Russia, alleged a Jewish conspiracy to achieve world domination and/or to destroy civilization. Best known as an example of a literary forgery and hoax, it was republished in 1905 by a Russian Orthodox priest, Sergius Nilus, in a book about the coming of the Antichrist. *Protocols* was promoted as the record of secret rabbinical conferences whose aim was to subjugate and exterminate Christians. Purporting to be a speech outlining a strategy for world domination—including plans to take control of the media and financial institutions—*Protocols* not only used text to support its conspiracy theory, but also graphic imagery. Nazi propaganda cartoons later employed some of this imagery, depicting Jews, for example, as an octopus encircling the globe. Monsignor Umberto Benigni, an official in Pius's Secretariat of State and his chief enforcer in purging the Church of modernist theologians, was one of the two principal distributors of *Protocols of the Elders of Zion* in Italy.

---

131   *Action Francaise* was founded in 1898 during the Dreyfus Affair, partly in reaction to the revitalization of liberalism (and leftist political parties) within France that materialized in defense of Alfred Dreyfus, launched by Emile Zola's *J'accuse* ("I accuse"). *J'accuse* was an open letter published on January 13, 1898, in the newspaper *L'Aurore.* In the letter, Zola addressed the president of France, Felix Faure, and accused the French government of anti-Semitism and the unlawful imprisonment of Dreyfus.

132   Henry Ford would fund the printing of five hundred thousand copies of *Protocols* that were distributed throughout the United States in the 1920s. Moreover, historian Norman Cohn suggested that Hitler used *Protocols* as the primary justification for initiating the Holocaust—his "warrant for genocide."

The Beilis Ritual Murder Trial

In 1913, Pius X refused to intervene in the (Menachem Mendel) Beilis trial, then taking place in Kiev, Ukraine, one of the twentieth century's most notorious cases of ritual murder. Beilis, who worked in a Jewish-owned factory, was arrested in 1911 and charged with killing a boy on factory grounds. Jewish leaders were particularly alarmed by the flood of articles in the Catholic press telling, in gruesome detail, of past ritual murders perpetrated by Jews. After a priest testified during the trial that ritual murders were historical fact, a number of influential English Jews asked the duke of Norfolk, a Catholic, to appeal to the pope to refute the libel. Pius, however, refused to intervene. According to David Kertzer: "By not taking this step (to refute the libel), the pope allowed the Catholic press, including that part of it viewed inside and outside the Church as communicating the pope's true sentiment, to continue to tar the Jews with the ritual murder charge."[133]

Notwithstanding that Pius X was canonized a saint in 1954 during the pontificate of Pius XII, becoming the only pope elevated to sainthood in modern history,[134] his pontificate, like those of Pius IX and of Pius XII, is considered among the most controversial in the modern history of the papacy.

Pope Benedict XV

Benedict XV (1914–22), born Giacomo Paolo Giovanni Battista della Chiesa, succeeded Pius X. His pontificate was overshadowed by World War I, hereinafter "WWI," the so-called "war to end all wars," which began in July 1914 and lasted until November 1918. According to Father Richard P. McBrien, Benedict's greatest accomplishment may have been putting the brakes on Pius X's aggressive anti-Modernist campaign against Catholic theologians. As world war became more and more likely, Benedict kept the Holy See strictly neutral, refusing to favor or condemn either side, resulting in both sides accusing him of partiality. It should be noted that Pius XII followed the same strategy in World War II, hereinafter "WWII," which his critics contend constrained him, in particular, and members of the clergy, in general, from speaking out against Nazi extremism. Additionally, it should be noted that Germany was the unprovoked aggressor in both

---

133   Kertzer, *The Popes against the Jews*, 232.

134   Popes Pius IX, Pius XII, and John XXIII were proposed for sainthood by John Paul II.

world wars, seeking in each to extend its territorial hegemony over other sovereign nations, clearly making both wars "unjust" pursuant to Catholic doctrine.

World War I

The underlying causes of WWI dated back, in part, to the unification of Germany in 1871 and the changing balances of power among the European Great Powers in the early twentieth century. These causes included the continuing French resentment over the loss of territory to Germany in the nineteenth century, the growing economic and military competition between Britain and Germany, and German desire for a "place in the sun" on the world stage equal to that of the more established countries of Europe.

The war was fought between two major alliances. The Entente Powers, a.k.a. the Allies, initially consisted of France, Britain, Russia, and their associated empires and dependencies. Numerous other states joined the alliance, most notably Japan in August 1914, Italy in April 1915, and the United States in April 1917. The Central Powers, so named because of their central location on the European continent, initially consisted of Germany and Austria-Hungary and their associated empires. The Muslim Ottoman Empire[135] joined the Central Powers in October 1914, followed a year later by Bulgaria. By the conclusion of the war, only the Netherlands, Switzerland, Spain, the Scandinavian countries,

---

135   Although Jews had the status of a protected minority (along with Christians and Zoroastrians) in the Ottoman Empire, this was only true as long as they remained visibly inferior to the Muslim majority. Once the Ottoman Empire broke up after WWI and the region was divided among the European victors, anti-Semitism began to rise in the Middle East. This was partly due to the influence of anti-Semitic literature from the West, feelings of inferiority vis-à-vis Jews (Jews were often middle men in colonial governments), and the rise of Arab nationalism. The Grand Mufti of Jerusalem, Haj Mohammed Effendi Amin el-Husseini, was a rabid anti-Semite, nationalist, and fervent Nazi supporter. During the 1930s and 1940s, the Nazis broadcast anti-Semitic propaganda in Arabic for the purpose of gaining valuable allies against the British and French, which administered Palestine pursuant to provisions of the Versailles Treaty. The establishment of the state of Israel in 1948 and the disastrous outcome of the Six Day War in 1967 further cemented resentment against Jews in the Arab Middle East. Today, many Arab governments are openly anti-Semitic. *The Protocols of the Elders of Zion* is a popular "nonfiction" book throughout the region. Anti-Semitism is also a core tenet among radical Islamist groups.

and Monaco remained officially neutral among the European countries, though several may have provided financial and material support to one side or the other. Austria-Hungary fielded eight million soldiers commanded by, among others, some twenty-five thousand Jewish reserve officers. Thirty years later, the nation-states that succeeded the empire, created by the Treaty of Versailles, would send most of their surviving Jewish officers to the gas chambers.

Most combat played out along several fronts that broadly encircled the European continent. The Western Front was marked by a system of trenches and fortifications separated by an area known as no man's land. These fortifications stretched 475 miles and precipitated a style of fighting known as trench warfare. On the Eastern Front, the vastness of the eastern plains and the limited railroad network prevented the stalemate that occurred on the Western Front, although the scale of the conflict was just as large. The Balkan, Middle Eastern, and Italian fronts also saw heavy fighting, and there was combat at sea and in the air.

WWI was remarkable for its extreme violence and slaughter. More than seventy million military personnel, including sixty million Europeans, were mobilized in one of the largest wars in world history. More than nine million combatants were killed, largely because of advances in firepower without corresponding advances in troop mobility, as fighting occurred mainly from trenches. The sixth-deadliest conflict in world history to that time, it provoked disruptive political change, including revolutionary changes, within combatant countries and in countries created by the Versailles Treaty. New weapons employed for the first time—among them, flamethrowers, airplanes, aerial bombs, machine guns, and poison gas—contributed to unprecedented carnage.

The signing of several treaties, most notably the Treaty of Versailles, brought the war to an end on June 28, 1919. The treaties led to a large redrawing of the map of Europe. All the Central Powers lost territory, and several new nations were created, including Poland, Finland, Austria, Hungary, Czechoslovakia, Yugoslavia, Estonia, Latvia, and Lithuania. The redrawn map of Europe sowed the seeds of WWII. The League of Nations, established after the war to prevent future wars by giving nations a means of solving their differences diplomatically, proved to be totally ineffective. WWI ended the world order that had existed since the end of the Napoleonic Wars, and paved the way, only twenty years later, for WWII.

In August 1917, Benedict XV proposed a seven-point peace plan, including renunciation of war indemnities and the return of all occupied territories, but both sides, more or less, ignored it. The Allies suspected him of favoring Germany because of Germany's promise to return the City of Rome to the Holy See after defeating Italy. Benedict also feared the expansion of Russian Orthodoxy if Russia and the Allies won the war. The Allies referred to him contemptuously as *le pape boche* ("the Kraut pope"), while the Germans referred to him as *der franzosische Papst* ("the French pope"). At war's end, Benedict XV pleaded for reconciliation among combatants and gave qualified support to the League of Nations. When the armistice was reached in 1919, however, Benedict was deliberately excluded from treaty negotiations in accordance with an agreement between the Allies and Italy.

The first so-called "modern" war, WWI aggravated the already deep divisions within German society. Over a quarter of a million Germans died in 1916 from starvation alone. Germany suffered millions of casualties, with only Russia enduring greater losses. During the war, German propaganda relentlessly stressed that victory was within reach. Until the very end in 1918, despite enormous casualties and sacrifices on the home front, Germany appeared to be winning the war. Then, in November 1918, seemingly without warning, the proverbial roof caved in. A sudden armistice and humiliating defeat left most Germans shocked, upset, and looking for a scapegoat. To make matters worse, following the abdication of Kaiser Wilhelm II, leftist and centrist outsider political parties created the Weimar Republic and imposed democracy on a people with no tradition of or preparation for it. The victorious Allies, moreover, compelled the newly created Weimar government to sign the Versailles Treaty of 1919,[136] with its preponderance of humiliating terms for Germany, thus beginning its political life carrying a staggering

---

136   One of the most controversial provisions of the Versailles Treaty was the "war guilt clause," which required Germany to accept responsibility for causing the war (along with Austria and Hungary). Other provisions required Germany, among other things, to disarm and pay heavy reparations. Total cost of reparations was assessed at 132 billion deutschmarks (then $31.4 billion) in 1921, roughly equivalent to $442 billion in 2011—a sum, at the time, deemed to be excessive, as it was projected that it would take Germany until 1988 to pay the debt in full.

financial debt of reparations. Written entirely by the victorious Allies, the treaty was universally hated by Germans. It required Germany, among other things, to relinquish its territories of Alsace, Lorraine, Poznan, West Prussia, and Upper Silesia, as well as its prized colonies in Africa. Additionally, Germany lost control of coal mines in the Saarland. One of the goals of Hitler's expansionist campaign would be to gain control of natural resources such as coal and oil to fuel his war effort, available in the East but not in Germany. Post-WWI conditions in Germany would set the stage for the rise of Nazism.

CHAPTER 5

Rise of Nazism

THE WEIMAR CONSTITUTION WAS QUITE progressive, containing a bill of rights, granting universal suffrage (including to Jews), and creating both a welfare state and a parliamentary system of government with proportional representation. This latter feature, however, led to proliferation of political parties, more than thirty-five by 1928, making governing particularly difficult. One of the parties, the Catholic Center Party,[137] served as a democratic counterweight to rightist parties like the extremist National Socialist German Workers' Party (a.k.a. the Nazi Party). Weimar's newly created centrist government, which tended toward coalitions and short-lived cabinets, not only had to deal with threats of revolution from within, but also with recession/runaway inflation, high unemployment, business failures, food shortages, lack of jobs, and civil strife.

At war's end, Benedict XV sent two talented young priests from the Vatican Curia, who would later become popes, on diplomatic missions: Achille Ratti (soon to be Pius XI) as apostolic visitor to Poland and Lithuania, and Eugenio Pacelli (the future Pius XII) as papal nuncio,

---

137   Founded in 1870 when Otto von Bismarck was chancellor of newly unified Germany, the Catholic Center Party in 1919 polled six million votes, second only to the Social Democrats. Occupying the contested middle ground of the Weimar Republic's political spectrum in the mounting chaos of the period, the Center Party provided five chancellors in the ten governments from 1919 to 1933. The Center Party opposed legislation aimed at Jews, and its leaders consistently rejected the gutter anti-Semitism that increasingly infected German public discourse as the German economy soured.

first to Munich, in Bavaria (where the majority of German Catholics resided), then to Berlin. With regard to the status of the Holy See within Italy, Benedict adopted a more moderate political course, allowing Catholics full participation in the political process and lifting the ban on official visits to the Quirinale Palace (previously the popes' summer residence, but, at the time, official residence of the King of Italy), by Catholic heads of state. He also authorized a secret meeting between Italy's fascist dictator Benito Mussolini and a curia representative to begin the process of regularizing the status of the Holy See within Italy. This effort would result in the Lateran Treaty of 1929.

The Russian Revolution (1917–18), which occurred during Benedict's pontificate, overthrew the Czarist monarchy with the executions of Czar Nicholas, his wife Alexandra, and their children. The revolution suppressed the Roman Catholic and Russian Orthodox Churches in the new Soviet state. As popes had feared since publication of the *Communist Manifesto* in 1848, organized religion was abolished in Russia and replaced with materialistic atheism. Making matters even worse, in October 1917, the Bolshevik regime issued a decree abolishing private ownership of landed estates and expropriating all church property. Church services were forbidden. The new government seized eleven million rubles on deposit with the Ecclesiastical College of the Czarist regime and all the land owned by the Roman Catholic Church of Russia. Jews were among the leaders and supporters of the Russian Revolution and, not surprisingly, many people linked Bolshevism with Judaism and came to see the two as the greatest existential threats facing the Church and European society. Also, not surprisingly, as noted previously, Hitler would soon begin to rail in his writings and speeches against Judeo-Bolshevism.

In 1917, Benedict XV promulgated a new Code of Canon Law. Benedict's predecessor, Pius X, gave the task of redrafting the code to two priests, one of whom was Eugenio Pacelli. The new code, which took ten years to complete, was intended to be the cornerstone of Pius X's program of centralizing church authority and giving the papacy unprecedented authority over every aspect of church life. Canon 218 defined the pope's authority as: "The supreme and most complete jurisdiction throughout the Church, both in matters of faith and morals and in those that affect discipline and Church government throughout the world."

Between 1919 and 1921, a third wave of anti-Semitic pogroms swept Poland and the Ukraine. Overall, more than sixty thousand Jews were killed, and several times that number were injured or wounded. In April 1920, Adolf Hitler, a corporal in the German army, was honorably discharged from military service having been awarded an Iron Cross first class for bravery, a medal he wore proudly until the day he died in April 1945. On March 21, 1921, anti-Jewish pogroms broke out in Jerusalem.

Father Eugenio Pacelli

Eugenio Pacelli, the future Pius XII, was ordained a priest in 1899, the year after Pope Leo XIII (1878–1903) condemned the heresy of "Americanism." Raised in a family with close ties to the Vatican, Pacelli's grandfather was one of the founders of *L'Osservatore Romano*; and his father, uncle, and brother worked in service to the Vatican. Clearly, the Pacelli family had a longstanding and deep devotion to the Holy See. Like his religious contemporaries, Pacelli was steeped in the Church's tradition of anti-Modernity, papal authoritarianism, and anti-Judaism. His seminary education concentrated in the study of canon law. In 1901, with little or no pastoral experience, Pacelli entered the Vatican Secretariat of State, where he and another priest were assigned the task of redrafting the Code of Canon Law. Distinguishing himself as a canon lawyer and diplomat, recognized for his work in redrafting the 1917 Code of Canon Law, Pacelli was elevated to the rank of cardinal in 1929 and appointed Vatican secretary of state in 1930. An admitted Germanophile who spoke fluent German, Pacelli lived in Germany from 1917, the year of his appointment as papal nuncio to Munich, until 1929, the last year of his appointment as nuncio to Berlin. John Cornwell, author of *Hitler's Pope* writes: "(Pacelli's) principal task in Germany was ... the imposition, through the 1917 Code of Canon Law, of supreme papal authority over ... Catholic bishops, clergy, and faithful."

While Pacelli was serving as papal nuncio to Munich, the city's chief rabbi asked him to use his influence with the Italian government to release a consignment of palm fronds grown in Italy, needed for the forthcoming celebration of *Sukkot* (Feast of Booths/Feast of Tabernacles), occurring in late September of that year. The fronds had been purchased but were being held up in the City of Como. Pacelli replied that, although he forwarded the request to Italian authorities, he feared that because of wartime delays and the fact that the Holy See had no diplomatic relations with the Italian Republic, it was unlikely that anything could be done in time. However, in a letter to the secretary of state, Cardinal Pietro Gasparri, Pacelli wrote: "It seemed to me that to go along with this would be to give the Jews special assistance not within the scope of practical, arm's-length, purely civil or natural rights common to all human beings, but in a positive and direct way to assist them in the exercise of their Jewish *cult*." (emphasis mine)

Weimar Germany

Postwar Germany was plagued with political and social instability as extremist parties on the left and the right vied with centrist parties in the middle for power. Aggravating the instability were revolutionary forces unleashed by the Russian Revolution, spearheaded by Germany's own Communist Party (one of the country's largest), many of whose members were Jewish. As had happened so many times before in history, the Jews were once again scapegoated for a natural or man-made disaster, this time for Germany's defeat in WWI (*Der Dolchstoff,* "Stab in the Back") and the ensuing chaotic conditions of the Weimar Republic. The conditions included: hyperinflation in 1923, which made the deutschmark virtually worthless; harsh economic stabilization measures of 1924; the worldwide Great Depression of 1929; and widespread popular discontent, often erupting into street riots between rival political parties and their bands of thugs.

In January 1923, French and Belgian armies occupied the industrial heartland of Germany, the Ruhr Valley, claiming that Germany had failed to make reparations called for in the Versailles Treaty. The National Socialist German Workers' Party, under the leadership of an obscure former army corporal from Austria, emerged out of the chaos and soon began to exploit the volatile situation. Among the tactics used to great effect were negative political campaigning and manipulative propaganda,[138] both pioneered by Joseph Goebbels, who would become Hitler's propaganda minister. Hitler and Goebbels were both baptized Roman Catholics.

---

138   Hitler said, prophetically, in 1921: "Propaganda is a truly terrible weapon in the hands of an expert."

Early in his political career, in 1923, Hitler proclaimed: "The Jew is a race, but not human."[139] According to his worldview, it was Germany's destiny to eradicate Jews from the face of the earth. Political leaders faced numerous assassination attempts during the 1920s, together with attempted *coups d'etat* on the left and the right, including Hitler's failed Beer Hall Putsch in 1923. After that abortive coup, he was convicted for treason and imprisoned in Landsberg fortress, where he wrote *Mein Kampf* ("My Struggles"), his autobiography and political manifesto. In it he expressed his radical ideas about history, race, politics, and the future of Germany, including the necessity to eliminate the Jewish menace, viewed as a Jewish conspiracy to rule the world. He also claimed that Germany's destiny was the acquisition of land in the East. Hitler blamed Germany's woes on the Reichstag, the Jews, Social Democrats, and Marxists, declaring that the parliamentary system had to be destroyed because it was, in principle, corrupt.

Hitler and the Nazis cleverly and calculatingly crafted their party platform to appeal to widespread popular discontent, promising, among other things, strong central leadership, a better way of life, and Germany's reascendance to its rightful place of prominence on the world stage. Despite repeated electoral failures in the 1920s, the Nazi Party in early 1933 won close to 30 percent of the electoral vote for Reichstag seats. On January 29, 1933, fearing continued social unrest and unable to envision a better solution, President Paul von Hindenburg, the eighty-five-year-old WWI hero, reluctantly appointed Hitler as chancellor of Germany. The proverbial die was cast. Almost immediately, Hitler began to fashion the Third Reich, his brutally totalitarian regime, which within six years would lead Germany and Europe into another cataclysmic world war and the Holocaust (*Shoah*).

---

139   Holding Jews responsible for Germany's social and economic problems, within ten years Hitler would begin to systematically remove all the civil, social, and economic rights they had gained just fifty years earlier when the North German Confederation declared in 1869 that "all existing limitations on civil right derived from a difference in religious persuasion are hereby eliminated." Two years later Bismarck united all German lands under the leadership of Prussia, and the new German Reich finally granted Jews the equality they had sought for so long.

Anti-Judaism Spawns Nazi Anti-Semitism

The term "anti-Semitism" purported to explain why Jews should be reviled as a race. Adopting an extreme version of anti-Semitism, Nazi propaganda depicted Jews as both an inferior race and a demonic one, whose threat could only be eradicated by their complete elimination from the Greater Third Reich, envisioned to encompass all of Europe including Great Britain. Admittedly, Nazi racist ideology differed from previous anti-Jewish tradition, but Hitler needed to build on that tradition in order for his virulent brand of racism to gain popular acceptance. Anti-Judaism (based on religion) not only spawned anti-Semitism (based on race), but spawned Nazi anti-Semitism.[140]

Hitler's particularly toxic brand of anti-Semitism, shamelessly laced with religiosity, revealed itself early on. In *Mein Kampf*, for example, he declared that "elimination of Jews from Europe" was his "sacred" mission. Additionally, he wrote, *inter alia*:

> Today, I believe that I am acting in accordance with the will of the Almighty Creator: by defending myself against the Jew, *I am fighting for the work of the Lord.*
>
> What we have to fight for ... is the freedom and independence of the fatherland, so that our people may be enabled to fulfill the mission assigned to it by the Creator.
>
> The founder of Christianity made no secret indeed of his estimation of the Jewish people. When He found it necessary, He drove those enemies of the human race out of the Temple of God.
>
> On the issue of German receptivity to Nazi anti-Semitism, Donald Niewyk, professor emeritus of history at Southern Methodist University, in a study entitled, "German anti-Semitism and the Road to the Final Solution," has written: "For the vast majority of those supporters of (the Nazi regime), for whom the 'Jewish problem' was anything but central, Nazi Jew-baiting seemed nothing dramatically out of the ordinary.

---

140   NB, The Holy See disputes the premise that anti-Judaism spawned anti-Semitism. In its official response to the Holocaust ("We Remember: A Reflection on the Shoah," published in 1998 by the Commission for Religious Relations with Jews), the Holy See asserted, "The Shoah was the work of a thoroughly modern neo-pagan regime. Its anti-Semitism had its roots outside of Christianity ..."

The old anti-Semitism had created a climate in which the 'new anti-Semitism' was, at the very least, acceptable to millions of Germans."

Pope Pius XI

Pope Pius XI (1922–39), born Achille Ratti, succeeded Benedict XV in 1922. As a former librarian and scholar, Pius XI was committed to the advancement of science and learning. His pontificate faced a number of significant problems including: the rise to power of Hitler and Mussolini, the anticlerical fury of the Spanish Civil War (1936–39) that killed thousands of clerics and laypeople, violence against the Church in Mexico, solidification of communist power in the Soviet Union, growth of the Communist Party in France, and anti-Semitic persecutions in various European countries.

In the early years of his pontificate, Pius XI viewed Hitler and Mussolini as defenders against Bolshevism. Not a fan of democracy, he, like his predecessors, believed that authoritarian governments were best suited to deal with societal problems. As dictators consolidated power in Europe, however, he began to see that their totalitarian policies threatened not only the Church, but, by the late 1930s, all humanity as well.

Father Richard P. McBrien enumerates as one accomplishment of Pius XI's pontificate the rehabilitation of a number of the liberal Catholic theologians who had been censured during Pius X's anti-Modernist campaign. Additionally, Pius XI authorized the installation of a radio station (Vatican Radio) in 1931 and was the first pope to use radio as a means of worldwide communication. He founded the Pontifical Academy of Sciences in 1936 and opened its membership rolls to scientists from many countries. Aided by two secretaries of state, Cardinal Pietro Gasparri (until 1930) and Cardinal Eugenio Pacelli (who succeeded him as pope in 1939), Pius XI concluded concordats[141] with twenty governments and improved relations with France. His

141 Concordats granted the Church freedom of practice within signatory countries, permitting it, for example, to organize youth groups; make ecclesiastical appointments; maintain a Catholic press; operate church schools, hospitals, and charities; and conduct religious services without state interference. They also ensured that canon law would be recognized within certain spheres (e.g., the validity of marriages and the status of converts to Catholicism). In return, the Church agreed to refrain from political activity.

most important political initiative was signing the Lateran Treaty[142] in February 1929 with Italy's fascist dictator, Benito Mussolini. By this treaty the Holy See finally recognized the Republic of Italy, almost sixty years after its founding, with Rome as its capital. The Italian government, in turn, compensated the Holy See for loss of the Papal States and recognized Catholicism as the only official state religion of Italy. Anticlerical laws were repealed and religious instruction in secondary schools became mandatory. Vatican City[143] was established as a sovereign city-state, independent of Italy.

A few days after the Lateran Treaty was concluded, Hitler warmly welcomed its signing, declaring:

> The fact that the Curia is now making its peace with Fascism shows that the Vatican trusts the new political realities far more than did the former liberal democracy with which it could not come to terms … The fact that the Church has come to an agreement with Fascist Italy proves beyond doubt that the Fascist world of ideas is closer to Christianity than those of Jewish liberalism or even atheistic Marxism, to which the so-called Catholic Center Party sees itself so closely bound, to the detriment of Christianity today and our German people.

As fascism[144] spread in Europe in the 1920s and '30s, the Holy See, by and large, remained aloof, occasionally challenging fascist ideology

---

142   Pacelli's brother, Francesco, was involved in the negotiation of the Lateran Treaty (1929) which became the model for the Reich Concordat (1933). A precondition of both treaties was dissolution of the Catholic Popular Party in Italy and the Catholic Center Party in Germany, respectively.

143   Vatican City is a landlocked political entity whose territory consists of a walled enclave within the city of Rome. It has an area of approximately 110 acres and a population of just over eight hundred, making it the smallest independent state in the world, both in area and population.

144   Fascism was founded in 1920 in Italy by Benito Mussolini. By the end of 1926, Italy had been transformed into a single-party dictatorial state. Fascist regimes eventually came to power in Germany, Romania, Slovakia, Croatia, Hungary, and Spain, but virtually every European country produced its own fascist political party. These regimes were nationalistic, antidemocratic, antiliberal and anticommunist. Heavily reliant on a cult of personality, no fascist regime survived the death of its founder.

when it impinged on church doctrine and practice or when it threatened the Church's institutional interests, but, for the most part, was unwilling to interfere with secular concerns. The Holy See found most aspects of right-wing regimes agreeable, appreciating their patronage of the Church, their opposition to socialism and communism, and their championing of a conservative (anti-Modernist) social vision. Fascist regimes were embraced as God-sent bulwarks against the socialist evil engulfing Europe. It should be noted that the Church, at that time, was still adhering to its static, classicist worldview and still warring against Modernism.

Opus sacerdotale Amici Israel ("Church Friends of Israel") was an international interfaith organization founded in Rome in February 1926, to pray for the conversion of Jews and to promote a favorable attitude toward them within the Church. An early proposal was that the word *perfidis* ("faithless"), used to describe Jews in the Prayer for the Jews during the Good Friday liturgy, be removed from the prayer. Pius XI was reportedly in favor of the move and asked the Congregation of Rites to review the matter. Traditionalist members of the Curia, however, reacted negatively to the proposal on the ground that if one change was made to the liturgy it would open the door to proposals for other changes. The Congregation for the Doctrine of the Faith, successor of the Holy Inquisition, dissolved *Opus sacerdotale Amici Israel* on March 25, 1928.

Knowledgeable about Nazi ideology, Secretary of State Cardinal Pacelli spoke little publicly about Hitler's racist theories. In 1929, however, Pacelli declared: "Hitler is capable of walking on corpses." In a 1935 speech, two years after Hitler became chancellor, Pacelli described the Nazis as "miserable plagiarists who dress up old errors with new tinsel." He added, "It does not make any difference whether they flock to the banners of the social revolution, whether they are guided by a false conception of the world and of life, or whether they are possessed by the superstition of a race and blood cult." Pacelli, speaking in 1937 to the American consul to Berlin, A. W. Klieforth, said: "Hitler is an untrustworthy scoundrel and fundamentally wicked person." In a report written in 1938 for President Franklin Roosevelt and given to the US ambassador to the Vatican, Joseph Kennedy, Pacelli asserted that the Church regarded compromise with the Third Reich as "out of the question."

In 1932, the Nazis established the Faith Movement of German Christians for the express purpose of encouraging German nationalism/ patriotism and undercutting the influence of the German Protestant Church. A key goal of the organization was to promote anti-Catholicism, anti-Bolshevism, and anti-Semitism. In January 1933, Austrian Bishop Johannes M. Gfollner of Linz wrote a pastoral letter to Catholics of his diocese declaring that it was their duty to adopt a "moral" form of anti-Semitism.

On January 30, 1933, President Paul von Hindenburg, as noted previously, appointed Hitler chancellor of Germany. The Nazis referred to Hitler's appointment as *Machtergreifung* ("seizure of power"). In February 1933, political demonstrations within Germany were banned: "Bloody Sunday" riots erupted in Berlin, leading to the death of one communist and injuries to hundreds of other citizens, including Jews; one hundred members of the Reichstag were arrested; and one Berliner was given fifty lashes for being a communist and fifty more for being a Jew.

Betrayal of the Rule of Law

In 1933, less than a month after he was appointed chancellor, Hitler used the pretext of a fire in the Reichstag building to suspend constitutional law in Germany, aggregating unlimited judicial authority in the new government to himself. After the fire, he proclaimed that certain "temporary" measures were required to stem this tide of terrorism. And who were the terrorists? Communists and Jews, of course. The communists were scapegoated for starting the fire. Accordingly several laws were quickly passed—one, to reform the Civil Service by ridding Jews from the judiciary and from the legal establishment. At first judges protested, but the head of the judicial conference, after meeting with Hitler, assured his fellow jurists that the measure was only temporary, relating: "I've been assured by the Führer that this will go away soon. These laws are necessary because we're living in a time of terror." Thus, according to Sol Wachler, former chief judge of the state of New York, a rare confluence of events caused a highly sophisticated, highly motivated legal and judicial system to become complicit with a totalitarian dictatorship bent on achieving racial purity and territorial conquest. Hitler was given enormous emergency powers, granting him license to do almost anything he wanted, in direct contravention of a democracy. Ten thousand German lawyers and judges thereupon took an oath of personal loyalty to him—the very antithesis of the Rule of Law.[145]

The primary governing procedure of German law during the Third Reich was the so-called Fuehrer Principle, under which Hitler had absolute discretion to make any ruling whatsoever in the interests of the Reich. Subordinate fuehrers (leaders) had wide discretion, limited only by what Der Fuehrer had commanded them to do. Over the next twelve years, the Nazi Party continued its subversion of constitutional safeguards until the German judiciary amounted to nothing more than a tool for the implementation of National Socialism. Early in their subversion of the Rule of Law, Nazi officials established special courts to deal with anyone the party deemed an enemy. In these courts there was no right to due process. Judges determined arbitrarily what evidence to consider. There was no right to cross-examine witnesses, no burden of proof beyond a reasonable doubt or by preponderance of the evidence, and no right of appeal. Once succeeding in concentrating all legal authority into his own hands, Hitler had what he needed to eliminate all perceived enemies of the Reich—Jews and political opponents in particular.

Before the Nazi era, Jewish lawyers and judges constituted a large percentage of Germany's legal community, causing resentment among many of their Christian counterparts. With Hitler's rise to power, however, Jews were forbidden to practice law. Eventually most of them would lose their lives, some by their own hand. A law enacted on April 7, 1933, forbade attorneys of non-Aryan descent from representing Aryan clients. Those who dared to disregard the law faced serious consequences: their names were published in the press, their practices were boycotted, and, eventually, their audacity even became a ground for divorce. Laws aimed at so-called "criminal types" allowed Hitler's courts to condemn enemies of the state, not based on what they had done, but on the sole basis of who they were. Ethnicity and race, in short, became status crimes. In 1934, the People's Court was established

---

145   See www.thirteen.org/openmind/history/hitlers-courts-betrayal-of-the-rule -of-law-in-nazi-germany-one-hour-special/1814/, Richard Heffner's interview of Sol Wachler, former chief judge of the state of New York entitled, "Hitler's Court: Betrayal of the Rule of Law in Nazi Germany," produced by Thirteen @2012 WNET.

to try defendants accused of political offenses. Eventually the court came under the presidency of Roland Friesler, an extremist who shocked even his fellow judges. Carl Schmidt, Hitler's legal theorist, described the Führer as Germany's "guardian of justice." Erwin Bumke, who drafted Hitler's emergency laws, and other senior officials of Hitler's courts empowered police to disband organizations, seize assets, make arrests, and determine on their own initiative what constituted a threat to the state.

The Nuremberg Laws of 1935 would reflect Nazi preoccupation with racial purity. Since Jews were defined as racially impure, marriage between Jews and non-Jews defiled the Aryan race and, therefore, was forbidden. Resourceful judges found other applications for the Nuremberg Laws by arguing, for example, that because Jews were no longer considered full human beings, they did not qualify for legal rights. Jews and other targeted minorities underwent civil death long before millions of them met physical death in the camps. During *Kristallnacht* in November 1938, thousands of Jewish men—nearly all the lawyers, former judges, prosecutors, and physicians remaining in Germany—would be arrested and dragged off to concentration camps. With the invasion of Poland and declaration of war in September 1939, Nazi lawmakers moved into high gear as thousands of so-called enemies of the Reich were arrested and tried in Hitler's courts. By 1939, roughly 60 percent of all law school professors were Nazi appointees engaged in training a new generation of lawyers and lawmakers, young zealots raised and educated under Nazi rule. And if some of this new generation harbored misgivings about the justice system in Germany, hardly any ever dared question the Nazi distortion of the Rule of Law.

In 1934, Dr. Lothar Kreyssig, a judge on the court in Brandenberg, objected to Hitler's euthanasia program and even attempted to prosecute Nazi officers for sending hospital patients to their death. Because he had been a respected jurist, he was encouraged to retire early. But such leniency was extremely rare. Dr. Johan von Donyanyi, at thirty-six the youngest member of the German Supreme Court, also dared to speak out against Nazi injustice, for which he was arrested and later executed. Sadly, the overwhelming majority of Germany's legal community cooperated with the Nazi regime. Postwar statistics estimate that by 1945 the number of death sentences handed down by Germany's various courts had exceeded fifty thousand, more than 80 percent of which were carried out.

Yet another blow to the Rule of Law would take place in September 1942, when the Reich Ministry of Justice empowered the SS to change any court decision it deemed overly lenient. Thousands of prisoners would be delivered to the SS at that time for summary execution. Moreover, lawyers accounted for more than half the participants at the January 1942 Wannsee Conference that promulgated the Final Solution. Reinhard Heydrich, who hosted the conference, was one of the cruelest mass murderers in Nazi Germany. Nicknamed the "Hangman," Heydrich said he was surprised that the lawyers and judges sitting around that table went along with other participants without raising any objection whatsoever, but by then, clearly, there was no justice in Germany. It had been perverted beyond recognition.

Minimizing the Jewish, and Christian, Threat

According to the census of June 1933, the Jewish population of Germany, including the Saar region (which at that time was still under the administration of the League of Nations), was approximately 505,000 out of a total population of 67 million, or somewhat less than 0.75 percent. That number represented a reduction from the estimated 525,000 Jews living in Germany in January 1933, the decrease due, in large part, to voluntary emigration after the Nazi takeover in January of that year. An estimated thirty-seven thousand Jews emigrated out of Germany by December 31, 1933. About 70 percent of German Jews lived in urban areas, with 50 percent living in the ten largest German cities. The largest Jewish population center was in Berlin (about 160,000 in 1925), representing less than 4 percent of the city's population. Jews were disproportionately represented in the German professions, particularly in higher education, law, the judiciary, and medicine, and in German business holdings, which, predictably, caused resentment within the far larger Christian population.

In a February 1933 speech to the Reichstag, Hitler, attempting to reassure skeptics of his religious bona fides, declared: "The churches will be an integral part of German national life ... The National Government will preserve and defend those basic principles on which our nation has been built up. It regards Christianity as the foundation of our national morality and the family as the basis of national life."

Despite his claim that churches would be foundational to German society, Hitler, nonetheless, viewed them as threats to National Socialism and fully intended to eliminate conventional churches from the Greater Third Reich. He planned to replace them with a Nazified Aryan Church, as defined and espoused by Hitler's theologians. This Nazified Aryan Church would embody the "positive Christianity"[146] of the Nazi Party platform. Ironically, what church leaders feared would happen if the Bolsheviks prevailed in Europe—namely, elimination of traditional churches from European society—undoubtedly would have happened if Hitler had won WWII.

Hitler's Religiosity

As demonstrated over and over again during his political career, Hitler, despite being thoroughly amoral, cloaked his writings and rhetoric with religiosity, knowing full well that doing so would resonate with Christians, German and non-German alike. Early in his career, beginning in April 1922, for example, he proclaimed:

> My feeling as a Christian points me to my Lord and Savior as a fighter. It points me to the man who once in loneliness, surrounded only by a few followers, recognized these Jews for what they were and summoned men to fight against them and who—God's truth!—was greatest, not as a sufferer, but as a fighter.
>
> Today, after two thousand years, with deepest emotion I recognize more profoundly than ever before the fact that it was for this that He had to shed his blood upon the Cross.
>
> As a Christian I have no duty to allow myself to be cheated, but I have the duty to be a fighter for truth and justice. And if there is anything which could demonstrate that we are acting

146 *Bekennende Kirche,* the "Confessing Church" (also translated "Confessional Church"), was a Protestant schismatic church that arose in opposition to government-sponsored efforts to Nazify the German Protestant church. The Confessing Church's opposition, however, was directed at the regime's ecclesiastical policy, not at its overall political and social objectives. Martin Niemoeller and Karl Barth were prominent members. A tenet of the Confessing Church was that "unquestioning obedience to the Third Reich was not compatible with the Christian faith."

rightly, it is the distress that daily grows. For as a Christian I have also a duty to my own people. And when I look on my people I see them work and work and toil and labor, and at the end of the week they have only for their wages wretchedness and misery.

In *Mein Kampf,* Hitler wrote:

I believe today that my conduct is in accordance with the will of the Almighty Creator.

What we have to fight for ... is the freedom and independence of the fatherland, so that our people may be enabled to fulfill the mission assigned to it by the Creator.

This human world of ours would be inconceivable without the practical existence of a religious belief.

And the founder of Christianity made no secret indeed of his estimation of the Jewish people. When He found it necessary, He drove those enemies of the human race out of the Temple of God.

In speeches, he said:

The National Government regards the two Christian confessions as factors essential to the soul of the German people. It will respect the contracts they have made with the various regions. It declares its determination to leave their rights intact. In the schools, the government will protect the rightful influence of the Christian bodies. We hold the spiritual forces of Christianity to be indispensable elements in the moral uplift of most of the German people. We hope to develop friendly relations with the Holy See.

The Government of the Reich regards Christianity as the unshakable foundation of the morals and moral code of the nation ... The rights of the churches will not be diminished.

National Socialism has always affirmed that it is determined to take the Christian Churches under the protection of the State. For their part the churches cannot for a second doubt that they need the protection of the State, and that only through the State can they be enabled to fulfill their religious mission. Indeed, the churches demand this protection from the State.

The Church's interests cannot fail to coincide with ours alike in our fight against the symptoms of degeneracy in the world of today, in our fight against the Bolshevist culture, against an atheistic movement, against criminality, and in our struggle for the consciousness of a community in our national life, for the conquest of hatred and disunion between the classes, for the conquest of civil war and unrest, of strife and discord. These are not anti-Christian, these are Christian principles.

I believe today that I am acting in the sense of the Almighty Creator. By warding off the Jews, I am fighting for the Lord's work.

Providence has caused me to be Catholic, and I know, therefore, how to handle this Church.

I believe that it was God's will to send a youth from here into the Reich, to let him grow up, to raise him to be the leader of the nation so as to enable him to lead back his homeland into the Reich. In three days the Lord has smitten them. And to me the grace was given on the day of the betrayal to be able to unite my homeland (Austria) with the Reich. I would now give thanks to Him who let me return to my homeland in order than I might now lead it into my German Reich. Tomorrow, may every German recognize the hour, and measure its import and bow in humility before the Almighty who in a few weeks has wrought a miracle upon us.

Impressed with the organization of the Papacy, Hitler was quoted as saying: "I learned much from the Order of the Jesuits; until now there has never been anything more grandiose on the earth than the hierarchical organization of the Catholic Church. I transferred much of this organization into my own party."[147]

---

147   Hermann Rauschning, *Hitler Said to Me*, 266–67.

CHAPTER 6

The Third Reich and the Church

THE REICHSTAG FIRE OF FEBRUARY 27, 1933, as noted previously, proved pivotal to Hitler's seizure of totalitarian control. On March 23, at Hitler's insistence, the Reichstag passed *Ermächtigungsgesetz*, the "Enabling Act," which gave him absolute power in Germany. The legislation, among other things, outlawed the German Communist Party, which he blamed for starting the fire. With the Enabling Act's passage, the Weimar Republic died, and the Third Reich was born. On March 27, Dachau, the first concentration camp, was opened only a few miles outside Munich in predominately Catholic Bavaria. By the end of 1944, the Nazis would build more than one thousand concentration camps in Germany and Occupied Europe.

In April 1933, little more than two months after his appointment as chancellor, Hitler met with two German Catholic clergymen, Bishop Hermann Wilhelm Berning of Osnabruck and Monsignor Wilhelm Steinman, advising them that his Jewish policy would mirror the Church's treatment of Jews over the centuries. To illustrate, he reminded them that the Church regarded Jews as dangerous and confined them in ghettos. He then boasted that his Jewish measures would do Christianity a great service. Bishop Berning and Monsignor Steinmann later described their discussion with him as cordial and to the point.

With its state-sponsored boycott of Jewish businesses in April 1933, the Third Reich began to systematically implement its Jewish policy. Throughout Germany, storm troopers, the *Sturmabteilung* (a.k.a.

"brown shirts," former specialist soldiers of the German army in WWI), and members of the SS, the *Schutzstaffel* ("Protection Squadron"), posted signs that read, "Don't Buy from Jews" and "The Jews Are Our Misfortune." They smeared the word *Jude* ("Jew") and painted the Star of David in yellow and black across thousands of doors and windows. Thugs stood menacingly in front of the offices of Jewish lawyers and doctors and at the entrances of Jewish-owned businesses. Passersby were discouraged from entering, while Jews were publically humiliated, harassed, beaten, and arrested.

Defending his refusal to condemn the boycott, Michael von Faulhaber, cardinal-archbishop of Munich, declared that it is: "a matter of economics, of measures directed against an interest group that has no very close bond with the Church." In a letter addressed to Secretary of State Cardinal Pacelli, Faulhaber wrote: "We bishops are being asked why the Catholic Church, as often in its history, does not intervene on behalf of the Jews. This is not possible at this time because the struggle against the Jews would then, at the same time, become a struggle against the Catholics, and because the Jews can help themselves, as the sudden end of the boycott shows."

Archbishop Faulhaber in 1933 resisted assaults on Hebrew scripture then being made by Hitler's theologians; he was careful, however, to explain that his concern was only with the "Israel of biblical antiquity," not Jews alive in his own day. His secretary added that the archbishop "had not taken a position with regard to the Jewish question of today." During a homily in 1937, Faulhaber boasted about the extent to which the Church had legitimized Nazism:

> At a time when the heads of the major nations in the world faced the new Germany with cool reserve and considerable suspicion, the Catholic Church, the *"greatest moral power on earth,"* through the Reich Concordat expressed its confidence in the new German government. This was a deed of immeasurable significance for the reputation of the government abroad. (emphasis mine)

Ironically, Faulhaber also asserted: "History teaches us that God always punished tormenters of ... the Jews. No Roman Catholic approves of the persecutions of Jews in Germany."

Sister Edith Stein

Edith Stein, a German Jewish convert to Catholicism, born into an observant Jewish family but an atheist by her teenage years, was baptized on January 1, 1922, and was received into the Discalced Carmelite Order as a postulant in 1934. Although the order relocated her out of Germany to the Netherlands to avoid Nazi persecution, Sister Teresia Benedicta (Edith Stein's monastic name) in 1942 was arrested, along with other Jews from the Netherlands, including Anne Frank, and sent to Auschwitz-Birkenau, where she died in a gas chamber. She was canonized as Saint Teresia Benedicta of the Cross by Pope John Paul II in 1998. In April 1933 (during Holy Week), she wrote a prophetic letter to Pope Pius XI,[148] in which she denounced the Nazi regime and asked him to denounce the regime as well, "to put a stop to this abuse of Christ's name." She wrote:

Holy Father! As a child of the Jewish people who, by the grace of God, for the past eleven years has also been a child of the Catholic Church, I dare to speak to the Father of Christianity about that which oppresses millions of Germans. For weeks we have seen deeds perpetrated in Germany which mock any sense of justice and humanity, not to mention love of neighbor. For years the leaders of National Socialism have been preaching hatred of the Jews. Now that they have seized the power of government and armed their followers, among them proven criminal elements, this seed of hatred has germinated.

But through boycott measures—by robbing people of their livelihood, civic honor, and fatherland—it drives many to desperation; within the last week, through private reports I was informed of five cases of suicide as a consequence of these hostilities. I am convinced that this is a general condition which will claim many more victims. One may regret that these unhappy people do not have greater inner strengthen to bear their misfortune. But the responsibility must fall, after all, on

---

148   See www.baltimorecarmel.org/saints/Stein/letter%20to%20pope.htm, letter of Saint Edith Stein to Pope Pius XI in 1933.

those who brought them to this point and it also falls on those who keep silent in the face of such happenings.

Everything that happened and continues to happen on a daily basis originates with a government that calls itself "Christian." For weeks not only Jews but also thousands of faithful Catholics in Germany, and, I believe, all over the world, have been waiting and hoping for the Church of Christ to raise its voice to stop this abuse of Christ's name. Is not this idolization of race and governmental power which is being pounded into the public consciousness by the radio open heresy? Isn't the effort to destroy Jewish blood an abuse of the holiest humanity of our Savior, of the most blessed Virgin and the apostles? Is not all this diametrically opposed to the conduct of our Lord and Savior, who, even on the cross, still prayed for his persecutors? And isn't this a black mark on the record of this Holy Year which was intended to be a year of peace and reconciliation?

We all, who are faithful children of the Church and who see the conditions in Germany with open eyes, fear the worst for the prestige of the Church, if the silence continues any longer. We are convinced that his silence will not be able in the long run to purchase peace with the present German government. For the time being, the fight against Catholicism will be conducted quietly and less brutally than against Jewry, but no less systematically. It won't take long before no Catholic will be able to hold office in Germany unless he dedicates himself unconditionally to the new course of action … (Signed) Dr. Edith Stein

Edith Stein's letter was written as the Reich Concordat was being negotiated by Eugenio Pacelli and Vice Chancellor Franz Von Papen. The Concordat was signed in July 1933. Her letter received no official reply from the Vatican, and it not known for certain whether Pius XI ever read it. Secretary of State Cardinal Pacelli, however, wrote a reply in German on the pope's behalf and sent it to Edith Stein's abbess, stating:

With special thanks I have confirmed to Your Grace (the abbess) the reception of your kind letter of April 12 and the attached document (Edith Stein's letter). I leave it to you to inform the sender (Edith Stein) in an opportune way that her letter has been dutifully presented to His Holiness (Pope Pius XI). With you, I pray to God that in these difficult times (God) may, in a special way, protect His Holy Church and grant all the children of the Church the grace of fortitude, and generous mentality, which are the presuppositions of our final victory. With the expression of my special estimation, and with my intimate wishes for the entire Archabbey, I am, Your Grace (the abbess), very devotedly, Eugenio Pacelli.

When Edith Stein was beatified in Cologne on May 1, 1987, the Church honored "a daughter of Israel," said Pope John Paul II, "who, as a Catholic during Nazi persecution, remained faithful to the crucified Lord Jesus Christ and, as a Jew, to her people in loving faithfulness." Although canonized a saint, she died a Jewish martyr, not a Christian one.

In May 1933, the Reich banned labor unions and similar associations. In July, the Nazis outlawed all political parties except the National Social Workers' Party. When President Hindenburg died in August 1934, the offices of president and chancellor were consolidated and Hitler assumed both. He assumed the title *Der Führer* ("The Leader") of the Nazi party and of Germany.

Book Burning

On the night of May 10, 1933, in *Opernplatz* ("Opera House Square") across from Humboldt University in Berlin, brown-shirted Nazi students and their professors burned more than twenty thousand books by Jewish and "Jewish inspired" authors. It was not an isolated incident; book burners in thirty other university towns purged "un-German" writings from libraries and shops, setting them on fire. They torched works by Albert Einstein, John Dos Passos, Thomas Mann, Karl Marx, Ernest Hemingway, Upton Sinclair, Emile Zola, H. G. Wells, Sigmund Freud, Helen Keller, Marcel Proust, Jack London, and Erich Maria Remarque, along with books by German poet Heinrich Heine who in 1820, prophetically, wrote: "Where books are burned, in the end people will be burned." Enthusiastic crowds witnessed the burnings, launched with torchlight parades and rousing speeches proclaiming the death of Jewish intellectualism and the purification of German culture.

Seven days later, Nazi opponents presented the Bernheim Petition (named for an imprisoned Silesian Jew named Franz Bernheim) to the League of Nations to protest German anti-Jewish legislation. In Norway, Vidkun Quisling established the Norwegian Fascist Party as well as the *Hirdmen* ("King's Men"), a collaborationist organization modeled on the Nazi storm troopers. On June 26, 1933, the *Akademie fur Deutsches Recht* ("Academy for German Law") was founded to rewrite the entire corpus of German law according to Nazi Party specifications.

On July 1, 1933, Reich authorities declared: "Reich Chancellor Hitler still belongs to the Catholic Church and has no intention of leaving it." Also on that day, the *Friedensbund deutscher Katholiken* ("German Catholic Peace Union"), founded by Father Franziskus Stratmann, OP, with a membership of over forty thousand, was officially dissolved by the Nazis. With its leadership scattered or imprisoned, its records confiscated or destroyed, the German Catholic Peace Union, a strong advocate for conscientious objection to participation in war, disappeared from the scene, leaving no trace.

The Reich Concordat between the Holy See and Nazi Germany was signed on July 20, 1933, only six months after Hitler's ascent to power. At the time, approximately thirty thousand people were interned in German concentration camps.

Communicating with Vatican Secretary of State Cardinal Pacelli in 1933, James McDonald, the League of Nations' high commissioner for refugees, raised the issue with Pacelli of Nazi mistreatment of Jews in the mineral-rich Saar region, a former borderline territory of Germany but at the time a Treaty of Versailles protectorate administered by France. McDonald wanted to help Jewish refugees from that region. Pius XII's defenders cite the future pope's intercession on behalf of these refugees as evidence of Pacelli's sympathy for their plight. According to McDonald, however, when he discussed the matter with Pacelli, "The response was noncommittal, but left me with the definite impression that no vigorous cooperation could be expected." Pacelli did intercede in January 1935, on their behalf, but only on condition that the US State Department encourage certain prominent American Jews to use their influence in Washington to pressure the Mexican government to not carry out its threat to confiscate church property in Mexico.

Outside the Circle of Vatican Concern

On September 2, 1933, Adolf Bertram, bishop of Breslau, wrote a letter to Cardinal Pacelli requesting that he intervene with Reich authorities on behalf of Jewish converts to Catholicism. Bishop Bertram wrote: "Will it be possible for the Holy See to put in a warm-hearted word for those who have been converted from Judaism to the Christian religion, since either they themselves, or their children or grandchildren, are now facing a wretched fate because of their lack of Aryan descent?"

Pacelli agreed to do so. His letter in defense of "non-Aryan Catholics" was careful to acknowledge, however, that the Holy See's concern was not with the fate of other non-Aryans (i.e., Jews). The letter began: "The Holy See (has) no intention of interfering in Germany's internal affairs." That is to say, the Holy See recognizes that the fate of non-Aryans is a matter *"outside the circle of Vatican concern"* (emphasis mine), with one exception:

> The Holy See takes this occasion, Pacelli wrote, to add a word in behalf of those German Catholics who themselves have gone over from Judaism to the Christian religion, or who are descended in the first generation, or more remotely from Jews who adopted the Catholic faith, and who, for reasons known to the Reich government, are likewise suffering from social and economic difficulties. (e.g., Sister Edith Stein)

The phrase (the fate of non-Aryans is a matter) "outside the circle of Vatican concern" in retrospect assumes portentous and unintended consequence.

Hitler's Theologians

Professor Robert Ericksen of Pacific Lutheran University terms three German Christian scholars—Paul Althaus, Gerhard Kittel, and Emanuel Hirsch—"Hitler's Theologians."

Althaus, author of *The German Hour of the Churches*, referred to Hitler's rise to power as "a gift and miracle of God"; to 1933 as "the year of Grace, an Easter moment"; and to Nazi Germany as "the new Israel."

Favorably comparing Hitler to Martin Luther and to Jesus himself, Althaus advocated that German Christians become "Nationalistic Christians," congregants of a new Nazified "Reich Church," the *Deutsche Christen* ("German Christian") Church.

Kittel, editor of the *Theological Dictionary of the New Testament*, was an apologist for anti-Semitism. He argued that Judaism and Christianity were perverted by Modernism and secularism and advocated for removal of Jews from German society because, among other reasons, their "over representation" in the professions was a threat to societal well-being. Kittel distinguished Old Testament ancient Jews, who were good, from modern secular Jews, who were evil. Persecution of modern secular Jews, therefore, was justifiable. He blamed liberals for the Jewish problem because they tolerated Jews.

Hirsch, dean of theology at Goettingen University, viewed the advent of Nazism as Germany's "rebirth as a nation," and the "sunrise of divine goodness." He compared the new German society to the "resurrection of Christ." His theology integrated the romantic concept of the German Volk with Christianity.

Nazi Racial Policy

Racial policy in Germany proceeded incrementally in five phases. The first phase, from 1933 to 1935, initiated legal discrimination against Jews. The second phase, 1935 to 1938, was characterized by passage of the Nuremberg Laws of 1935 that further legitimized discrimination and institutionalized racial profiling. Nazi race policy in these years focused on *Entjudung*, pressuring Jews to emigrate from Germany. A third, more violent and sinister, phase started with *Kristallnacht* in November 1938. The fourth phase began in 1939 with Germany's unprovoked invasion of Poland and the beginning of WWII. In 1941, the Nazis and their allies forced Jews in the East to live in many hundreds of inner-city ghettos. The final and most diabolical phase began in 1942 as ghettos were liquidated and their inhabitants—men, women, children, and babies—transported to killing camps, where industrialized mass murder took place.

Foundation Stone of the Holocaust

On July 20, 1933, only six months after Hitler became chancellor of Germany, Secretary of State Cardinal Pacelli, on behalf of Pius XI, signed the Reich Concordat with Vice Chancellor Franz Von Papen, also a Roman

Catholic. Von Papen assured Pacelli that the rights of the Church in the Third Reich would be respected. Although Pius XI and Pacelli were skeptical of that assurance, believing that Hitler might violate certain provisions of the Concordat, they hoped that the agreement, on balance, would stabilize the Church's position in Germany, restoring it to the more favorable status it enjoyed before the onset of WWI, particularly from 1878 to 1890. According to Carroll, Hitler prized the Vatican's endorsement because it established his legitimacy at home and abroad:

> In these early months of 1933, Catholic leaders went from being Hitler's staunch opponents to his latest allies. This transformation was dramatically symbolized by the fact that, in 1932, the Fulda Episcopal Conference, representing the Catholic hierarchy of Germany, banned membership in the Nazi Party and forbade priests from offering communion to anyone wearing the swastika; then, on March 28, 1933, two weeks after Pacelli offered his overture to Hitler, the same Fulda conferees voted to lift the ban on Catholic membership in the Nazi Party. The bishops expressed, as they put it, "a certain confidence in the new government, subject to reservations concerning some religious and moral lapses.[149]

Pacelli would later express regret for signing the Concordat, but at the time he was quoted in *L'Osservatore Romano* as saying that it was "a triumph for canon law and a victory for the Holy See" and that he had been seeking such a concordat with Germany for years. In June 1941, Pacelli, by then Pius XII, commenting in a letter to the bishop of Passau on the regime's continuing violations of the Reich Concordat wrote: "The history of the Reichskonkordat shows that the other side lacked the most basic prerequisites to accept minimal freedoms and rights of the Church, without which the Church simply cannot live and operate, formal agreements notwithstanding."

Hitler, an astute politician, was well aware of the Reich Concordat's symbolic value. In a letter dated July 23, 1933, he wrote: "The fact that the Vatican is concluding a treaty with the new Germany means the acknowledgement of the National Socialist state by the Catholic Church. This treaty shows the whole world clearly and unequivocally

149   Carroll, *Constantine's Sword*, 498.

that the assertion that National Socialism is hostile to religion is a lie."

John Cornwell relates that at a meeting with his ministers after its signing, Hitler listed the advantages of the Concordat and emphasized, in particular: Vatican recognition of the one nationalist German state, and the banning of Catholics from membership in political organizations. Moreover, Hitler asserted, the disbanding of the Catholic Center Party could be regarded as final. Hitler opined that the Concordat had created an atmosphere of confidence that would be *especially significant in the urgent struggle against international Jewry."*[150] (emphasis mine)

Demise of the Catholic Center Party

In his New Year's message on January 1, 1934, following abolition of the liberal Catholic Center Party, Hitler declared:

> While we destroyed the (Catholic) Center Party, we have not only brought thousands of priests back into the Church, but to millions of respectable people we have restored their faith in their religion and in their priests. The union of the Evangelical Church in a single Church for the whole Reich (the Deutsche Christen Church), the Concordat with the Catholic Church, these are but milestones on the road which leads to the establishment of a useful relation and a useful cooperation between the Reich and the two Confessions.
>
> I know that here and there the objection has been raised: Yes, but you have deserted Christianity. No, it is not that we have deserted Christianity; it is those who came before us who deserted Christianity. We have only carried through a clear division between politics, which has to do with terrestrial things, and religion, which must concern itself with the celestial sphere. There has been no interference with the doctrine of the Confessions or with their religious freedom, nor will there be any such interference. On the contrary the State protects religion, though always on the one condition that religion will not be used as a cover for political ends.

---

150   John Cornwell, *Hitler's Pope*, 152.

There may have been a time when even parties founded on the ecclesiastical basis were a necessity. At that time Liberalism was opposed to the Church, while Marxism was anti-religious. But that time is past. National Socialism neither opposes the church, nor is it anti-religious, but on the contrary, it stands on the ground of a real Christianity.

Clergy Loyalty Oath

Article 16 of the Reich Concordat required Catholic bishops and priests to swear an oath of allegiance to the Third Reich. It read:

> Before bishops take possession of their dioceses they are to take an oath of fealty either to the Reich Representative of the State concerned, or to the President of the Reich, according to the following formula: "Before God and on the Holy Gospels I swear and promise as becomes a bishop, loyalty to the German Reich and to the [regional] State of ... I swear and promise to honor the legally constituted Government and to cause the clergy of my diocese to honor it. In the performance of my spiritual office and in my solicitude for the welfare and the interests of the German Reich, I will endeavor to avoid all detrimental acts which might endanger it."

As the Reich subsidized church functions in Nazi Germany, priests were subject not only to their diocesan bishop's authority, but, as civil servants, were subject to Reich authority as well. Accordingly, when it was ordered in July 1933 that all civil servants were required to offer the *Seig Heil* ("Heil Hitler") salute, priests and bishops were also required to comply. It should be noted that anti-Judaism, the clergy loyalty oath, the Reich Concordat, and the Vatican's policy of neutrality during WWII, coupled with church leaders' own feelings of nationalism/patriotism and fear of Bolshevism, constrained them from speaking out against escalating evil in the Third Reich—an unintended consequence.

The Reich Concordat,[151] patterned after the Lateran Treaty of 1929, was one of four concordats Pacelli concluded with various German

---

151   Pius defender Jose M. Sanchez terms the Reich Concordat a "pragmatic and morally defensible measure to protect German Catholics and the relative freedom of the Catholic Church in Germany." See Sanchez, *Pius XII and the Holocaust: Understanding the Controversy.*

states. State concordats were necessary because the Weimar constitution gave authority to states in matters of education and culture, thereby diminishing church influence in these areas. The Reich Concordat granted freedom of religious practice to German Catholics and granted to the German Catholic Church, among other things, freedom to operate parochial schools, religious associations, and a Catholic press, without state interference. In return, the Church agreed not to interfere in political matters, which, in effect, banned organized Catholic political activity in the Third Reich. Pius's critics contend that by entering the Concordat, the Church granted German Catholics its imprimatur to cooperate with the new regime, and even to join the Nazi party.[152]

John Cornwell contends that Pacelli's primary interest in negotiating the Concordat was to advance the Church's institutional interests, in general, and to enhance papal power, in particular. Cornwell further contends that by entering the Concordat, the Church imposed a moral duty on Catholics to obey their Nazi rulers. He described the Concordat's effect:

> Seeking a concordat between the Reich and the Vatican, Pacelli betrayed the millions of Catholic supporters of the Catholic Center Party by signing an agreement with Hitler that resulted in a ban on political activity by members of the church. It was the only democratic party left in Germany and with its disbanding, Hitler became the supreme leader of the country. Nothing stood in his way; the Vatican had even become the first state to recognize his odious regime, giving it tacit approval by its Reich Concordat.[153]

Regarding Vatican concordats, Heinrich Bruning, Hitler's predecessor as chancellor (1930–32) wrote in his diary: "All success (Pacelli believed) could only be attained by papal diplomacy. The system of concordats led him and the Vatican to despise democracy and the

---

152 Prior to 1933, some German clerics warned the faithful against Nazi racism. In certain dioceses Catholics were forbidden to join the Nazi party; some priests and bishops even refused to administer the sacraments to party members (excommunication). Relatively few Catholics voted for Hitler or Nazi party candidates during parliamentary elections between 1930 and 1933.

153 Cornwell, *Hitler's Pope*, 162.

parliamentary system ... Rigid governments, rigid centralization, and rigid treaties were supposed to introduce an era of stable order, an era of peace and quiet."

Pius's critics, John Cornwell and James Carroll among them, speculate that if the liberal Catholic Center Party had continued to exist in Germany, Hitler's rise to absolute power might have been delayed or, perhaps, even prevented. Additionally, Cornwell charges that the Concordat ensured that whatever Catholic resistance to Nazism arose would be "isolated and impotent"; and thus the way was clearer for the Nazi regime to pursue, unfettered, its racist policies and virtual conquest of Europe. The Concordat for Hitler was a diplomatic and strategic victory. It made him, in the colorful language of the German term, *"salonfähig"* ("fit for association with decent people").

James Carroll, as noted previously, argues that, in the 1870s, Pius IX ordered German Catholics to passively resist antichurch legislation enacted during *Kulturkampf* and threatened to excommunicate any Catholic who obeyed it. On that occasion, Carroll continues, the German Catholic Church not only survived the threat to its institutional interests, but prospered in newly unified Germany. Therefore, in negotiating and signing the Concordat, Carroll charges, the future Pius XII capitulated to Hitler, and thereby enabled Nazism to rise unopposed by "the most powerful Catholic community in the world." Carroll concludes that Pacelli elevated Catholic institutional self-interest above Catholic conscience, acting more like a politician than a prophet.

Race Attestation

The "Law for Preventing Overcrowding in German Schools and Schools of Higher Education," which took effect[154] on April 25, 1933, two months after Hitler's ascent to power, became a vehicle for German Catholic complicity in the Holocaust. The law required thousands of priests across Germany to disclose blood purity details from marriage and baptismal registries in order to implement a quota system for restricting Jewish access to German schools and universities, and entry of Jews into the medical and legal professions. After passage of the Nuremberg Laws in 1935, attestation information would be used to ensure that only German citizens who could prove their Aryan lineage would hold civil service positions.

---

154   Similar extralegal discrimination against Jews by imposition of quotas to universities also existed in the United States and other countries.

Attestation compliance, which continued until the Third Reich collapsed in 1945, connected the Catholic and Protestant churches with the death camps, according to Daniel Jonah Goldhagen, author of *Hitler's Willing Executioner*—another unintended consequence. Regarding clergy race attestation, Guenter Lewy has written:

> The Church cooperated as a matter of course, complaining only that priests already overburdened with work were not receiving compensation for this special service to the state. The very question of whether the Church should lend its help to the Nazi state in sorting out people of Jewish descent was never debated … And the cooperation of the Church in this matter continued right through the war years (i.e., from 1939 through 1945), when the price of being Jewish was no longer dismissal from a government job and loss of livelihood, but deportation and outright physical destruction.[155]

On January 26, 1934, Germany and Poland signed a ten-year nonaggression pact, which Hitler would flagrantly violate on September 1, 1939, when Germany invaded Poland. On January 30, 1934, Hitler declared publicly that Germany would not be deterred from rearming militarily, even though it would violate the Versailles Treaty. On February 17, Britain, France, and Italy warned that Austria's independence must be maintained inviolate. In April 1934, the Reich established *Volksgericht* ("People's Court") to deal with enemies of the state. On April 7, several thousand Americans attended a pro-Nazi rally in Queens, New York. And on October 1, 1934, Hitler secretly ordered a rapid buildup of the army and navy, and creation of an air force, the *Luftwaffe*.

Also in 1934, Hitler approved for publication "Twenty-Five Points of the German Religion," written by Nazi ideologue Ernst Bergmann. It asserted, among other things, that Christ was not a Jew but a Nordic warrior put to death by Jews whose death spared the world from Jewish domination and that Adolf Hitler was the new messiah sent to earth to save the world from Jews and Bolsheviks. For his most ardent followers, that Hitler would survive forty-two assassination attempts served to bolster his aura of invincibility and divine favor. On May 1, 1934, the

---

155   Guenter Lewy, *The Catholic Church and Nazi Germany*, 282.

widely read Nazi weekly newspaper *Der Stürmer* ("The Stormer," or, more accurately, "The Attacker"), published by rabid anti-Semite Julius Streicher, reminded readers that throughout history Jews had been guilty of committing ritual murder of Christian children and using their blood for religious rituals. That and similar lies were repeated over and over again in every form of media, including movies[156] and radio. Pervasive and repeated use of blatantly false and manipulative propaganda by the Nazis would be largely responsible for the word "propaganda" acquiring a negative connotation.

On March 16, 1935, Germany initiated military conscription, another violation of the Versailles Treaty, but once again there was no public protest from the governments of France, Britain, or the United States. In a sermon on August 25, Lutheran Pastor Martin Niemoller, a leading Protestant anti-Nazi, declared that Jewish history is "dark and sinister" and that the Jewish people are forever "under a curse" because they not only "brought the Christ of God to the cross" but they also bear the responsibility for the "blood of all the righteous men who were ever murdered."

The Nuremberg Laws

In September 1935, two measures were announced at the annual Nazi Party Rally in Nuremberg, which would become the Nuremberg Laws. The first, "Law for the Protection of German Blood and German Honor," prohibited marriages and extramarital intercourse between Jews (the name now officially used in place of "non-Aryans") and Germans, prohibited employment of German females under forty-five in Jewish households, and authorized the forced sterilization of the unfit, *lebensunwertes leben* ("life unworthy of life"). The second, "The Reich Citizenship Law," stripped Jews of their German citizenship and introduced a new distinction between "Reich citizens" and "nationals." The Nuremberg Laws formalized the unofficial measures taken by the Reich against Jews up to 1935. Nazi leaders made a point of stressing the consistency of the legislation with the party's platform demanding that Jews be deprived of their right to live in new Germany. Neither the Holy See nor the German Catholic Church protested the Nuremberg Laws.

---

156   Two especially popular movies vilifying Jews were *Eternal Jew* and *Jud Suss* (A Jew named Suss).

In November 1935, German Protestant churches also began to collaborate with the Nazis by supplying information from their church records—to be used to differentiate Jews from non-Jews.

On March 7, 1936, in defiance of the Versailles Treaty and other international agreements, German troops entered and occupied the Rhineland, a region on both banks of the Rhine River in central Europe. Although publicly denouncing the incursion, the governments of France, Britain, and the United States, nonetheless, capitulated to Hitler, in yet another attempt to appease him. This latest attempt at appeasement would only encourage Hitler to engage in further provocations in Europe. On March 9, 1936, Jews were injured and killed during a pogrom in Przytyk, Poland. In April 1936, French conservatives condemned French Socialist leader Leon Blum because of his Jewish ancestry and anti-Nazi orientation. A popular slogan at the time disparaged the future premier of France: "Better Hitler than Blum." On July 3, 1936, Stefan Lux, a German Jew, killed himself in the assembly room of the League of Nations in Geneva, Switzerland, to protest persecution of German Jews. In 1936, Jewish teachers were banned from teaching Aryan children.

Mit brennender Sorge
Between 1933 and 1936, the Holy See lodged thirty-four official protests regarding violations of the Reich Concordat, most of which went unanswered. Pius XI considered terminating the Concordat, but, critics contend, Secretary of State Pacelli and other prominent members of the Curia, who feared the impact of such an action on German Catholics, dissuaded him from doing so. After the war, Pacelli would acknowledge his role in convincing Pius XI not to terminate the Concordat. Finally, in 1937, Pius XI issued *Mit brennender Sorge* ("With Searing Anxiety"), his encyclical denouncing the violations and condemning Nazism as fundamentally racist and anti-Christian. He might have been influenced to speak out by Sister Edith Stein's letter to him written in 1933. The encyclical written in German, rather than the customary Latin, was authored largely by Michael von Faulhaber, cardinal-archbishop of Munich.

Mit brennender Sorge named specific Reich violations of the Concordat, among them: harassment of parochial school teachers; arrests of priests and religious; closing convents, monasteries, and schools; suppressing Catholic associations; and shutting down religious presses. Smuggled into Germany from Italy, the encyclical was read in all churches on Palm Sunday, 1937. The encyclical not only indicted the regime for violating the Reich Concordat, but warned against the "deification of race, nation, and state," and accused Hitler of "deceiving Germans and the international community." It mentioned "God-given rights," invoked "human nature that went beyond national borders," and warned that rejection of the Old Testament was blasphemous. It charged that Hitler was "perfidious, untrustworthy, dangerous and determined to take the place of God." It condemned, in particular, "the paganism of the national-socialism ideology, the myth of race and blood, and the fallacy of their conception of God." Apparently caught off guard by the encyclical, an enraged Hitler ordered the burning of as many copies as could be confiscated.

Mit brennender Sorge, the first official denunciation of Hitler made by any major institution, resulted in increased persecution of German Catholics, which included a number of staged trials of clergy on morals charges. Pius XII's defenders point to this and similar retaliatory measures taken by the Reich after official church protests of Nazi policies as proof that making condemnatory public statements was counterproductive.

Hitler, speaking to Cardinal Archbishop Faulhaber[157] on November 4, 1936, said: "Think, my Lord Cardinal ... and discuss with other church leaders how you want to support the great task of National Socialism ... and how you want to establish friendly relations with the state. Either National Socialism and the Church will win together or they will both go under."

---

157   Archbishop Faulhaber ordained Joseph Ratzinger to the priesthood in 1951. Ratzinger, who in 2005 became Pope Benedict XVI, succeeded Faulhaber as archbishop of Munich. "What's moved me deeply about him (Faulhaber)," Ratzinger wrote after the war, recalling his experience as a seminarian, "was the awe-inspiring grandeur of his mission, with which he had become fully identified." James Carroll, in *Practicing Catholic*, contends, on the other hand, that Ratzinger as Pope Benedict XVI remains devoted to Faulhaber's memory, but "this and numerous other statements on the subject show, Ratzinger remains equally devoted to the proposition that the German Catholic Church was a consistent center of resistance to the Nazis. Whatever accounts for Ratzinger's memory, it is not true. What Catholic resistance showed itself in Germany was exceptional ..." (*Practicing Catholic*, 263).

Poland

Anti-Semitism in Poland, as in other Eastern European countries, was widespread and deeply embedded in society. In July 1934, the anti-Semitic organization *Oboz Narodowo-Radykalny* was banned by Polish dictator Marshal Jozef Pilsudski, three months after its founding. Following Pilsudski's death on May 12, 1935, Jews in Poland experienced an uptick of anti-Semitism. On June 9, 1935, anti-Jewish riots broke out in the city of Grodno (now located in Belarus). Jewish-owned businesses and homes were set on fire during a pogrom in the city of Minsk Mazowiecki in June 1936. The same year, riots erupted in Polish universities where Jewish students were restricted to special seating. Pogroms, rallies, boycotts of Jewish businesses, and an anti-Semitic legislative agenda, modeled on Nazi Germany's, exacerbated Polish-Jewish relations in the mid-1930s. Germany's growing economic and military strength convinced many Poles that the time was ripe to settle differences with their "troublesome" Jewish minority.

The right-wing, anti-Jewish weekly publication *Samoobrona Naradu* ("National Self-defense") lobbied extensively to remove all Jews from Poland. Urging Poles to pay heed to their Jewish problem, the paper led a campaign to "clear Poland of its Jews." "Jobs and bread for the Poles!" read one of its headlines as it attempted to arouse national pride, solidarity, and unity. Jews were attacked throughout Poland between 1935 and the fall of 1939; tens of thousands of them fled to Holland, France, Belgium, and Palestine.

Archbishop August Hlond

In August 1936, Poland's Ministry of Commerce ordered all Polish small businesses to publicly display their owners' names as the names appeared on birth certificates. The directive was intended to identify Jewish-owned businesses.

August Hlond, archbishop of Poznan and Gniezno, primate of the Polish Catholic Church, publicly advocated in favor of discrimination against Jews unless they converted to Catholicism. Thought to be less anti-Semitic than many of Poland's other bishops, Hlond's 1936 pastoral letter on the Jewish question, criticizing Jews for their "harmful morality," revealed the growing influence of Nazi racist ideology in Catholic Poland. In that letter, urging Catholics to boycott Jewish businesses in Poland, Bishop Hlond wrote:

It is a fact that Jews fight against the Catholic Church, they are free-thinkers, and constitute the avant-garde of atheism, Bolshevism, and revolution ... (I)n the schools the Jewish youth is having an evil influence, from an ethical and religious point of view, on Catholic youth. The Jews have a disastrous effect on morality and their publishing houses dispense pornography. It is true that Jews commit fraud, usury, and are involved in trade in human beings ... Not all Jews are like this, however, there are very many Jewish faithful who are honest, just, compassionate, and charitable. Hlond concluded, One should protect oneself against the influence of Jewish morals ... but it is inadmissible to assault, hit or injure Jews. In a Jew you should also respect and love a human being and your neighbor.

Also in 1936, Archbishop Hlond[158] declared: "There will be a Jewish problem as long as Jews remain in Poland." Some Poles understood this statement to mean "unless and until Jews were eliminated from Poland." When pogroms broke out in Poland that same year, Archbishop Hlond condemned Jewish "usury, fraud and white slavery." According to John Cornwell, Archbishop Hlond's anti-Jewish views provided religious cover for a variety of Polish anti-Semitic groups. Despite the pastoral letter's attempt to qualify his condemnation of Jews, Hlond's words clearly gave a "patina of legitimacy" to a virulent anti-Semitism that was to reach its most horrific reality on Polish soil in the death camps to come.

---

158   In January 1940, Vatican Radio broadcast a number of reports from Archbishop Hlond detailing Nazi atrocities then being perpetrated against Polish Jews and Catholics. These reports were included in documents submitted by the Polish government to Nuremberg Trial prosecutors after the war. In August 1941, Archbishop Hlond advised Vatican Secretary of State Cardinal Luigi Maglione that Polish Catholics felt abandoned by the Church, citing Pope Pius XII's failure to speak out against Nazi persecution of Polish Catholics. Pius XII, however, continued his silence, failing to condemn the murder of approximately two million Polish Catholics (including 2,935 members of the clergy) by the Nazis and the murder of approximately one million Polish Catholics by the Soviets. Hlond was elevated to the rank of cardinal by Pius XII in 1946.

Angel of Death

In January 1937, a twenty-five-year-old doctor, Josef Mengele, began his research assistantship at the University of Frankfurt's prestigious Institute of Hereditary Biology and Racial Hygiene. He soon joined the Nazi Party and SS, and six years later, in May of 1943, his career in service of Nazi Germany's racial purity ideology reached its zenith when he was assigned to the Auschwitz-Birkenau death camp. During his twenty months there Dr. Mengele conducted medical experiments and presided at "selections" to determine who would be gassed. In his medical experiments, victims were placed into pressure chambers, tested with drugs, castrated, frozen to death, and injected with lethal germs. They were forced to undergo sex change operations; their organs and limbs were removed—often without anesthesia. Children were also exposed to experimental surgeries performed without anesthesia; as well as to transfusions of blood from one child to another, isolation endurance, and reaction to various stimuli. In one experiment, Dr. Mengele injected chemicals into the eyes of children in an attempt to change their eye color. He carried out twin-to-twin transfusions, stitched twins together, and castrated or sterilized twins. Many twins had limbs and organs removed in macabre surgical procedures. When it was reported that one cell block within the death camp was infected with lice, he solved the problem by gassing all the 750 women assigned to it. Self-identified as Roman Catholic, for his diabolical activity Dr. Mengele earned the nickname, "Angel of death."[159]

Crusade against Bolshevism

On January 3, 1937, a New Year pastoral letter from the bishops of Germany was read from pulpits. Noting that a "fateful hour" had arrived, the bishops warned:

> Russian Bolshevism has started its march toward Europe. The Fuehrer and Chancellor of the Reich, Adolf Hitler, has sighted the advance of Bolshevism from afar and his thoughts and aspirations aim at averting the horrible danger from our German people and the entire occident. The German bishops consider it their duty to support the head of the German Reich by all those means which the Church has at its disposal. Cooperation

---

159   Josef Mengele was one of a number of Nazi war criminals who, after the war, fled to safety in a Vatican-sanctioned ratline.

in repelling this threat is a religious task. We do not intend to intrude into the political realm or yet to call for a new war. But we must mobilize all the spiritual and moral forces of the Church in order to strengthen confidence in the Fuehrer.

The German bishops' 1937 New Year pastoral letter, in retrospect, strikes a number of discordant chords. Among them: it named Bolshevism as an existential threat to all of Europe; invoking religion and patriotism, linking civic and moral duty, it called, in effect, for a crusade against Bolshevism; it proclaimed Hitler leader of the crusade; it exhorted the faithful to cooperate with and support Hitler "by all means possible," while Germany was marching inexorably toward an unjust war.

Lesser of Two Evils

Garry Wills,[160] author of *Papal Sin*, is among Pius's critics who maintain that Pacelli was a leading exponent of the then prevailing view within the Vatican that Bolshevism posed the gravest threat to the Church and European society, second only to Judaism. The Nazis, under this view, might try to manipulate institutional churches, but at least they allowed them to exist. Bolshevists, on the other hand, abolished churches altogether. Even when Nazism began to look evil, it remained, according to Wills, not only "the lesser of two evils, but a bulwark against the greater one." Wills concludes that this mind-set, among other things, helps explains why the Vatican, when it criticized the Nazi regime, used language that was "cautious and negotiatory."

In October 1937, the "Aryanization" of Jewish-owned businesses began (i.e., Jewish-owned businesses were expropriated under process of law and transferred to Aryans). In November 1937, the German Museum in Munich mounted the *Der Ewige Jude* ("The Eternal Jew") exhibition, linking Jews with Bolshevism.

By January 1938, about 200,000 of the approximately 525,000 Jews who had resided in Germany five years earlier had emigrated elsewhere—the lucky ones escaped Europe altogether. In January, the first issue of *Judisches Nachrichtenblatt* ("Jewish Newsletter") was published to keep

---

160   Garry Wills is a Pulitzer Prize-winning author, journalist, and historian, specializing in American history, politics, and religion, as well as the history of the Roman Catholic Church.

German citizens apprised of Nazi regulations regarding Jews. Right-wing Catholic priest Jozef Tiso became the fascist dictator of Slovakia, a state created by the Versailles Treaty, and immediately established ties to Nazi Germany.[161] Work to enlarge the Dachau concentration camp began, and the government of Romania stripped Romanian Jews of their citizenship rights. Also in January 1938, at an International Eucharistic Congress held in Budapest, while the Hungarian legislature was considering passage of proposed anti-Jewish legislation patterned after the Nuremburg Laws of 1935, Cardinal Pacelli, as presiding papal legate, addressed the Congress, referring to Jews "whose lips curse (Christ) and whose hearts reject him even today."

In 1938, Hitler informed Hans Frank, his minister of justice, that it was his (Hitler's) destiny to fulfill the curse imposed by Jews on themselves in the New Testament.[162] In addition to exploiting Roman Catholicism, Hitler exploited Protestantism as well. As noted previously, he took great satisfaction in quoting from German native son and "Father of the Protestant Reformation" Martin Luther, whose anti-Semitic treatise *On the Jews and Their Lies,* was always on display at party rallies.

On March 12, 1938, the German army marched into Vienna, Austria. Without a single shot being fired, Germany annexed Austria (the *Anschluss*) into the Third Reich and Austria became subject to all anti-Semitic laws in effect in Germany. On March 31, just a few weeks after the *Anschluss*, the Polish parliament passed legislation making it possible to revoke the citizenship of Poles living abroad. Both before and after that date, the Polish government took steps aimed at preventing the return to Poland of thousands of Polish Jews living in Germany.

One month later, on April 26, Jews living in Germany were ordered to register their real estate holdings and other assets exceeding five thousand marks in value with Reich authorities, the first step toward expropriation of Jewish property. On the same day, Jews were ordered to apply for identity cards to be shown to police on demand. In May, Jewish men and women in Occupied Austria were forced to scrub streets with small brushes and with the women's fur coats. Carl von Ossietzky, an anti-Nazi German journalist and winner of the 1935 Nobel Peace

---

161   Tiso would be executed for war crimes after the war.

162   "His (Jesus's) blood be upon us and upon our children" (Matthew 27:25).

Prize, died at age fifty, after five years' captivity in a concentration camp. In June, a Munich synagogue was destroyed; in August, male Jews were required to use the middle name of "Israel," and females, the middle name of "Sarah"; and an October decree required special identification cards for German Jews—their passports were marked with a large red "J."

Manifesto della Raza

In July 1938, Mussolini, under pressure from Hitler, initiated an anti-Jewish campaign entitled *Manifesto della Raza* ("Manifesto of Italian Racism"), declaring that Italians were part of the pure race. Racial laws, similar to the Nuremberg Laws, were enacted in Italy, in Occupied Austria, Vichy France, Slovakia, Croatia, and Hungary. *Manifesto della Raza*, among other things, forbade Jews to marry Catholics (miscegenation), barred them from attending or teaching in public schools and universities, prohibited them from serving in the military or holding public service positions, stripped them of their Italian citizenship, and deprived them of property, which, it should be recalled, also happened to Italian Jews during the pontificate of Pope Paul IV in the sixteenth century. After *Manifesto*, foreign Jews living in Italy as refugees were rounded up and confined in internment camps, similar to camps for Japanese-Americans in the United States. The Holy See made no protest against *Manifesto della Raza*, except regarding provisions impacting specific church functions like the solemnization of marriages or status of converts to Catholicism (i.e., functions/interests within the "circle of Vatican concern").

German Clergy Call for Obedience

Adolf Bertram, archbishop of Breslau (now part of Poland), in a 1938 address to the thirty thousand Catholics of his diocese, invoked scripture to encourage obedience to Reich authority. "There is no need to urge you to give respect and obedience to the new authorities of the German state," he said. "You all know the words of the apostle (St. Paul): 'Let every man be subject to the powers placed over him.'"[163]

This passage from St. Paul's Letter to the Romans, "Let every man be subject to the powers placed over him," was clearly misused by the Nazis and others to justify unquestioning obedience to the Fuehrer, the

---

163   Romans 13:1.

Nazi Caesar,[164] who was the very personification of evil. It is noteworthy that misuse of scripture to justify immoral behavior has occurred over and over again throughout history, and will, no doubt, continue to occur.

Gordon C. Zahn, author of *German Catholics and Hitler's Wars*, accused Catholic clergy of functioning as cheerleaders of the German war effort. He wrote:

> The German Catholic supported Hitler's wars not only because such support was required by the Nazi rulers but also because his religious leaders formally called upon him to do so; not only because the actions and opinions of his fellow citizens made him feel obligated to share the nation's burdens and sorrows but also because, by example and open encouragement, the Catholic press and Catholic organizations gave their total commitment to the nation's cause; not only because of deep-felt fears of the terrible price nonconformity would bring or the warm surge of satisfaction accompanying nationalistic or patriotic identification with the war effort, but also because his most cherished religious values have been called into play to encourage him to take his post "on the field of honor" in the "defense of Volk and Vaterland" (people and fatherland).

Each member of the Wehrmacht (German military) was required to render unconditional obedience to Hitler personally by swearing a military oath, which read: "I swear before God this sacred oath that I will render unconditional obedience to the Führer of the German nation and Volk, Adolf Hitler, the Supreme commander of the armed forces, and that, as a brave solider, I will be ready at all times to stake my life in fulfillment of this oath."

Pius XI Condemns Anti-Semitism

On September 6, 1938, Pius XI told a group of Belgian pilgrims, once again perhaps influenced by Sister Edith Stein's letter: "Anti-Semitism is a hateful movement, a movement that we cannot, as Christians, take any part in … Anti-Semitism is inadmissible." In concluding his remarks he said:

---

164   "Render to Caesar the things that are Caesar, and to God the things that are God's" (Mark 12:17).

Mark well that in the Catholic Mass, Abraham is our Patriarch and forefather. Anti-Semitism is incompatible with the lofty thought which that fact expresses. It is a movement with which we Christians can have nothing to do. No, no, I say to you it is impossible for a Christian to take part in anti-Semitism. It is inadmissible. Through Christ and in Christ we are the spiritual progeny of Abraham. Spiritually, we are all Semites.

Pius XI's September 1938 statement to the Belgian pilgrims that "spiritually, we are all Semites," was not published in *L'Osservatore Romano*, in *Civiltà Cattolica*, or any other Catholic publication.

CHAPTER 7

The Holocaust

IN LATE OCTOBER 1938, REICH authorities ordered the deportation of Polish Jews living in Germany to Poland, but Polish authorities refused them entry. The family of Herschel Grynszpan, age 17, was among the Polish Jews who, because they were barred from returning to Poland, ended up in a concentration camp in Germany. Living in Paris at the time, Grynszpan found out that his family had been forced to leave their home in Hanover, Germany. In angry reprisal, he went to the German Embassy in Paris on November 7, 1938, and shot Ernst vom Rath, third secretary of the German Legation, who died two days later. Seizing the opportunity, Hitler used the shooting as his pretext to authorize the implementation of a long-planned state-sponsored pogrom which became known as *Kristallnacht* ("Night of Broken Glass").

The Holocaust began on November 9, 1938, with *Kristallnacht* across Germany and Occupied Austria, but quickly spread to all of Europe. The attacks included breaking windows, looting, and destruction of Jewish-owned businesses. Jews were beaten and killed. Male Jews were arrested and sent to concentration camps, though most would be released within a few weeks. Synagogues were desecrated and destroyed (almost all the synagogues of Germany and Austria). SS chief Heinrich Himmler instructed security agencies to burn synagogues unless German lives or property would be endangered. Accordingly and quite anomalously, firefighters stood by, not to put out the fires of burning synagogues, but to protect German-owned properties from collateral damage. On November 15, Jewish children were banned from public schools.

Guenter Lewy,[165] author of *The Catholic Church and Nazi Germany*, described the Holy See's reaction to *Kristallnacht*:

The hands-off policy of the Church stood out especially in the fateful days of November 1938 … During the night of November 9–10, the display windows of Jewish shops all over Germany were shattered, about twenty thousand male Jews were arrested and herded into concentration camps, 191 synagogues were set on fire and 76 others completely destroyed … 36 Jews were killed during this well-organized action; a much larger number succumbed to the sadistic treatment meted out to them in Buchenwald and other concentration camps where they were imprisoned. (The reaction of the Church was that) bishops remained silent in the face of the burning temples and the first round-up of the Jews.[166]

On December 8, 1938, Jews were banned from teaching in German universities and institutions of higher education and research.

On January 30, 1939, in a ceremony commemorating the sixth anniversary of the Nazi rise to power, Hitler proclaimed that in the event of war, Jews would need to be annihilated. Also in January 1939, two months after *Kristallnacht*, following passage of Manifesto of Italian Racism, *L'Osservatore Romano* published an Italian bishop's homily which referenced the newly enacted Italian legislation. He stated:

The Church has always regarded living side by side with Jews, as long as they remain Jews, as dangerous to the faith and tranquility of Christian people. It is for this reason that you find an old and long tradition of ecclesiastical legislation and discipline intended to break and limit the action and influence of the Jews in the midst of Christians, and the contact of Christians with them, isolating the Jews and not allowing them

---

165   Guenter Lewy is a German-born author, political scientist, and professor emeritus at the University of Massachusetts. His works span several topics, but he is most often associated with his 1978 book on the Vietnam War, *America in Vietnam*, and several controversial works that deal with the applicability of the term "genocide" to various historical events, including the Armenian genocide.

166   Lewy, *The Catholic Church and Nazi Germany*, 284.

the exercise of those offices and professions in which they could dominate or influence the spirit, the education, the customs of Christians.

A 1939 issue of B'nai B'rith *National Jewish Monthly* featured Pius XI on the front cover. In the accompanying article, the author wrote: "Regardless of their personal beliefs, men and women everywhere who believe in democracy and the rights of man have hailed the firm and uncompromising stand of Pope Pius XI against fascist brutality, paganism, and racial theories. In his annual Christmas message to the College of Cardinals, the great Pontiff vigorously denounced Fascism … The first international voice in the world to be raised in stern condemnation of the ghastly injustice perpetrated upon the Jewish people by brutal tyrannies was Pope Pius XI." On March 15, 1939, in violation of the Munich Pact of September 29, 1938, Germany invaded Czechoslovakia.

Pius XII

Eugenio Pacelli became Pope Pius XII on March 2, 1939, six months before Germany's unprovoked invasion of Poland. On that same day, German troops were massing on the Czechoslovakian border, preparing to invade the German-speaking Sudetenland in violation of the Versailles Treaty. On March 6, Pius XII personally drafted and sent a letter to Hitler, written in German. It read, in pertinent part:

> To the illustrious Herr Adolf Hitler, Führer and Chancellor of the German Reich! Here at the beginning of Our Pontificate We desire to express the wish to remain united by the bonds of profound and benevolent friendship with the German people who are entrusted to your care … We pray that Our great desire for the prosperity of the German people and for their progress in every domain may, with God's help, come to full realization.

Hidden Encyclical

Upon becoming pope, Pius XII faced a momentous decision: what to do with the deceased Pius XI's draft encyclical, *Humani Generis Unitas*[167] ("On the Unity of the Human Race"), in which, for the first time, the Church would publicly and explicitly condemn Nazi anti-Semitism and call for an end to Jewish persecution. Father John La Farge, SJ, had written a draft of the encyclical at the pope's request in late 1938. According to Daniel Jonah Goldhagen, a former associate professor of political science and social studies at Harvard University, Pius XII decided to bury it in the Vatican archives. The encyclical, now referred to as the "Hidden Encyclical," was never issued. Although choosing not to issue it, Pius used selected parts of it in his inaugural encyclical, *Summi Pontificatus* (subtitled "On the Unity of Human Society"). His critics contend that *Humani Generis Unitas* is a significant example of a lost opportunity that might have pressured the regime to stop or, at least, mitigate its persecution of Jews.

Humani Generis Unitas read, in pertinent part: "It becomes clear that the struggle of racial purity ends by being uniquely the struggle against the Jews. Save for its systematic cruelty, this struggle is no different in true motives and methods from persecutions everywhere carried out against the Jews since antiquity."

Regarding the Hidden Encyclical, Daniel Jonah Goldhagen writes:

> That (Pius XII) began his papacy burying this remarkable document in defense of the Jews, now known as the Hidden Encyclical, in the "silence of the Vatican archives" and that the Vatican for half a century tried to hide Pius XII's act of suppression and the encyclical itself, tells us a great deal about Pius XII, and about the dissimulations that have surrounded that Pope's and the Church's relationship to the Holocaust.[168]

---

167   It is alleged that the leader of the Jesuit Order, Superior General Wlodimir Ledochowski, deliberately kept the Hidden Encyclical from Pius XI who, at the time, was in failing health.

168   Goldhagen, *A Moral Reckoning*, 39–40.

Unprovoked Invasion of Poland

On September 1, 1939, one week after the signing of the Molotov-Ribbentrop Pact, the Wehrmacht without provocation[169] invaded Catholic Poland[170] from the west, north, and south. The invasion marked the start of WWII. While Poles struggled valiantly to repel the German advance from the west, the Soviet army on September 17, 1939, under terms of the Molotov-Ribbentrop Pact,[171] invaded from the east, occupying the eastern part of the country. By then Germany already occupied the western two-thirds of Poland with its approximately 2.1 million Jews. On September 17, the balance, approximately 1.2 million Jews, came under Soviet rule. By October 6, Nazi Germany and Soviet Russia divided and annexed the whole of Poland, beginning a reign of terror for the Polish people, Jews and Catholics alike, who were trapped in a vice between competing political ideologies, Nazi fascism and Soviet Bolshevism.

At the start of the invasion, Hitler proclaimed: "I have issued the command ... that our war aim does not consist in reaching certain lines, but in the physical destruction of the enemy ... Accordingly, I have placed ... orders to send to death mercilessly and without compassion, men, women and children of Polish derivation and language.[172] Only thus shall we gain the living space (*lebensraum*) that we need."

The German bishops' response to the invasion was to urge Catholics to support the war effort by faithfully discharging their religious, patriotic, and civic duty. This attitude was characterized by Military Vicar General Buchwieser, who on September 17, 1939, declared:

---

169   On the evening of August 31, 1939, Nazi SS troops wearing Polish uniforms staged a phony invasion of Germany, damaging several minor installations on the German side of the border. They also left behind a handful of dead German prisoners in Polish uniforms to serve as further evidence of the alleged Polish attack, which Nazi propagandists publicized as an unforgivable act of aggression. Hitler used the staged event as the pretext to invade Poland the next day.

170   Roman Catholics comprised approximately 90 percent of Poland's population.

171   NB, Hitler, anointed by German bishops to lead Europe's crusade against Bolshevism, in effect, made a pact with the devil, Josef Stalin, to partition and subjugate Catholic Poland—an unintended consequence.

172   Later, Heinrich Himmler would say: "All Poles will disappear from the world ... It is essential that the great German people should consider it as its major task to destroy all Poles."

The Fatherland has entered upon a fateful hour of decision. Responding to the seriousness of the hour, the faithful are being summoned to lift their hands trustingly to God, the Ruler of all history, that He may protect the People and Fatherland in their present emergency and danger; that He may stand by their responsible leaders in the hour of life-and-death decision; that He may strengthen our soldiers and accompany them along the difficult paths of war; that He may comfort the families who are sorely anxious over members and providers; that He may lend His strength and help to all those who will be hit the hardest by the trials of war.

In such difficult times, when everything is at stake, *it is absolutely imperative that everyone faithfully discharge his religious, patriotic and civic duties at whatever post he is assigned*; and that one and all stand side by side in the spirit of true Christian charity and consciousness of community." (emphasis mine)

Hitler, addressing the Reichstag on January 30, 1939, declared: "Today I will once more be a prophet! If the international Jewish financiers inside and outside Europe should again succeed in plunging the nations into a world war, the result will not be the Bolshevization of the earth and thus victory of Jewry, but the *annihilation* of the Jewish race throughout Europe."

On October 29, 1939, Cardinal Michael von Faulhaber called upon the faithful to support the national *Winterhilfswerk* collection for charitable donations. The annual appeal, however, was given a new wartime dimension. He said:

We owe it to the relatives of those who stand at the battle front and risk their lives for the Fatherland that they be protected against need, hunger, and cold. It will be truly special comfort to the fighting men in the field to know that their loved ones at home are spared from worry and care through the active assistance provided by the *Winterhilfswerk* whenever needed. Therefore, the voice of the Church is joined with the government's appeal in pursuance of the direct commission she [the Church] has received from her Lord and Master to regard every man[173] in need as a brother and to feed, clothe, and shelter him ...

On September 1, 1939, Poland had the highest concentration of Jews in Europe, approximately 10 percent of the population. Warsaw was one of Eastern Europe's centers of Jewish culture. Polish Jews, however, were the least assimilated of European Jewry because, among other things, of their distinctive dress, grooming styles, mannerisms, and customs. They made up about 65 percent of the Polish Communist Party membership. Jews had lived in Poland since the eleventh century, when, ironically, they fled Germany to avoid persecution.

Beginning in October 1939, Polish Jews *and* Catholics[174] were stripped of their citizenship rights. Jews were forced to wear a Star of David and were forcibly conscripted into slave labor. In November, the first ghetto was established in Piotrkow Trybunalski. Young Catholic Polish men were forcibly conscripted into the German army. All secondary schools and colleges were closed. The Polish press was shut down, libraries and bookshops were vandalized, Polish art and cultural treasures were destroyed, churches and synagogues were burned. Priests were arrested and sent to concentration camps. The Polish language was forbidden; only the German language was allowed. Street signs were changed to German names; cities and towns were renamed in German. The name of the city of Oświęcim, for example, was changed to Auschwitz, soon to become home of the notorious killing camp of the same name. Hitler's expressed goal was to obliterate all traces of Polish history and culture. Polish community leaders, mayors, local officials, teachers, lawyers, judges, doctors—most of Poland's intelligentsia—were targeted for execution.

Within five weeks of the invasion, Poland lost approximately seventy thousand combatants. The Holy See, despite repeated entreaties by the British and French ambassadors to protest, according to John Julius Norwich, author of *Absolute Monarchs*, offered not a word of sympathy

---

173   Jews and other victims of Nazi injustice excepted?

174   "First they came for the socialists, and I did not speak out, because I was not a socialist. Then they came for the trade unionists, and I did not speak out—because I was not a trade unionist. Then they came for the Jews, and I did not speak out—because I was not a Jew. Then they came for me—and there was no one left to speak for me" (Pastor Martin Niemoller).

or regret, still less of denunciation. The "deafening silence" continued until the third week of October, when Pius XII published his first encyclical, *Summi Pontificatus*. His refusal to speak out was regarded as betrayal by many Polish Catholics, including members of the clergy. When in May 1942, Pius appointed Hilarius Breitinger as apostolic administrator for the Wartheland,[175] Poles viewed the appointment as implicit recognition of the breakup of Poland. British minister to the Holy See, Sir D'Arcy Osborne, following the invasion, annexation, and partition of Poland, wrote: "The Holy Father appears to be ... adopting an ostrich-like policy toward these notorious atrocities. It is felt that as a consequence of this exasperating attitude, the great *moral authority* enjoyed by the Papacy throughout the world under Pius IX has today been notably diminished." (emphasis mine)

In *Summi Pontificatus*, Pius XII finally addressed publically[176] the invasion, occupation, and partition of Poland. It read, in pertinent part:

> The blood of countless human beings, even noncombatants, raises a piteous dirge over a nation such as Our dear Poland, which, for its fidelity to the Church, for its services in the defense of Christian civilization, written in indelible characters in the annals of history, has a right to the generous and brother sympathy of the whole world, while it awaits, relying on the powerful intercession of Mary, Help of Christians, the hour of resurrection in harmony with the principles of justice and true peace.

Summi Pontificatus warned against theories that deny the unity of the human race and warned against the deification of the state, all of which Pius saw as leading to an "hour of darkness." *Summi Pontificatus*, however, is more significant for what it did not say (i.e.,

175 Wartheland is the name given by the Nazis to the territory of Greater Poland, which was occupied, annexed, and directly incorporated into the Greater Third Reich after defeating the Polish army in 1939.

176 Although Pius XII addressed the deplorable situation in Poland in an encyclical written in Latin, its impact was minimal compared to what a forceful and forthright address to the world in German or Italian, weeks earlier on Vatican Radio, might have been.

it did not condemn Nazi anti-Semitism, nor call for the cessation of Jewish persecution, or even specifically mention Jews by name).

In November 1939, Hitler survived an assassination attempt in Munich. The official Catholic reaction was noted in a local news report published in boldface type:

> On November 12, in conjunction with Solemn High Mass in the Cathedral (of Munich) a *Te Deum* was held in order to thank Divine Providence in the name of the archdiocese for the Führer's fortunate escape in connection with the criminal attempt made upon his life. With grateful hearts, the assembled congregation joined in the hymn of thanksgiving and jubilation. We Catholic Christians are united with the entire German Volk in the burning wish that God may protect for Führer and Volk.

T-4 Euthanasia Program

In the fall of 1939, guided by principles of racial hygiene, purity, and national health, the Reich inaugurated *Euthanasie Programme* ("Euthanasia Program"), headquartered at *Tiergartenstrasse* 4 in Berlin. Code name for the program, derived from its street address was Aktion T-4, or "Operation T-4." Its purpose—to eliminate *lebensunwertes leben* ("life unworthy of life") (i.e., Jews and others, including the mentally defective, severely handicapped, incurably insane, and incurably sick). Between December 1939 and August 1941, approximately fifty thousand to sixty thousand Germans, children and adults, were taken from medical facilities and secretly killed by lethal injections or in gassing installations designed to look like shower stalls.

The euthanasia program proved to be a precursor of atrocities to come in the killing camps. SS Major Christian Wirth, for example, was transferred from his duties at a euthanasia center to take over supervision of Chelmno, the first of six extermination camps in Poland to become operational. Expertise in large-scale extermination was a major consideration for his transfer. Wirth later served at Belzec, Treblinka, and Sobibor. In 1940, Austrian-born SS Major Franz Stangl was transferred from another euthanasia center to Sobibor, where he served as camp commandant. Stangl performed so well there that he was transferred in the summer of 1942 to Treblinka. Viewing Jews as "objects" of his work rather than as people, and regarding his job the same as he would any job, Stangl wrote: "That was my profession. I enjoyed it. It fulfilled me. And yes, I was ambitious about that, I won't deny it." In 1970, Stangl was extradited from Brazil[177] to West Germany to stand trial. Found guilty for the murder of nine hundred thousand Jews, sentenced to the maximum penalty of life imprisonment, he died of heart failure six months later.

Holocaust by Bullets

The first mass execution of WWII took place in Poland on December 27, 1939, in Wawer, near Warsaw, when 107 Polish Catholic men were taken by force from their homes in the middle of the night and shot, beginning a series of street roundups and mass executions that continued until war's end. As is well documented, the Soviets too committed atrocities against Polish Catholics.[178] The Nazi goal was to terrorize Poles into subservience to the German master race. Persecution of Jews, particularly in urban areas, began almost immediately after the invasion. In the first year and a half, Jews were stripped of their property, herded into ghettos (the seven largest of which all had populations over 25,000), and ordered to perform forced labor in war-related industries. With the German invasion of Soviet Russia in June 1941, SS *Einsatzgruppen* mobile killing squads began operating behind front lines to shoot "dangerous elements" (i.e., Jews and Bolsheviks). It should be noted that approximately two million Jews were shot and buried in mass graves, many in areas of eastern Poland annexed

---

177   SS Major Franz Stangl was one of the Nazi war criminals who, after the war, fled to safety in South America through a Vatican sanctioned ratline.

178   The Katyn Forest Massacre, for example, was a mass murder of Poles carried out by the Soviet secret police in April-May 1940 under order of Josef Stalin to execute all members of the Polish officer corps. Katyn Forest was a wooded area near Gnezdovo, a short distance from Smolensk in Russia. The total number of victims was estimated at about twenty-two thousand Poles murdered in the Katyn Forest, in the Kalinin, in Kharkov prisons, and elsewhere in Poland by the Soviets. About eight thousand were officers taken prisoner during the Soviet invasion of Poland; the rest were Polish doctors, professors, lawmakers, police officers, factory owners, lawyers, and priests. The Soviets denied culpability for the massacre, blaming the Nazis, until after the fall of the Soviet Union in 1989.

by the Soviets. This Holocaust by Bullets[179] occurred *before* the killing camps came into full operation in 1943.

Tykochen, a village in the Bialystok region in northeast Poland, was captured by the Nazis in June 1941. On August 25, all the Jewish residents, whose ancestors had resided there since 1522, were ordered to assemble in the market square, then taken to a church basement. Fourteen hundred of them were transported to large pits in a forest outside the village and murdered. A few survivors found temporary shelter in the Bialystok ghetto but later perished. Today there are no Jews in Tykochen, and its one synagogue is a museum.

Pius's critics contend, as noted previously, that the Vatican's response to worsening conditions for Jews in Germany, beginning soon after Hitler's rise to power in 1933 and continuing throughout WWII into 1945, was characterized by prudence and reserve. For example, there was no public protest against the Reich-sanctioned boycott of Jewish businesses in April 1933, the Nuremburg Laws of 1935, or the Reich-sponsored pogrom of *Kristallnacht* in November 1938. And prudence and reserve would continue to characterize the Vatican's response even when death camps reached full killing capacity. Pius became more proactive only when it became clear in late 1943 that the Allies would likely win the war, according to the pope's critics. Among his goals during the war were to limit the global conflict where possible and protect the influence and standing of the Church as an independent worldwide voice. Apprehensive of schism, Pius also worked to maintain the loyalty of Catholics in Germany, Italy, Poland, and elsewhere. Fearful of threats to the Church from the outside and fearing he might be kidnapped or assassinated, Pius did not confront the Nazis or Italian fascists directly.

Christianity in Europe

Religious affiliation in Nazi Germany in January 1933 was 94 percent Christian—40 percent Roman Catholic and 54 percent Protestant. Jews

---

179   Before construction of the death camps, where most of the mass killing took place, over 1.5 million Jews were executed, one bullet at a time, in what has been termed "Holocaust by Bullets." To date, the work of Father Patrick Desbois and his team of the *Yahad-In Unum* Association has identified over eight hundred mass gravesites and other execution sites located in the Ukraine. Jews were also murdered in mobile killing vans, utilizing the vehicles' exhaust fumes.

comprised less than 1 percent of the population, approximately 525,000. Organized into twenty-five dioceses, each headed by a Vatican-appointed bishop, the German Catholic Church numbered over twenty thousand priests for twenty million Catholics, as against sixteen thousand pastors for forty million Protestants. The same organizational structure existed in other European countries where Christian populations likewise predominated. Religious affiliation in the Greater Third Reich was 43 percent Roman Catholic. Papal nuncios served in every country, providing the Vatican with an extensive information gathering and dispensing network.

Catholic and Protestant churches were the official state churches in Nazi Germany; the Reich collected a tax earmarked for church functions, including parochial schools. Religious instruction was part of the public school curriculum; chaplains[180] provided spiritual guidance to military personnel; theology was taught in state universities. Article 24 in the Nazi Party Program professed "positive Christianity" as the foundation of the German state.

Like Hitler and Goebbels, Heinrich Himmler (SS chief and overseer of death camps), Reinhard Heydrich (principle planner of the Final Solution), and Rudolf Hoess (architect and SS commandant of Auschwitz-Birkenau) were also baptized Catholics. Catholics comprised a third of Germany's military, police, and security forces (22 percent of the SS), judiciary, civil service, medical, and concentration/killing camp staff. The balance was Protestant.

---

180   Hundreds of priests were among the chaplains assigned to minister to the spiritual needs of the Wehrmacht and occupation forces in Eastern Europe by, among other things, holding religious services, hearing individual confessions, and giving spiritual counsel. Serving in the thick of the killing operations, how did these priests respond to questions of conscience posed to them by perpetrators, collaborators, and bystanders? How did they square Jesus's commandment to love others unconditionally, especially the least of his brother and sisters, with the unmitigated evil happening all around them? Daniel Jonah Goldhagen writes:

> Of an estimated one thousand Catholic and Protestant clergy serving as military chaplains, fewer than ten cases (most are Catholic priests) have come to light—some of which are dubious—where it can be said that the chaplains conveyed disapproval of or urged resistance to the mass murder ... That Catholic priests in the thick of the mass murder greeted the annihilation of the Jew with silence or worse should come as no surprise, since the Catholic military bishop, Franz Justus Rarkowski, the spiritual leader of the priests assigned to the Wehrmacht, was deeply Nazified (*A Moral Reckoning*, 63).

Joseph Goebbels, drawing on his Catholic upbringing, opined: "Christ is the genius of love, as such the most diametrical opposite of Judaism, which is the incarnation of hate. The Jew is a non-race among the races of the earth … Christ is the first great enemy of the Jews … that is why Judaism had to get rid of him. For he was shaking the very foundations of its future international power. The Jew is the lie personified. When he crucified Christ, he crucified everlasting truth for the first time in history."

Nazism arose phoenixlike from the ashes of WWI, leading inexorably to the cataclysm of WWII. WWII's *fifty-five* million victims included combatants and noncombatants alike throughout Western and Eastern Europe who lost their lives in military operations, political purges, or the Holocaust, and many, many more who were grievously injured, physically and emotionally, as well as those who endured the privations of postwar recovery and dislocation.

The Holocaust was the systematic, state-organized persecution and murder of at least six million Jews, including 1.5 million children, by Nazi Germany and its puppet or partner regimes. Not only were two-thirds of European Jewry and one-third of world Jewry annihilated, but so too were at least five million non-Jews, including Roma and Sinti (Gypsies), Poles and other Slavic people, Soviet POWs, homosexuals, the mentally and physically disabled, Jehovah's Witnesses, and political dissidents. Anyone deemed unfit to live among the Aryan master race in the Greater Third Reich, or anyone opposed to the Nazi regime, was targeted for elimination.

The uniqueness of the Holocaust is rooted in the form and function of the racist ideology that helped spawn it. Adopting an extreme version of anti-Semitism based on late nineteenth and early twentieth century racial theory, Nazi ideology depicted Jews as a genetically inferior race, threatening to pollute the purity of the racially superior Germanic people. Jews, however, were not the only threat to racial purity. So too were the mentally and physically disabled, homosexuals, and habitual criminals. And when German hegemony began to spread throughout Europe after the invasion of Poland in September 1939, Poles, Ukrainians, Lithuanians, Latvians, Russians, and other Slavic peoples, as members of inferior races, were also targeted. Inferior races, apart from the Jews, existed only to serve the master race. But Jews, as carriers of absolute evil in their genes and blood, were beyond redemption. They headed the target list. Condemned by their DNA, not even conversion to Christianity could save them.

Approximately three million Polish Jews were murdered in the six death camps on Polish soil or perished from starvation and disease in overcrowded ghettos or were executed in the Holocaust by Bullets before ever reaching the death camps. The total number of Jews killed in Poland exceeded four million; however, because so many were deported to its extermination camps from elsewhere in Europe—in particular, from France, Greece, Italy, Hungary, Belgium, the Netherlands, Lithuania, and Germany—Poland was Hitler's biggest "killing field." Furthermore, of the six million Polish citizens murdered during the Holocaust, 20 percent of its population, three million were Jews and three million were Christians, the vast majority Roman Catholic.

Hitler's racial policy, his desire to create lebensraum ("living space") for the German people, and his crusade against Judeo-Bolshevism were all connected. Ultimately, Hitler wanted to create an economically independent Greater German Reich with access to natural resources unavailable in Germany, and to the slave labor of racially inferior people. He envisioned a political division of the world among four leading empires. Germany would dominate the European continent, including Russia. Britain would continue its empire. The United States would be the dominant power in the Western Hemisphere, but Hitler believed it would eventually collapse because of racial heterogeneity. Japan would dominate Asia.

Nazi Propaganda

Hitler's propaganda machine relentlessly bombarded the German people with negative messages—in feature films, faked newsreels, phony documentaries, fabricated news stories, radio plays, even in children's books—demonizing, dehumanizing, and scapegoating Jews for just about every problem of German society. Public demonstrations were regularly choreographed and mass rallies were staged to vilify them. All news was carefully controlled, censored, and always upbeat. Newspapers, radio, and newsreels spewed forth a steady stream of orchestrated information emphasizing the regime's positive achievements, particularly its successes in foreign affairs. The official view of Nazi society was one of happy farmers, workers, and middle-class Germans working together in a classless society, a *Volksgeminschaft*, or "people's community." Hitler was glorified by many Germans with semireligious fervor; revered as savior of the Aryan nation. Clearly, however, Hitler feared the power of the Church and from the beginning of the Third Reich worked to neutralize it, first in Germany and then in Occupied Europe.

The unending propaganda barrage was accompanied by state-imposed terror designed to crush opponents and to quash dissent. The notorious Gestapo (secret police) intentionally made arrests at night using brutally repressive tactics to instill fear and docility, a policy known as "Fog and Night." Although, obviously, there were Germans who disapproved of Nazi excesses, few were willing to speak out, especially when it became clear that they and their entire families would be severely punished, even killed. Regularly and routinely, opponents of the regime disappeared without a trace and were never heard from again. Neighbor spied and informed on neighbor. Children, indoctrinated from early age by ideologues of the Nazi Youth Movement,[181] informed on their parents. Opposition to the regime soon became sporadic and isolated. Catholic clergy, members of religious orders, and the laity, even Jewish converts to Catholicism, despite guarantees to the contrary in the Reich Concordat, were persecuted, as were their Protestant counterparts. Many non-Jews also were deported to concentration and killing camps.

Cloaking himself and his regime with religiosity, Hitler's insidiously effective propaganda machine was able to tap effortlessly into the poisonous groundwater of anti-Judaism, based on religion, and easily blend into Nazi anti-Semitism, based on race. When Nazi racist ideology defined the Jew as a demonic "other," it was building on an aspect of the European psyche firmly in place for close to two millennia. In short, Nazi anti-Semitism had two parents—neopagan anti-Semitism *and* Christian anti-Judaism. The Holy See acknowledged the first parent, but not the second.

In pursuit of a racially pure society, the Nazis abandoned the fundamental commandment of traditional morality, "Thou shall not kill." Hitler stressed this point when he proclaimed: "The Ten Commandments have lost their validity ... Providence has ordained that I should be the greatest liberator of humanity. I am freeing man

---

181   *Der Giftpilz* (*The Poisonous Mushroom*) was one of many anti-Semitic books written for German children. Highlighting the theme of Jews as Christ-killers, it urged children: "Whenever you see a cross, then think of the horrible murder by the Jews on Golgotha."

from the restraint of any intelligence that has taken charge; from the dirty and degrading self-mortification of a chimera called *conscience and morality*, and from the demands of a freedom and personal independence which only a few can bear ..." (emphasis mine)

Nazi Terrorism

The Gestapo, founded by Hermann Göring in April 1933, was placed under the administration of Heinrich Himmler as chief of German police in 1934. It specialized in extracting information by gruesome torture methods at its Berlin headquarters on *Prinz Albrechtrasse* ("Prince Albert Street"). Ironically, some of the Gestapo's interrogation and surveillance techniques were pioneered by the Holy Inquisition. The Gestapo offered a bounty to anyone who denounced Jews in hiding: a quart of liquor, four pounds of sugar, a carton of cigarettes, or small cash payments. For wartime civilians subject to rationing, such a bounty provided a powerful incentive to cooperate with the Reich, one made even more palpable by widespread anti-Semitism. Anyone discovered hiding Jews was summarily executed. At the height of the war, when living space, food, sanitation facilities, and medicine were in short supply, rescuers of Jews sacrificed a great deal, indeed, in addition to risking their lives.

The equally hated SS (Nazi Party Police), also headed by Heinrich Himmler, was both the chief instrument of Nazi terrorism and torchbearer of its racial ideals. Himmler developed the group into an elite brotherhood, complete with cultlike rituals and Teutonic symbols. Dabbling in occultism, he believed himself to be the reincarnation of a medieval German king who had conquered eastern territories. Himmler grew up in a respectable middle-class Catholic family. His father, Gebbard, taught Greek and Latin at the renowned Wilhelm Grammar School in Munich, and his son Heinrich was a diligent student. Peter Longerich, in a book entitled *Heinrich Himmler*, wrote that Himmler read anti-Semitic and astrological tracts in an effort to integrate the most important elements of radical right-wing ideology— anti-Semitism, extreme nationalism, racism, hostility to democracy— into a more comprehensive worldview. Himmler married a blonde, blue-eyed nurse named Margarete Boden whose credo was, "A Jew is always a Jew!"

Reinhard Heydrich, nicknamed "Hitler's Hangman," also grew up in a respectable middle-class Catholic family. His father, Bruno, was a gifted composer who ran a conservatory in the city of Halle and ensured that his son enjoyed a rigorous musical education, including playing the piano and violin by age six and attending Wagner[182] operas. Allegations of a Jewish pedigree in the Heydrich family tree plagued Reinhard throughout his career. For Himmler and Heydrich, the Nazi party afforded career opportunities and the chance to play important roles in what was intended to be the "Thousand Year Reich." Both men, driven by ideological hatreds, became skillful operatives who ascended to the very top of Nazi leadership.

According to Daniel Jonah Goldhagen, Nazi terrorism alone did not induce ordinary people to become complicit in mass murder, to, in his words, become "Hitler's willing executioners" (the title of one of his books). Rather it was Christianity's long history of Jew hatred. It was anti-Judaism that enabled Christians to assent willingly to Nazi eliminationist anti-Semitism, which caused many of them to make this morally conflicted choice—"allowing or abetting the Germans' and their helpers' persecution of Jews and even letting Jews die was preferable to intervening on their behalf."

Among the causes of the Holocaust:

- An evil, amoral, and charismatic leader
- Chaotic post-WWI conditions
- Popular discontent
- Masterful use of propaganda
- A brutal totalitarian regime
- State sponsored terrorism
- Territorial expansionism
- The fog of war[183]

---

182   Under a pseudonym, Richard Wagner in 1850 published an essay, *Das Judenthum in der Musik* ("Judaism in Music"). The essay attacked Jewish contemporaries (and rivals) Felix Mendelssohn and Giacomo Meyerbeer, and accused Jews of being a harmful and alien element in German culture. Wagner asserted, among other things, that the German people were repelled by Jews' alien appearance and behavior: "with all our speaking and writing in favor of the Jews' emancipation, we always felt instinctively repelled by any actual, operative contact with them."

183   The "fog of war" is a term used to describe the level of ambiguity in situational awareness experienced by participants in military operations, which, among other things, diminishes cultural taboos, for example, against theft, torture, rape, and murder.

- Sadism
- Careerism
- Anti-Judaism/anti-Semitism
- Fear of Judeo-Bolshevism
- Extreme nationalism/patriotism
- Paralysis of will
- Unquestioning obedience to authority
- Lack of moral guidance
- Failure of conscience
- Widespread culpability, complicity, and indifference

It is important to know that Hitler became chancellor of Germany in 1933 under process of law, his Nazi party winning 37 percent of the popular vote in a parliamentary democracy, not in a coup d'état. And, within three months of assuming power, his racist policy began to unfold. To illustrate, in April 1933, Jewish medical doctors, pharmacists, dentists, and dental technicians were forbidden to serve in German hospitals, clinics, and public health centers. In September 1935, the Nuremberg Laws transformed Jews into "denizens" of the Third Reich, stripping them of their civil and human rights. Subsequent legislation excluded them from attending public schools and universities, from holding positions in the judiciary[184] or civil service, and from entering public parks or using public transportation. Personal items such as radios and bicycles were confiscated from them. Jewish doctors were forbidden to treat non-Jewish patients, all actions intended to marginalize them within German society. The prime target of Nazi fanaticism was, at first, the relatively small German Jewish population that considered itself German and well assimilated into German society. Ironically, before the advent of Nazism, Germany was considered a safe haven for Eastern European Jews.

Similarly, Jews in Italy considered themselves well assimilated into Italian society. Prior to 1938, fascist Italy had no official policy regarding

---

184   All professional associations involved with the administration of justice were merged into the National Socialist League of German Jurists. A law enacted in April 1933 purged Jewish and socialist judges, lawyers, and other court officers from their professions. Further, the Academy of German Law, and Nazi legal theorists such as Carl Schmitt, advocated for the Nazification of German law, cleansing it of "Jewish influence." Judges were enjoined to let "healthy folk sentiment" (*gesundes Volksempfinden*) guide them in their decisions.

Jews and their treatment by Mussolini's regime was relatively benign. Jews had resided in Rome since before the time of the apostles Peter and Paul, and it was not uncommon, for example, for Jews to marry Catholics. Most Italians considered Jews as friends and neighbors. Some Jews even joined the Italian Fascist Party. In July 1938, however, with the passage of *Manifesto della Raza*, life for Italy's Jews began to deteriorate.

Evian Conference

From February 1933 until October 1941, Reich policy encouraged Jewish emigration out of Germany, and many Jews such as Albert Einstein and Billy Wilder, did, in fact, leave Germany, especially following the boycott of Jewish-owned business in April 1933. Gradually, however, the Nazis sought to deprive Jews fleeing Germany of their property by levying an increasingly heavy emigration tax, restricting the amount of money that could be transferred abroad from German banks, and limiting how much property could be taken out of Germany. Only a few countries, including Britain,[185] Canada, and the United States, would accept them as political refugees. In July 1938, at the invitation of President Franklin D. Roosevelt, delegates of thirty-two nations convened at a seaside resort in Evian-les-Bains, France, to discuss the international refugee problem. Although delegates at the Evian Conference expressed sympathy for Jewish refugees, except for the Dominican Republic, the borders of their countries, outside existing quotas, remained closed. The noose for Europe's Jews was tightening.

After *Kristallnacht*, many more Jews within Germany and Occupied Austria decided to flee.[186] Because immigration policies in potential host countries had become more restrictive, however, those remaining

---

185   As the situation worsened in Nazi Germany beginning in 1933, approximately 250,000 Jews fled to Palestine, a British protectorate under terms of the Versailles Treaty. The influx of Jewish refugees unsettled the tense political situation there, leading to Arab revolts beginning in 1936. In an attempt to placate the Arabs and guarantee access to Middle Eastern oil, British authorities restricted immigration. Accordingly, in May 1939, four months before the outbreak of WWII, pursuant to the MacDonald "White Paper," it was decreed by the British government that only seventy-five thousand Jewish immigrants would be admitted in Palestine over the course of the next five years, trapping hundreds of thousands of Jews in Europe, an unintended consequence.

186   Ninety percent of the 214,000 Jews still remaining in Germany in 1939 were killed during the war.

faced a more difficult time. By 1939, not only were visas required to enter other countries, but money was needed to leave Germany, and the red tape required to obtain permission from the Nazis to leave was formidable. For some, unfortunately, visas were acquired too late. The voyage of the SS *St. Louis* seemed to present a last hope for at least some to escape.

Voyage of the Damned

On May 13, 1939, the SS *St. Louis*, a refugee ship, part of the Hamburg-America Line, sailed from Europe to Cuba with 937 Jews on board. The ship arrived in Cuba, but was refused entry into port; only twenty-nine passengers were allowed to disembark, and a few committed suicide. For thirty-six days, the *Saint Louis* sailed from port to port, including to the United States,[187] Canada, Mexico, and Jamaica, but the ship, in each

---

187 In the 1930s and early '40s, with the United States still in the throes of the Great Depression, the mood among Americans was isolationist. Additionally, anti-Semitism, as elsewhere in the world, was prevalent there, including among prominent Americans like Charles Lindbergh and Henry Ford and among Catholic clergy like Father Charles Coughlin. Father Coughlin, an American priest, is a notorious example of a Nazi sympathizer and rabid anti-Semite. During the 1930s, his popular radio program reached a mass audience, estimated at times to rise to as much as a third of the population, also including listeners in Europe. His office received up to eighty thousand letters per week. Historians consider Coughlin to be one of the major demagogues of the twentieth century for being able to influence politics through radio broadcasting without holding political office himself. Fond of quoting Joseph Goebbels, he once said during a broadcast: "When we get through with the Jews in America, they'll think the treatment they received in Germany was nothing."

After the 1936 presidential election, Coughlin increasingly expressed sympathy for the fascist policies of Hitler and Mussolini as "an antidote to Bolshevism." On November 20, 1938, two weeks after *Kristallnacht*, Coughlin, referring to the millions of Christians killed by Bolshevists, said, "Jewish persecution only followed after Christians first were persecuted." On December 18, 1938, two thousand of Coughlin's followers marched in New York City protesting potential changes to the asylum law that would allow more Jews into the United States, chanting, "Send Jews back where they came from in leaky boats!" and "Wait until Hitler comes over here!" Not until May 1942 did his religious superior, the archbishop of Detroit, Most Rev. Edward Mooney (the former bishop of Rochester, New York), finally order him to stop engaging in political activities, but not before Coughlin's vitriol influenced many people, Catholic and non-Catholic alike. Critics of Pius XII charge that the Vatican wanted Coughlin silenced sooner, but it feared causing schism within the US Church.

instance, was ordered back to Europe. No doubt feeling rejected by the world, the passengers returned to Europe in June 1939. The governments of Britain, France, Holland, and Belgium finally agreed to accept some of them, dividing those accepted among each country. Of the 908 passengers who returned to Europe, 254 (nearly 28 percent) died in the Holocaust; 288 found refuge in Britain. Of the 620 who returned to the continent, 366 (just over 59 percent) survived the war. A 1974 book, *Voyage of the Damned,* written by Gordon Thomas and Max Morgan-Witts, and a 1976 film of the same title, portrayed the fate of passengers onboard the SS *St. Louis.*

Restricted Immigration
Tens of thousands of Jews sought to enter the United States, like those onboard SS *St. Louis,* but they were barred by a restrictive immigration policy.[188] The relatively small quota of visas available often went unfilled, although the number of applicants was many times the number available. Temporary admission, a relaxation of stringent entry requirements, and later, the bombing of Auschwitz-Birkenau, were among the practical measures that might have aided Jewish rescue.

The governments of Britain, Canada, and the United States made few attempts between 1933 and 1939 to mitigate the worsening situation for Jews in Europe. Hitler and Goebbels, unfortunately, interpreted the reluctance of countries outside Europe to accept Jewish refugees as license to radicalize Nazi racist policy. They eventually would conclude that widespread public indifference and the "the fog of war" would provide them the cover they needed to get away with genocide.[189] No doubt, Hitler was also emboldened by the lack of public outrage over of the Armenian genocide, perpetrated by Ottoman Turks during WWI, in which up to 1.5 million lost their lives.

Between September 1939 and the spring of 1940, no significant fighting took place in Western Europe. In April 1940, Germany invaded Norway and Denmark. In May 1940, Germany invaded France,

188 In 1998 Stuart Eizenstat, US Undersecretary of State in the Clinton administration, admitted that: "America's response to the early stages of the Holocaust was largely one of indifference ... No country, including the United States, did as much as it might have or should have done to save innocent victims of Nazi persecution."

189 "Genocide" is defined as "the deliberate and systematic extermination of a national, racial, political, or cultural group."

Belgium, and the Netherlands, and quickly vanquished the French army, which wrongly believed itself secure behind the Maginot Line. The Battle of Dunkirk ended with surviving British forces driven back across the English Channel. The surprisingly easy victory over France marked the high-water mark of Hitler's popularity at home. In June 1940, fascist Italy entered WWII on the side of Germany. In July 1940, Germany began planning the invasion of Britain ("Operation Sea Lion") and launched an air assault ("Battle of Britain"). Britain, however, proved to be a tougher foe than France, as the Royal Air Force defeated the *Luftwaffe* in a series of air battles. In September 1940, Italy, Germany, and Imperial Japan signed the Tripartite Pact, which became known as the Axis alliance.

Tightening the Grip on European Jewry

After completing its successful military campaign in the West, Nazi Germany tightened its grip on European Jewry. In less than two years from the invasion of Poland in September 1939 to the beginning of its campaign against the Soviet Union ("Operation Barbarossa") in June 1941, Germany managed to conquer most of Europe. Norway, Denmark, Belgium, France, the Netherlands, Yugoslavia, and Greece fell after only brief military operations. Southeastern Europe—Italy, Slovakia, Hungary, Romania, and Bulgaria—was incorporated willingly into the Greater Third Reich.

As military conquest in the East brought new territory and millions more Jews under Nazi domination, it became apparent that solving the Jewish problem would require a more robust plan. At first the plan called for forcibly deporting Jews to Madagascar, an island off the coast of Africa and, when that proved unfeasible, to restricted areas in Eastern Europe. Soon after the invasion of the Soviet Union in June 1941, however, as even more Jews came under Nazi control, the word "deportation" assumed a horrific connotation.

In 1941, the Reich issued a decree dissolving all German monasteries and abbeys, many of them to be occupied and secularized by the SS. However, in July 1941, *Aktion Klostersturm* ("Operation Monastery") was cancelled because Hitler feared that protests by German Catholics might undermine the war effort on the Eastern front, demonstrating that fear of protest could, indeed, influence Hitler to alter his course.

Tragically, a significant number of Europeans bought into Nazi fanaticism against Jews, as evidenced by the words of Roberto Farinacci, a member of Mussolini's Fascist Grand Council, who, while speaking in 1939 on "The Church and the Jews" declared: "We fascist Catholics consider the Jewish problem from a strictly political point of view ... But it comforts our souls to know that if, as Catholics, we became anti-Semites, we owe it to the teachings that the Church has promulgated over the past twenty centuries."

The Final Solution

In October 1940, the Warsaw Ghetto was established in Poland with a residency of approximately four hundred thousand Jews. About 30 percent of Warsaw's population was forced to live in about 2.4 percent of the city's usable land space under deplorable conditions. Other major ghettos in Poland were established in Krakow, Lotz, Lvov, Lublin, Lida, Bedzin, Bialystok, Kovno/Kaunas, Grodno, Radom, and Riga. There were at least one thousand ghettos in Occupied Poland and countries of the Soviet Union. During 1942 and 1943 the Nazis liquidated the ghettos and their residents—men, women, children, and infants—were deported to the six death camps on Polish soil.

In May 1940, Rudolf Hoess became commandant of Auschwitz, a former army barracks located near the city of the same name. During his three-year tenure there, Auschwitz was upgraded to extermination-camp status, eventually becoming the largest of the killing centers, Auschwitz-Birkenau. As commandant, Hoess was guilty of the deaths of more than a million people in gas chambers, and an additional half-million by starvation and disease. He performed his duties so efficiently that his superiors commended him as a "true pioneer in his field." Yet, he insisted he never personally hated Jews, rationalizing his behavior on the ground that Jews were enemies of the German people and claiming his sense of duty compelled him to carry out Hitler's orders. His Catholic parents wanted him to become a priest, but Hoess decided instead to join the SS.

Unconditional Obedience

Writing about his religious upbringing and of his intent to become a priest, Rudolf Hoess repeatedly referred to his "duty to obey orders without question." He wrote: "I can still remember how my father, who on account of his fervent Catholicism was a determined opponent of the Reich government and its policy, never ceased to remind his friends that, *however strong one's opposition might be, the laws and decrees of the state had to be obeyed unconditionally."* (emphasis mine)

Wannsee Conference

In a magnificent villa on Lake Wannsee outside Berlin on January 20, 1942, fifteen high-ranking Nazi Party and German government officials, including Adolf Eichmann,[190] a majority of whom were lawyers, gathered for a conference chaired by Reinhard Heydrich. At this Wannsee Conference during a ninety-minute working lunch, the Third Reich revised its plan for resolving the Jewish problem. Entitled "Final Solution," the plan called for deporting European Jews to six industrialized killing centers, to be located in Poland—Chelmno, Belzec, Sobibor, Treblinka, Majdanek, and the largest, Auschwitz-Birkenau—where they would be exterminated. The goal was the complete annihilation of European Jewry (8.86 million people, including Jews in the Soviet Union and Great Britain). After the conference, Himmler declared that the extermination of Jews was a "moral right," a "historic task," and "a page of glory in German history."

"The Jews," declared Hitler in a radio broadcast on February 9, 1942, "will be liquidated for at least a thousand years." Within a month of the Wannsee Conference, implementation of the Final Solution was under way in Poland, Germany, Austria, Hungary, Croatia, Slovakia, and France. Between 1942 and 1943, the Nazis liquidated the Polish ghettos and exterminated the inhabitants. To honor Reinhard Heydrich, the name chosen for the Polish operation was *Aktion Reinhard* ("Action Reinhard"). Sadly, the world's response to the rapidly deteriorating situation for European Jewry was disappointingly muted, including the responses of most national governments, international aid organizations, and institutional churches.

The Holy See was well aware of what was happening in Europe through its worldwide network of nuncios and from other sources. John Julius Norwich relates that on April 21, 1942, the British minister to the Holy See, Sir D'Arcy Osborne, wrote a letter to his friend Bridget McEwen, in which he stated, in pertinent part: "Yesterday being Hitler's birthday, I wore a black tie in mourning for the millions he has massacred

---

190   Eichmann was charged by Reinhard Heydrich with the task of facilitating and managing the logistics of mass deportation of Jews to ghettos and eventually to extermination camps.

and tortured. The pope could hardly have worn a black tie, but he could have spoken out against the continuing atrocities."

On July 31, 1942, Osborne wrote to Mrs. McEwen:

> It is very sad. The fact is that the *moral authority* of the Holy See, which Pius XI and his predecessors had built up into a world power, is now sadly reduced. I suspect that H.H. (His Holiness) hopes to play a great role as peacemaker and that it is partly at least for this reason that he tries to preserve a position of neutrality as between the belligerents. But, as you say, the German crimes have nothing to do with neutrality ... and the fact is that the Pope's silence is defeating its own purpose because it is destroying his prospects of contributing to peace.[191] (emphasis mine)

In September 1942, President Roosevelt dispatched a personal envoy to request that the pope speak out against German war crimes, but Pius declined to do so. His secretary of state, Cardinal Luigi Maglione, reiterated that the Holy See was doing all it could do. On December 17, 1942, the Allies issued a condemnation of Nazi atrocities entitled "German Policy of Extermination of the Jewish Race," declaring that perpetrators would be brought to justice after the war. Pius was requested to join in the condemnation, but he again declined to do so. It should be noted that by December 1, 1942, 3.8 million Jews had already been murdered, 2.7 million in 1942 alone. His critics contend that, throughout the war, the most Pius would do was issue vague appeals against the oppression of unnamed racial and religious groups and try to ease the plight of Jewish converts to Catholicism.

On Christmas Eve 1942, the pope was scheduled to make a broadcast to the world on Vatican Radio in which he would address wartime conditions in Europe. It was an historic moment that many millions of people across the globe had been waiting for. The address, however, failed to measure up to expectation. According to his critics, it was overly long, opaque, equivocal, cautionary, and far from a clarion

---

191   Norwich, *Absolute Monarchs*, 444.

call to prophetic action.[192] Calling on men of goodwill to make a solemn vow "to bring back society to its center of gravity, which is the law of God," Pius declared:

> Mankind owes that vow to the countless dead who lie buried on the field of battle. The sacrifice of their lives in the fulfillment of their duty is a 'holocaust' offered for a new and better social order. Mankind owes that vow to the innumerable sorrowing host of mothers, widows, and orphans who have seen the light, the solace and support of their lives wrenched from them. Mankind owes that vow to those numberless exiles whom the hurricane of war has torn from their native land and scattered in the land of the stranger, who make their own lament of the Prophet: "Our inheritance is turned to aliens, our house to strangers." Mankind owes that vow to the hundreds of thousands of persons who, without any fault on their part, "sometimes only" because of their nationality or race, have been consigned to death or to a slow decline.

His critics fault Pius for what he failed to say in his 1942 Christmas Eve address. Once again there was no mention of Jews, of Nazis, or even of Germany. Although Pius spoke the word "holocaust," it was not in the context of genocide. According to John Julian Norwich, author of *Absolute Monarchs*, Pius toned down the racial aspect of the mass killing by using equivocal words like "sometimes only"; and by reducing the number of victims—up to four million Jews killed by Christmas 1942—to "hundreds of thousands." When Mussolini heard the address, he reportedly said to his minister of foreign affairs (and brother-in-law),

---

192   In Rolf Hochhuth's play, *The Deputy*, which premiered in Germany in 1963, Hochhuth's pope says:
   "Secretly ... silently, cunning as serpents—that is how the SS must be met." Pius's fictionalized advisor, Father Fontana, responds:
   "Your Holiness, may I ask in all humility: Warn Hitler that you will compel five hundred million Catholics to make Christian protest if he goes on with these mass killings!"
To which the pope replies,
   "Fontana! An advisor of your insight! How bitter that you too misunderstand Us. Do you not see that disaster looms for Christian Europe unless God makes Us, the Holy See, the mediator?"

Count Gian Galeazzo Ciano: "This is a collection of platitudes which might better have been made by the parish priest of Predappio."

Most victims of the Holocaust lived in countries with large Roman Catholic populations and/or heads of state (e.g., Germany, Austria, Italy, Poland, Spain, Lithuania, France, Hungary, Slovakia, and Croatia). In Poland, as noted previously, victims included not only 88 percent of Polish Jews, but also three million Polish Roman Catholics. And in the former Yugoslavia (Croatia, Bosnia, Slovenia, and Serbia), not only 80 percent of Yugoslav Jews were murdered, but so too were 750,000 Orthodox Catholic Serbs.

CHAPTER 8

Christian Culpability

As NAZI GERMANY'S SPHERE OF influence spread through territorial expansion, it found tens of thousands of willing accomplices in its campaign to eliminate European Jewry among the populations of Western and Eastern Europe. Following the invasion and occupation of France in May 1940, for example, German officers expressed surprise at the eagerness of some French nationals to please their occupiers. It was the local police, the *gendarmerie*, who conducted roundups of French Jews, most of whom went along willingly, trusting that their fellow countrymen would not harm them.[193] With the invasion of the Soviet Union (Operation Barbarossa) in June 1941, this pattern of local complicity surfaced to an even greater degree as local and national police organizations, militias, security forces, auxiliaries, and ordinary citizens participated in roundups and executions. In Romania, to cite another example, the enthusiasm of volunteer ethnic German and Romanian army units taking part in the mass shootings surprised even the coldhearted SS men. Hitler's order regarding Operation Barbarossa called for waging total war, including executing members of the Polish intelligentsia and officer corps, and Soviet officers and commissars. Additionally, the order called for executing all Jews and enslaving all Soviet POWs.

As the mobile killing squads of the SS *Einsatzgruppen* entered Eastern Europe in 1941 alongside German army units, the comparatively thin ranks of the killing squads were augmented by units of Estonian, Latvian, Lithuanian, Belorussian, and Ukrainian nationalist collaborators.

---

193   The roundup of French Jews is described in the historical novel, *Sarah's Key*, by Tatiana De Rosnay.

These killing squads came directly to the home communities of Jews and massacred them. Entire Jewish populations of towns and villages were wiped out.[194] The particularly brutal *Hilfspolizei*, the Ukrainian[195] auxiliary police, hunted down Jews escaping from ghettos and murdered them. Shamefully, the killing was done with the willing collaboration of many thousands of Germans and non-Germans, including Father Jozef Tiso, priest and fascist leader of Slovakia; Father Miroslav Filipovic, priest and death camp commandant in Croatia; and Cardinal Alojzije Stepinac, Vatican-appointed primate of Croatia. All of them were convicted of war crimes after the war (Tiso and Filipovic were executed).

The Catholic Church and Protestant churches, by and large, offered weak resistance to Nazi extremism, both before and during the war. Most, with the notable exception of the Danish Lutheran Church and the Jehovah Witnesses, failed to measure up to the high ethical standard demanded in Jesus's Gospel of Love. Most churches buckled under pressure when their functions were restricted, their schools and printing presses closed down, and the courageous few of their members who resisted Nazi tyranny sent to prisons or death camps. In an attempt to ensure institutional survival and minimize retaliation against their congregants, most churches chose accommodation with Hitler over confrontation. To illustrate, the Vatican, as a sovereign city-state, continued to adhere to its wartime policy of neutrality,[196] despite

---

194   In August 1941, at Kamenets-Podolski in the Ukraine, for example, members of the SS *Einsatzgruppen* and local Ukrainian nationalists murdered about twenty-five thousand Jews at the edge of huge open pits. Victims included five thousand local Jews as well as nearly twenty thousand Jews "deported" from Hungary. As noted previously, 1.5 million Jews were slaughtered in this manner before the death camps became operational. Additionally, many died while crowded into mobile killing vans, forced to breathe deadly vehicle exhaust fumes as they were driven through the countryside.

195   Cf. the Chmielnicki Massacres of 1648–56, when Catholic Ukrainians (Cossacks) slaughtered more than one hundred thousand Jews in cities and towns across Poland. The uprising resulted in the greatest loss of Jewish lives until it was surpassed by the Holocaust.

196   "If you are neutral in situations of injustice, you have chosen the side of the oppressor" (Bishop Desmond Tutu).

"There may be times when we are powerless to prevent injustice, but there must never be a time when we fail to protest" (Elie Wiesel).

"The hottest places in hell are reserved for those who in a period of moral crisis maintain their neutrality" (Dante).

repeated violations of the Reich Concordat, including provisions meant to protect Jewish converts to Catholicism. The signing of the Concordat, not only demoralized German Catholics, who, for the most part, had stood with their bishops in opposing National Socialism from the early 1920s until the Concordat's signing in July 1933, but also undercut the Church's capacity to advocate for justice —a primary function of religion. Pius XII, sadly, made only minimal efforts to save Jewish lives, and, with a few exceptions, such as Bishop Angelo Roncalli,[197] the future Blessed Pope John XXIII, and Monsignor Angelo Rotta,[198] members of the Vatican diplomatic corps did little better. As with the churches, the response of the Allies and worldwide organizations such as the International Red Cross[199] was similarly weak. To cite another example, not until January 1944, the year before the war ended, was an agency, the War Refugee Board, created for the express purpose of saving Jewish lives.

In August 1941, August Hlond, bishop of Poznan and Gniezno and primate of the Church in Poland, as noted previously, advised Vatican Secretary of State Cardinal Maglione that Polish Catholics felt abandoned by the Church, citing Pius's failure to speak out against Nazi persecution of Polish Catholics. Wladislaw Raczkiewicz, president of the Polish government-in-exile, personally appealed to Pius XII in January 1943, to denounce publicly Nazi atrocities against Jews and

---

197   Bishop Angelo Roncalli is credited with saving thousands of Hungarian, Bulgarian, and Slovakian Jews from deportation by, among other things, encouraging priests to issue false baptismal certificates and urging British authorities to grant transit visas to Palestine. Pius XII defenders contend that Roncalli interceded to rescue Jews at Pius's explicit request. Hannah Arendt, a noted German American political theorist, reported, however, that when Roncalli in 1963, by then Pope John XXIII, was asked what was to be done about *The Deputy* and its controversial portrayal of Pius XII, Pope John responded: "*Do against it? What can you do against the truth?*"

198   Rotta has been recognized as a Righteous Gentile by the Israeli government at Yad Vashem, the Holocaust Memorial and Museum in Jerusalem. Roncalli's nomination for this recognition is still pending.

199   Despite its commitment to worldwide humanitarian initiatives, the Swiss-based International Committee of the Red Cross made only sporadic efforts to aid European Jewry. Similar to the Vatican's policy position, Red Cross officials feared that public condemnation of Nazi atrocities would backfire and jeopardize the organization's relief work on behalf of POWs and non-Jewish civilian internees.

Catholics in Poland. Pius, however, did not speak out, at that time or later, despite the murder of two million Polish Catholics (including more than twenty-nine hundred clergy and religious) by the Nazis and the murder of another one million Polish Catholics by the Soviets.

Pius XII's "silence" in response to the Holocaust has been the subject of controversy since 1963, when the play, *Der Stellvertreter* (*The Deputy*) by Rolf Hochhuth, premiered in Germany. *Deputy* evokes the title vicar of Christ, implying, among other things, that by not publicly challenging Nazi racist policies, Pius failed in his role as prophet.[200] His detractors accuse Pius of everything from anti-Semitism to collusion with the Nazi regime, and from cowardice to hedging his bets in case Hitler won the war. One of them, John Cornwell,[201] even referred to him as "Hitler's Pope."

Guenter Lewy, author of *The Catholic Church and Nazi Germany*, writes that when the correspondent of *L'Osservatore Romano* in Berlin, Dr. Eduardo Senatro, asked Pius XII whether he would not protest the extermination of the Jews, the pope answered:

> "Dear friend, do not forget that millions of Catholics serve in the German armies. Shall I bring them into *conflicts of conscience?*" The Pope knew that German Catholics were not prepared to suffer martyrdom for their Church; still less were they willing to incur the wrath of their Nazi rulers for the sake of the Jews whom their own bishops for years had castigated as a harmful influence in German life. In the final analysis ... the Vatican's silence only reflected the deep feeling of the Catholic masses of Europe, those of Germany and Eastern Europe in particular. *The failure of the Pope was a measure of the Church's failure to*

---

200   "Pius XII and the Jews ... The whole thing is too sad and too serious for bitterness ... a silence which is deeply and completely in complicity with all the forces which carry out oppression, injustice, aggression, exploitation, war" (Thomas Merton OCSO).

201   Five years after the publication of *Hitler's Pope,* however, Cornwell stated: "I would now argue, in the light of the debates and evidence following *Hitler's Pope,* that Pius XII had so little scope of action that it is impossible to judge the motives for his silence during the war, while Rome was under the heel of Mussolini and later occupied by Germany."

convert her gospel of brotherly love and human dignity into living reality. (emphasis mine)

First published in 1964, Lewy's book has proven both controversial and influential. *The Deputy* had premiered only a year earlier, indicting the Vatican for failing to act to save Jewish lives during the Holocaust. Amid the Vatican's outrage with the play, Lewy's text continued in the same vein: "One is inclined to conclude that the Pope and his advisers—influenced by the long tradition of moderate anti-Semitism so widely accepted in Vatican circles—did not view the plight of the Jews with a real sense of urgency and moral outrage. For this assertion no documentation is possible, but it is a conclusion difficult to avoid."

Pius's critics focus on the quintessential evil that Nazism presented and contend that his moral leadership in Christian Europe, as head of the oldest, largest, and most powerful Christian faith community on earth, should have been clear, forthright, and outspoken. Neutrality for someone of his religious stature, during a time of egregious injustice, was simply not an option. Explicit condemnation of Nazi extremism, they argue, would have inspired more people of faith to act righteously on behalf of victims, who, at least, would have had the comfort of knowing that the world was not indifferent to their plight. Further, critics contend, his role as leader of a sovereign city-state with international interests conflicted with his role as the world's preeminent spiritual leader, causing him, like many of his predecessors, to be more concerned with politics than conscience.

Pius's defenders, on the other hand, contend that, among other things, issuing condemnatory public statements would have been ineffectual and resulted in reprisals, making matters even worse for Jews and Catholics alike. It is, indeed, true that Nazi reprisals followed public condemnations, but if condemnations had begun early on, during the boycott of Jewish businesses in April 1933, for example, later condemnations of even worse behaviors might not have been necessary. The same can be said of attempts at appeasing Hitler, which only emboldened him to ever more provocative actions, until his unprovoked invasion of Poland in September 1939 finally went too far. "Of all the words of tongue or pen," wrote John Greenleaf Whittier, "the saddest are these: 'what might have been.'"

Obviously, not every Christian was responsible for the Holocaust, but the vast majority of those who were responsible were Christian. In reflecting on the issue of culpability, Franklin H. Littell, a pioneer of Holocaust studies who traced his engagement with the subject to the revulsion he experienced as a young Methodist minister witnessing a large Nazi party rally in 1939, wrote:

> Those comparatively few Christians who maintained their integrity during the Holocaust did in fact challenge the dominant culture, some perished. A good many more suffered persecution as a counterculture[202] to totalitarian creeds and systems. But that does not excuse the rest of us, who wittingly or unwittingly accommodated; certainly it does not cover the apostasy of the millions who collaborated. The majority of those who suffered martyrdom as witnesses to the truth of God in the twentieth century were Jews.

Unquestioning Obedience to Authority

There were, admittedly, additional reasons besides anti-Judaism for Christian culpability in the Holocaust. German Catholics, like their Protestant counterparts, for example, were motivated by nationalism/patriotism and Germany's long tradition of respect for authority, the latter, reinforced by scripture and tradition. Ultranationalism and extreme patriotism, coupled with excessive respect for authority, however, became excuses for unquestioning obedience to unjust authority, an unintended consequence.

Regarding obedience to authority, Primo Levi, a Holocaust survivor, wrote: "Monsters exist, but they are too few in number to be truly dangerous. More dangerous are the common man, the functionaries ready to believe and to act without asking questions."

At the Nuremburg Trials (1945–46), a commonly heard defense to charges of war crimes was, "I was only following orders." Charles Dubost, a French prosecutor, in an opening argument before the Nuremberg Tribunal in 1946 stated:

---

202   Before Emperor Constantine's conversion, Christianity was a countercultural force in the Roman Empire.

[Nazi Germany] allowed itself to be robbed of its conscience and its very soul. Evil masters came who awakened its primitive passions and made possible the atrocities which I have described to you. In truth, the crime of these men is that they caused the German people to retrogress more than twelve centuries.

It should be noted that history is replete with examples of unspeakable evil perpetrated by tyrants when ordinary people fail to resist or blindly follow unjust authority, prompting Edmund Burke to opine: "All that is required for the triumph of evil is for good people to do nothing." Another significant twentieth century example, which predates the Holocaust, is the *Holodomor* (Ukraine, "Killing by hunger"), a man-made famine in Soviet Russia between 1932 and 1933, in which between 2.4 million to 7.5 million Ukrainians died of starvation during peacetime. The Holodomor was engineered by Soviet dictator Josef Stalin, who like Hitler was a personification of evil. A third example, which also predates the Holocaust, is the Armenian Genocide,[203] killing between one million and 1.5 million people. Perpetrated in 1915 during WWI by the leadership of the Ottoman Empire, the Armenian Genocide[204] consisted of massacres, deportations, and forced marches. How many more times will humanity be forced to relearn the same lesson of history?

Clergy Complicity

LIKE GERMAN LAITY, CATHOLIC (AND Protestant) clergy also approved of many of Hitler's policy goals, for example, his opposition to socialism

203   Hitler, a week before the invasion of Poland, on August 22, 1939, is reputed to have told his Wehrmacht commanders: "Who, after all, speaks today of the annihilation of the Armenians?"

204   The Republic of Turkey, successor state of the Ottoman Empire, continues to deny that genocide is an accurate description of what happened. According to Taner Akcam, an associate professor of history at Clark University, recently declassified documents from government archives in Istanbul clearly demonstrate that Ottoman demographic policy from 1913 to 1918 was genocidal. Professor Akcam asserts that the phrase "crimes against humanity" was coined as a legal term and first used on May 24, 1915, in response to the genocide against Armenians and other Christian civilians. See Taner Akcam, "The Young Turks' Crime Against Humanity: The Armenian Genocide and Ethnic Cleansing in the Ottoman Empire," *Human Rights and Crimes Against Humanity* (Princeton, NJ: Princeton University Press, 2012).

and communism and his championing of a conservative social vision. Clergy members, too, prided themselves in Hitler's foreign policy successes, including the reoccupation of the Rhineland, the bloodless annexation of Alsace-Lorraine and Austria, the bloodless takeover of, first, the German-speaking Sudetenland, and then all of Czechoslovakia.²⁰⁵ Members of the clergy, like the general populace, took pride in, among other things, the improved national economy, the restoration of public order, Germany's ascendency as a world power, and Hitler's many public works projects such as the autobahn.

But some of the clergy who supported Hitler were also blatantly anti-Semitic. Garry Wills, author of *Papal Sin*, charged that Archbishop Cesare Orsenigo, papal nuncio to Berlin during the war, was a Nazi sympathizer, and "far from the only friend of the Nazis in the hierarchy." Wills cites, as another example, the rector of the German College in Rome, Archbishop Alois Hudal, who, after the war, was instrumental in assisting Nazi war criminals like Adolf Eichmann, the "architect of the Holocaust";²⁰⁶ Klaus Barbie, the Gestapo "Butcher of Lyon"; Franz Stangl, commandant of Sobibor and Treblinka; and Dr. Josef Mengele, the "Angel of Death," to escape prosecution through Vatican-sanctioned ratlines.

Ratlines

Ratlines (*Rattenliniens*) were a system of escape routes for Nazis and other fascists fleeing Europe at the end of WWII. These escape routes mainly

---

205   Hitler's foreign policy successes were due, in part, to a "paralysis of will" (to stop him) by the victorious WWI allies. Britain and France, in particular, had suffered huge losses in WWI (i.e., Britain lost one million soldiers dead; France lost 1.5 million dead, with both countries suffering many more severely wounded). Also adversely affected by the worldwide Great Depression, France and Britain sought to avoid a second world war with Germany at all costs. Hitler capitalized on their reluctance to risk another world war by engaging in ever more provocations in Europe until his invasion of Poland finally became the last straw.

206   Eichmann, who arrived safely in Argentina, decided to designate himself in his new passport as "Catholic," even though he was Protestant. He explained: "I recall with deep gratitude the aid given to me by Catholic priests in my flight from Europe and decided to honor the Catholic faith by becoming an honorary member." In 1960 Eichmann was captured by Israeli Mossad operatives in Argentina and abducted to Israel to face trial on fifteen criminal charges, including crimes against humanity and war crimes. Found guilty, he was executed by hanging in 1962.

led to safe havens in South America, particularly Argentina, Paraguay, Brazil, Uruguay, and Chile. Other destinations included the United States, Canada, and the Middle East. There were two primary routes, one from Germany to Spain, then Argentina; the other from Germany to Rome or Genoa, then to South America.

The origins of the first ratlines were connected to various developments in Vatican-Argentine relations before and during WWII. According to Michael Phayer, author of *Catholic Church and the Holocaust, 1930–1965,* as early as 1942, Secretary of State Cardinal Maglione contacted Ambassador Llobet, inquiring as to the "willingness of the government of the Argentine Republic to apply its immigration law generously, in order to encourage at the opportune moment European Catholic immigrants to seek the necessary land and capital in your country." Afterward, a German priest, Father Anton Weber, head of the Rome-based Society of Saint Raphael, traveled to Portugal, continuing to Argentina to lay the groundwork for future Catholic immigration. This was to be a route which fascist exiles would use "without the knowledge of the Catholic Church," says Phayer, who asserts that "this was the innocent origin of what would become the Vatican ratline."

In his memoirs Archbishop Alois Hudal wrote: "I thank God that He (allowed me) to visit and comfort many (German) 'victims' in their prisons and concentration camps and to help them escape with false identity papers." As justification for his actions, Hudal explained: "The Allies' War against Germany was not a crusade, but the rivalry of economic complexes for whose victory they had been fighting. This so-called business … used catchwords like democracy, race, religious liberty and Christianity as bait for the masses. All these experiences were the reason why I felt duty bound after 1945 to devote my whole charitable work mainly to former National Socialists and Fascists, especially to so-called 'war criminals.'" Hudal's phrase, "so-called 'war criminals,'" is an early example of Holocaust denial.

Brown Bishops

Another complicit member of the German clergy was Konrad Grober, archbishop of Freiburg, known as the "brown bishop" (brown being the official color of the Nazi movement), because of his enthusiastic support of the Nazis. Grober was a sponsoring member of the SS who blamed Jews for the death of Jesus and asserted that the fate of Jews under National

Socialism was not only justified but a "self-imposed curse." "No German bishop," he declared, "would want to bring harm to the 'beloved Volk and Vaterland.'" In 1943, while the killing camps were at maximum operation, Grober urged his fellow bishops to remain loyal to the Reich. After the war, however, he claimed to have been such an opponent of the Nazis that they planned to "crucify him on the door of Freiburg Cathedral."

In 1935, Archbishop Grober wrote a book in which he reaffirmed the Church's traditional teaching on just war, a reaffirmation which included an explicit rejection of pacifism[207] and a willingness to surrender the final determination of a war's justice or injustice to the secular ruler. He wrote:

> In her almost two thousand years of existence, the Church has never yet absolved her members from military duty, as have several sects—for instance, the Manichaeans and the followers of Wycliffe. She has, on the contrary, rejected the extreme and helpless pacifism which sees war as something forbidden and unchristian and thereby surrenders power to the unjust ... Catholic theologians have always distinguished between the just and unjust war and have never left it to the judgment of the individual, with all his shortsightedness and emotionalism, to decide the justice of any given war. Instead, the final decision has been left to the legitimate authority.[208]

Willingness to surrender the final determination of a war's justice or injustice to a secular leader without qualification, most enlightened and sane people would agree, led to catastrophic (and unintended) consequences in the case of Adolf Hitler and WWII.

A third example of complicity is Adolf Bertram, bishop of Breslau, who like Archbishop Grober denied knowledge of the existence of death camps. To lend credence to his claimed ignorance, Bertram cut off contact with members of the Jewish community in his diocese. The Church during the Third Reich, in his view, needed to exercise restraint in order to avoid jeopardizing national unity and to fulfill its central role of administering the sacraments. When in 1938 Bertram addressed the

207   NB, Jesus was a pacifist.

208   Conrad Grober, *Kirche, Vaterland und Vaterlandsliebe* (Freiburg, Herder, 1935), 108.

people of his diocese, as noted previously, he invoked scripture (St. Paul's letter to the Romans) to urge support of the Reich, saying: "There is no need to urge you to give respect and obedience to the new authorities of the German state. You all know the words of the apostle: 'Let every man be subject to the powers placed over him.'"[209]

In April 1940, Bishop Bertram sent a birthday letter to Hitler, assuring him of the sincere good wishes of his Catholic subjects. In April 1945, after Hitler committed suicide in his Berlin bunker, Bertram presided at a solemn requiem Mass in commemoration of the Führer's life. Like Pius XII, Bishop Bertram did not, however, preside at a solemn requiem Mass for the millions of Hitler's victims.

Michael Buchberger, bishop of Regensburg, claimed that Nazi racism directed at Jews was "justified self-defense" in the face of "overly powerful Jewish capital." Antonius Hilfrich, bishop of Limburg, opined that the true Christian religion "made its way not from the Jews but in spite of them." He wrote in a 1939 pastoral letter: "The Jewish people were guilty of the murder of God and have been under a curse since the day of the crucifixion."

Gordon C. Zahn[210] charged that official German Catholic support for the war reached its peak of dedication and enthusiasm in Catholic Military Bishop Franz Josef Rarkowski. "Here," Zahn wrote, "we find all the ultra-nationalist clichés and symbols that constitute the 'myths men kill by' in their fullest expression." For example, at the beginning of the war, Bishop Rarkowski, in words filled with nationalistic fervor, declared:

---

209   In retrospect, Bishop Bertram's invocation of scripture in 1938 to support Reich authority, as war clouds were gathering over Europe, demands closer scrutiny.

210   Gordon C. Zahn was an American sociologist, pacifist, and teacher who taught at Loyola University and the University of Massachusetts. During WWII, he was a conscientious objector and served in a Civilian Public Service camp established by the Catholic Worker Movement. Zahn authored several books and articles, often focusing on the topics of conscience and war, among them, *Military Chaplains*, based on interviews with RAF chaplains who had served during the war. He then wrote *German Catholics and Hitler's Wars*, in which he accused priests of preaching that it was a combatant's religious duty to fight for the Fatherland. Later he wrote *In Solitary Witness: The Life and Death of Franz Jägerstätter*, about a little known Austrian conscientious objector who refused to fight in Hitler's army. Zahn was cofounder of Pax Christi USA.

Comrades! In this serious hour when our German Volk must undergo the trials of a test by fire in a struggle for its natural and God-given right to live … I turn to you soldiers who stand ready at the front and who bear the great and honorable responsibility of guarding and defending with the sword the life of the German nation.

Each of you knows what is at stake for our Volk in these stormy days; and, in whatever is asked of you, each sees before him the shining example of a true warrior, our Führer and Supreme Commander, the first and most valiant soldier of the Greater German Reich, who is even now with you at the battlefront. We will never forget that first day of September when he issued his formal call to arms to the entire Volk. You, too, were somewhere out there—on the borders of the Reich or in the barracks or already marching forward on that memorable morning. Your ears and hearts were witness to that historic moment when the Führer stepped before the whole Volk in his old military cloak of army gray. You heard his words and sensed in them that your Supreme Commander's love and concern—though devoted as always to the entire Volk—is in a special sense with you soldiers of the German army in these trying hours. Thus the example of the Führer stands before you in brilliant glory.

Bishop Rarkowski's rabid nationalism infused with religiosity was still evident during Lent of 1944, even as Germany's defeat on the battlefield appeared more and more likely. He wrote:

One must be clear about what this phrase means "to serve God." It would be completely wrong to interpret it as a turning away from the world. In order to serve God and to be able to do everything for God, there is certainly no need to flee from the world. Service to God is performed there, wherever one stands, wherever one has his job to do. It is a matter of seeing God's will and a God-given task in whatever burden is placed upon one and the mastering of that task. In that all of us today, on the battlefront and in the Heimat (love and attachment to the homeland), do our very best in this hour of critical need in the service of our Volk; that each of us serving his Vaterland dedicates his heart, his thoughts, his every power to the service of his Volk; that the soldier loyally and bravely follows the path set before him—therein lies the realization of the principle: "I wish to serve God."

At least two German bishops, on the other hand, spoke out against Nazi extremism. Konrad von Preysing, bishop of Berlin,[211] chaired a group, the Kreisau Circle, opposed to the Reich's race policies. In November 1942, Bishop Preysing preached a homily in which he declared that every person has the right to life, including Jews. The following month Josef Frings, bishop of Cologne, wrote a pastoral letter cautioning the faithful not to violate the rights of others without exception. Preaching at the Cathedral in Cologne, Bishop Preysing said: "No one may take the property or life of an innocent person just because he is a member of a foreign race." Both bishops were accused by the Gestapo of attacking the state.

St. Clemens August Graf von Galen, bishop of Münster, was also noteworthy for his opposition to Nazism. At first Bishop Galen hoped the Nazis would restore Germany to its former position of prominence lost in its defeat in WWI. But, disenchanted with the regime's anti-Catholic propaganda and racism, Galen soon became a critic of the regime, frequently complaining directly to Hitler regarding violations of the Reich Concordat. When in November 1936, Nazis in the City of Oldenburg in the State of Saxony removed crucifixes from schools, Galen's protest sparked a public demonstration, and the order was rescinded. In July and August 1941, Galen preached against the lawlessness of the Gestapo, the confiscation of religious property, and the T-4 euthanasia program. In part because of Galen's public protest, the T-4 program was formally halted but continued on in secret.

---

211   In June 1940, following Bishop Bertram's birthday letter to Hitler, Bishop Preysing, who thought the letter inappropriate, informed Pope Pius XII of his inclination to resign as bishop of Berlin. Guenter Lewy, in *The Catholic Church and Nazi Germany*, described the pope's response: "Pius XII, exhibiting the diplomatic skill for which he was known, did his best to conciliate all parties to the dispute. He resolutely rejected the idea of Preysing's resignation, reassuring him of his full support, while at the same time he praised the leadership of Bishop Bertram."

Documents discovered after the war showed that the Nazis were close to executing Galen but decided to wait until victory was achieved. Bishop Galen was named a cardinal on February 18, 1946. He was canonized a saint by Benedict XVI on October 9, 2005, largely because of his role in opposing the T-4 Program.

Brown Priests

There were at least 138 priests—109 diocesan priests from Germany, nineteen ordained members of religious orders, and ten priests from dioceses outside Germany—who actively promoted National Socialism.[212] Known as "brown priests," some of them joined the Nazi Party and fully embraced Hitler's policies. Father Richard Kleine, one of the brown priests, wrote:

> Since I was a child a burning love for my German Volk and fatherland has been part of me ... the relationship between the Church and Germany has been especially important to me. I am one of those who firmly believed that the National Socialist movement stood for the national and social future of my Volk and was altogether the superior alternative to the Communist-Bolshevist ideology. I trusted ... that Christian presence and cooperation in this movement could enhance Christian thought.

Daniel Jonah Goldhagen speculates about what role Catholic clergy could have played in Nazi Germany. He wrote:

> If Pius XI and Pius XII, church leaders and lower clergy had used their pulpits and their enormous number of newspapers and diocesan publications with their huge, faithful readerships in Germany and around Europe to declare anti-Semitism a vicious delusion and to denounce the persecution of the Jews as a grievous crime and sin, then the political history of Europe would have been different, and the fate of the Jews much better.[213]

---

212   See Kevin P. Spicer, *Hitler's Priests: Catholic Clergy and National Socialism.*

213   Goldhagen, *A Moral Awakening*, 44.

In a 1939 editorial in the Hungarian fascist party newspaper *Arrow Cross*, an unnamed Hungarian priest wrote:

In places where priests are murdered, the educated are slaughtered, and churches are burnt; that is where the Jew is to be found. Even if no Jew is actually there in a physical sense, his presence is represented there by his venomous literary works. Like naked spirits they drift all over the world, and by means of their filthy moral concepts, their distorted philosophy, and their base artistic schools, they spread their revolting ideas. Their sullied views corrupt the world.

Another unnamed Hungarian priest, at the height of the 1944 killing frenzy in Hungary, wrote: "Ever since the Jews crucified Jesus, they have been the foes of Christianity. May the Jews be expelled from Hungary, and then the Church, too, will be able to breathe more freely."

Conditional Love

In May 1941, an article written by a priest entitled, "Why Are the Jews Persecuted?" appeared in the diocesan newspaper of Croatian bishop Ivan Saric. It stated:

The descendants of those who hated Jesus, persecuted him to death, crucified him and persecuted his disciples, are guilty of sins greater than (those of) their forebears. Jewish greed increases. The Jews have led Europe and the world towards disaster—moral and economic disaster. Their appetite grows till only domination of the world will satisfy it … Satan aided them in the invention of Socialism and Communism. *There is a limit to love*. The movement of liberation of the world from the Jews is a movement for the renewal of human dignity. Omniscient and omnipotent God stands behind this movement. (emphasis mine)

The phrase "there is a limit to love" is a sad commentary indeed, especially when uttered by a priest, because Jesus espoused *unconditional* love, which by definition excludes no one—not even Jews.

When the occupation regime in the Netherlands ordered all Dutch citizens with at least one Jewish grandparent to register with Nazi authorities, the archbishop of Utrecht, Johannes de Jong, failed to protest, even though urged to do so by Protestant Reformed Church leaders who did protest. When the regime ordered that all government officials sign a statement declaring themselves to be members of the Aryan race, Jan Koopmans, a Dutch Reformed Church minister, wrote Archbishop de Jong asking him to speak out against the decree: "difficult as this might be in view of the fact that the Pope had blessed Italian Arms and the attitude of some German bishops." Archbishop de Jong, however, declined to speak out.

German Bishops Bless an Unjust War

In December 1941, a month before the Wannsee Conference, the German Catholic Bishops directed that a special war prayer be read at the beginning and end of all Masses. This prayer asked God to bless the Wehrmacht with victory and to protect the lives and health of all German combatants. The bishops also directed priests of their dioceses to preach, at least once a month, about the war, mentioning German soldiers on land, on sea, and in the air in a favorable light. German Catholics, thereupon, began to pray publicly at the beginning and end of Masses for a Nazi victory in an *unjust* war. Remember that Germany, without provocation, started the war with announced goals that included: territorial conquest of sovereign nations, enslavement of captured populations, brutalization and killing of innocent civilians, and genocide—all clear violations of the Catholic Just War Doctrine.[214] Preaching from the pulpit about the war, mentioning German combatants in a favorable light, also violated the Just War doctrine. Both practices obviously led to unintended consequences, not the least of which was prolonging the war and its unprecedented level of carnage, especially in 1944, when the Wehrmacht was clearly losing the war.

Bishops Invoke Patriotism

A joint pastoral letter from the bishops of Cologne and Paderborn in March 1942, reaffirmed the natural rights of life, liberty, and property, and decried the arbitrary detention and killing of innocents. It concluded, however, with a rousing endorsement of German nationalism/patriotism and this challenge:

---

214 Regarding the Just War Doctrine, first espoused by St. Augustine, see current edition of the *Catechism of the Catholic Church*, n.s., 2302–2317.

That which we bishops had to tell you today with grievously moved soul may not however serve anyone as an excuse to neglect his national duties. On the contrary! With the full authority of our holy office we urge you again today: In this time of war fulfill your patriotic duties most conscientiously! Don't let anyone surpass you in willingness to make sacrifices and readiness to do your share! Be faithful to our people!

Catholic bishops in Slovakia, ruled by fascist dictator and priest Father Josef Tiso, issued a pastoral letter in 1942 in which they justified the persecution of Jews, declaring:

The influence of the Jews (has) been pernicious. In a short time they have taken control of almost all the economic and financial life of the country. Not only economically, but also in the cultural and moral spheres, they have harmed our people. The Church cannot be opposed, therefore, if the state with legal regulations hinders the dangerous influence of the Jews.

No Mercy
A priest in Kowel (Ukraine) preached a homily in May 1942 in which he excused Catholics from performing Corporal Works of Mercy[215] for Jews. He stated: "Dear merciful people, I beg you and warn you, do not give a piece of bread to a Jew ... No trace of a Jew is to remain. We should erase them from the face of the earth. When the last Jew disappears from the face of the earth, we shall win the war."

Pope Urges Caution
In April 1943, with the killing camps working at full capacity, Pope Pius XII, in a letter to Konrad Preysing, bishop of Berlin, wrote:

We give to the pastors who are working on the local level the duty of determining if and to what degree the danger of reprisals

---

215   The Corporal Works of Mercy are actions Catholics perform that extend God's compassion and mercy to those in need (i.e., feed the hungry, shelter the homeless, clothe the naked, visit the sick and imprisoned, bury the dead, and give alms to the poor). Excluding suffering Jews from God's compassion and mercy is, obviously and unequivocally, blasphemy.

and of various forms of oppression occasioned by episcopal (church) declarations … *ad maiora mala vitanda* ("to avoid worse") … seem to advise caution. Here lies one of the reasons, why We impose self-restraint on Ourselves in our speeches; the experience, that we made in 1942 with papal addresses, which We authorized to be forwarded to the Believers, justifies our opinion, as far as We see … The Holy See has done whatever was in its power, with charitable, financial and moral assistance. To say nothing of the substantial sums which we spent in American money for the fares[216] of immigrants.

In August 1943, members of the Kreisau Circle, a Berlin resistance group, drafted a letter regarding deportations to death camps. Intended to be sent to Hitler under the signatures of German bishops, it read, in pertinent part:

> With deepest sorrow—yes, even with holy indignation—have we German bishops learned of the deportation of non-Aryans in a manner that is scornful of human rights. It is our holy duty to defend the unalienable rights of all men guaranteed by natural law … Shocking reports reach us regarding the awful, gruesome fate of the deported …

The draft letter made specific requests including: humane living and working conditions, access to friends and relatives, admission of chaplains and of a visitation committee into camps, a list of where deportees were detained, a list of all evacuees, and an accounting of their whereabouts. Unfortunately, the letter was never sent. It was rejected in favor of "small successes" (i.e., it was feared that taking public action would make it more difficult for rescuers hiding Jews).

Guenter Lewy charged that with the exception of Konrad Preysing, bishop of Berlin, (elevated to the rank of cardinal by Pius XII in 1946):

---

216   Pius used his own personal funds to help defray the cost of Jewish refugees fleeing to Brazil.

All German bishops until the very last days of the conflict called on the faithful to do their patriotic duty. This position, we may assume, represented sincerely felt loyalty to their country. The fact that Germany was ruled by the Nazis who harassed and persecuted the Church and were guilty of untold other crimes, made no difference.[217]

Most bishops of Poland, as elsewhere in Europe, were passive during the Holocaust. For example, three councils of Polish bishops occurred during German occupation, and none of them issued a statement even alluding to the mass murder taking place on Polish soil. Moreover, correspondence between Polish bishops and the Holy See contained little expression of concern over the plight of Jews.

France

Before the onset of WWII, France, a predominately Roman Catholic country, was one of the more accommodating European countries in welcoming Jewish refugees from Poland, Romania, and Germany. In June 1940, there were approximately 350,000 French Jews, more than half of them refugees from Germany. The treatment of Jews in France at the hands of the Nazis is a poignant reminder of the fragility of democracy. Though French Jews were emancipated and granted citizenship rights for the first time in European history in 1790 during the French Revolution and were reasonably well integrated into French society, their fate changed drastically in 1942.

A month after invading Denmark and Norway, on April 9, 1940, the Wehrmacht marched into France, Belgium, Luxembourg, and the Netherlands. Only the massive sea evacuation of some 338,000 British, French, and Belgian troops from Dunkirk in France at the end of May prevented the Germans from decisively destroying the military forces that opposed them in Western Europe. On June 5, 1940, Germany launched its final assault against France. Paris fell with little resistance on June 14. Two days later, Marshal Phillipe Petain,[218] the aging French hero of WWI, took over as head of the French government and quickly petitioned for an armistice, signed on June 22. The armistice resulted in a two-zone division of France and annexation by Germany of the

---

217   Lewy, *The Catholic Church and Nazi Germany*, 232.

218   After the war, Petain was convicted of war crimes.

eastern provinces of Alsace and Lorraine (taken from Germany under the Versailles treaty). The Nazis occupied the northern two-thirds of the country, including Paris. Southern France, with governmental headquarters in the resort town of Vichy, remained unoccupied until early 1942. The Germans allowed a collaborationist puppet government to exist there, led by Petain, in exchange for its cooperation. The cooperation demanded by the Nazis for allowing Petain's Vichy regime to exist included exploitation of French natural resources, approval of labor brigades to be sent to work in German factories, and anti-Jewish measures.

In 1941, the Vichy regime informally inquired whether the Holy See would object to passage of anti-Jewish laws in France, then under consideration in the national legislature. Pius XII, through his secretary of state, Cardinal Maglione, responded that although the Church condemned racism, it did not repudiate every rule affecting Jews. When Petain's puppet government introduced the legislation, *Statut des Juifs* ("Jewish Statutes"), the Vichy ambassador to the Holy See informed Petain that the Vatican did not consider the legislation in conflict with Catholic teachings, as long as it was carried out with "charity and justice." The legislation, among other things, excluded Jews from public life in France. It barred them from civil service positions, from the military and commerce, and from participation in various professions, including medicine, law, and education. Neither the French Catholic Church nor the Holy See issued any public protest against *Statut des Juifs*.

The Catholic hierarchy in France welcomed the Vichy government not only because it seemed to represent a degree of independence from state interference, but also because it promised to repudiate certain liberal values against which the Church had long fought in France. The right to divorce, for example, was abolished. Additionally, religious education was approved in state schools and some confiscated church property (i.e., the Grotto at Lourdes) was returned to the French Church. As Cardinal Pierre-Marie Gerlier of Lyon said in an interview, "No one supports more zealously than I the policies of Marshal Petain."

In July 1941, consistent with the *Statut des Juifs*, the Vichy regime inaugurated a program of Aryanization by, among other things, confiscating Jewish-owned property and setting up internment camps for foreign Jews. Thousands were sent to internment camps, such as Gurs near the Spanish border. Four thousand were eventually deported from Gurs to Auschwitz-Birkenau. Elsewhere in France, internment camps were located in Saint-Cyprien, Rivesaltes, Le Vernet, and Les Milles. Foreign Jews fared particularly badly in France. Roundups of "undesirable refugees" netted some thirty thousand Jews. Confined in these camps, three thousand of them died because of deplorable conditions. At Gurs, 1,167 died of starvation, dysentery, and typhoid.[219] At Rivesaltes, where children were imprisoned apart from their mothers, mortality rates were equally high. Deplorable sanitary conditions; lack of food, water, and adequate shelter from the cold; and sadistic harassment by guards were common features of French internment camps.

Preparations began in early 1942 to include Western European Jews in the Final Solution. The Vichy regime cooperated in the roundup and transport of Jews to death camps in Poland. Deportations started that summer, with French police responsible for carrying out roundups. Early on a Thursday morning in July 1942, more than four thousand Gendarmes set out in pairs through the streets of Occupied Paris, carrying arrest orders for scores of Jewish men, women, and children. Within days, 13,152 people were rounded up, herded off, and interned for several days in the Velodrome d'Hiver sports arena, where they were held without food or water until deportation to Auschwitz-Birkenau. No more than one hundred would survive. Throughout France, Jews were seized from their homes, herded into camps, loaded onto cattle cars, and sent to the Drancy transit camp northeast of Paris. During 1942 more than sixty separate transports left Drancy, the last stop before dying for at least sixty-two thousand Jews. It should be noted that the mass arrests, the largest in wartime France, were planned and carried out not by the Nazi occupiers but by the predominately Roman Catholic French.

The last transport to Auschwitz-Birkenau left in August 1944, eight months before the war would end. Over seventy-seven thousand Jews deported from France were murdered in Nazi death camps. Of these, one-third were French citizens, and over eight thousand were children under the age of thirteen. Seventy-four percent of French Jewry survived

---

219 NB, Anne Frank, rounded up in Amsterdam, died of typhus at Bergin-Belsen.

the Holocaust. The high survival rate was attributable to a number of factors, including dispersal of Jews in many localities, minimal German police presence, the few church leaders who protested deportations, Christians who engaged in rescue and resistance, and the relatively small number of bystanders.

Not all clerics in France were silent concerning *Statut des Juifs*, particularly after the roundups began. One notable exception was Father Pierre Marie-Benoit, who was recognized as a Righteous Gentile by the Yad Vashem Holocaust Martyrs' and Heroes' Remembrance Authority in Jerusalem. Father Marie-Benoit declared: "The law (under which the Jews were being arrested) is immoral. Accordingly, we must not overlook such laws and are duty-bound to resist them actively ..."

The French Church's affinity to the Vichy regime and its long history of anti-Judaism and anti-Semitism (e.g., the Dreyfus Affair) constrained church leaders from protesting against anti-Jewish measures. One church leader who did eventually protest was Bishop Delay of Marseilles, but his remarks early on were less than charitable:

> We do not ignore the fact that the Jewish question poses difficult national and international problems. We are well aware that our country has the right to take all appropriate steps to defend itself against those who, especially in recent years, have done her so much harm and to punish those who abuse the hospitality that has so liberally been extended to them.

There were some French bishops, particularly in unoccupied southern France, who publicly protested deportations. For example, Archbishop Jules-Gerard Saliege of Toulouse, in a pastoral letter read in the churches of his diocese said:

> That children, that women, fathers and mothers be treated like cattle, that members of a family be separated from one another and dispatched to an unknown destination, it has been reserved for our own times to see such a sad spectacle ... the Jews are real men and women. Foreigners are real men and women ... They are a part of the human species. They are our brothers like so many others.

One effect of Archbishop Saliege's pastoral letter was to encourage other bishops to issue similar declarations condemning anti-Jewish measures. His opposition to the deportations and to the persecution of Jews helped bring about a change in public opinion. As a result, more Jews found hiding places in French homes, demonstrating the positive impact that a "shepherd" could have on his flock. Bishop Pierre-Marie Théas of Montauban wrote in a pastoral letter: "I give voice to the outraged protest of Christian conscience, and I proclaim that all men, Aryans or non-Aryans, are brothers created by the same God; that all men, whatever their race or religion, have the right to be respected by individuals and by states." Others who wrote pastoral letters urging compassion and tolerance for Jews included Cardinal Pierre-Marie Gerlier of Lyon, and the bishops of Bayonne, Albi, and Marseilles. Some bishops spoke out in public protest of persecution occurring in Vichy, France, setting an example for how people "of conscience" ought to respond to injustice.

The Netherlands

In 1939 approximately 140,000 Jews lived in the Netherlands (1.4 percent of the population), including twenty-five thousand German-Jewish refugees who fled from Germany in the 1930s. A poor and middle-class minority, Jews were seemingly well integrated into a Dutch society that exhibited little overt anti-Semitism. Roman Catholics made up 30 percent of the population. When Germany invaded and occupied the Netherlands in May 1940, Queen Wilhelmina fled to Britain to form a government in exile, but the Dutch bureaucracy continued to function under the occupying regime.

Anti-Jewish policy in the Netherlands evolved gradually, starting with elimination of Jews from civil service positions in September 1940, followed by the compulsory registration of Jewish-owned corporations and the registration of all Dutch Jews under race laws enacted by the occupation regime. Soon the policy took on an increasingly radical turn when Jews were forced to wear the Star of David, and preparations began for their deportation to death camps. By war's end, 107,000 Jews had been deported. Of these, only five thousand survived, another thirty thousand managed to survive in hiding or by other means. Over

76 percent of Dutch Jews perished at the hands of the Nazis, including 14-year-old Anne Frank[220] and most of her family.

Deportation from the Netherlands to death camps began in July 1942. In February 1943, Archbishop de Jong issued a public protest and ordered that a pastoral letter be read in all churches of his archdiocese in which he offered prayers for "the people of Israel" and their sufferings. Catholics were advised that cooperation with the deportations was morally unacceptable. The Nazis retaliated by speeding up the deportation process,[221] even arresting Catholic converts from Judaism, including Sister Edith Stein, then residing in a Dutch convent. She and other religious and clerics were among those deported to Auschwitz-Birkenau.

Approximately twenty-four thousand Jews were rescued by "people of conscience" in the Netherlands, which has the second largest number of Righteous Gentiles (after Poland) recognized by Yad Vashem, the Holocaust Martyrs' and Heroes' Remembrance Authority in Jerusalem—4,376, including Corrie ten Boom, a member of the Dutch Reformed Church, whose defiance of the Nazis led to her internment in a concentration camp. She and her family publically protested Nazi persecution of Jews as an "injustice to humanity" and an "affront to God." Joop Westerweel, a Dutch educator and pacifist, set up a clandestine network to rescue Jewish youth, accompanying them through Occupied Belgium and France to the Spanish border. Westerweel was eventually apprehended and executed. Johannes Bogard, a religiously devout Dutch farmer, rescued scores of Jews by hiding them on his farm and in nearby residences.

---

220   Otto Frank, the only survivor of the Frank family, returned to Amsterdam after the war to find that Anne's diary had been saved, and his efforts led to its publication in 1947. It was translated from its original Dutch and first published in English in 1952 as *The Diary of a Young Girl*. It has since been translated into many languages. The house where the family hid at the *Prinsengract* in Amsterdam is now a museum. She wrote in February 1944: "I looked out of the open window, over a large area of Amsterdam, over all the roofs and on to the horizon, which was such a pale blue that it was hard to see the dividing line. As long as this exists, I thought, and I may live to see it, this sunshine, these cloudless skies, while this lasts I cannot be unhappy."

221   Pius XII defenders cite this instance of Nazi retaliation to support their claim that public protests by the pope would have been counterproductive.

Much of Dutch resistance to the Nazis could be characterized as either passive resistance or nonviolent active resistance. For example, immediately following the Nazi occupation, American and British films were banned from theaters, replaced with German movies and newsreels. Dutch patrons, however, walked out or booed during the newsreels. Although forbidden to listen to BBC radio and broadcasts from the Dutch government in exile, many listened in defiance. In 1943, over one million radios were confiscated by the Nazis in retaliation. When university students were required to sign an oath of allegiance to the occupation regime, over 85 percent refused to comply. Underground newspapers flourished and were particularly useful after the confiscation of radios and loss of electricity during the later years of the war.

Dutch resistance groups were organized to serve a variety of functions, including rescue and shelter, creating false documents, providing couriers to act as messengers, or engaging in acts of sabotage. It is estimated that fifty thousand to sixty thousand people were directly involved in resistance activities with hundreds of thousands more offering assistance. More than ten thousand resisters lost their lives.

Hungary

Historians term the Austro-Hungarian Empire, from the end of the nineteenth century to the beginning of WWI, a "Golden Age" for Jews. It was a time characterized by openness to both Jewish emigration and assimilation, for which the Austro-Hungarian monarchy (the House of Hapsburg) enjoyed the support and loyalty of its Jewish population. Austro-Hungary was considered, like Germany before Hitler, a safe haven for Jews. The situation began to deteriorate, however, when Austro-Hungary, allied with Germany, was likewise defeated by the Allies in WWI. Under terms of the Versailles Treaty, Austria and Hungary became separate countries with republican forms of government. Like Germany, neither country had a tradition of or preparation for participatory democracy. Accordingly, political instability soon ensued in both Hungary and Austria, as it did in Weimar Germany, also aggravated by economic woes. In all three countries, the ever present undercurrent of anti-Semitism surfaced, became enflamed by right-wing agitators, and led to the scapegoating of Jews.

Germany invaded Hungary in March 1944, late in the war, and installed a puppet regime controlled by the national fascist party, *Arrow Cross*, under the leadership of fascist dictator Ferenc Szálasi. Two-thirds of the population was Roman Catholic. In the first six weeks of German occupation, Hungarians made over thirty-five thousand denunciations of their Jewish neighbors, who had been stripped of their citizenship rights in the 1930s. At the height of what was soon to become a killing frenzy of unprecedented proportion, an unnamed priest wrote an article for the *Arrow Cross* Party newspaper in which he declared: "Ever since the Jews crucified Jesus, they have been the foes of Christianity. May the Jews be expelled from Hungary, and then the Church, too, will be able to breathe more freely."

Before the invasion, Hungarian Jews had been spared deportation because, although allied with Germany in WWII, Hungary's national government, like Italy's, resisted Nazi requests to deport Jews. After the invasion and occupation, however, as happened in Italy in October 1943, after Mussolini's fall from power, Jews were left unprotected. Almost immediately, Hungarian Jews were rounded up, marched to the banks of the Danube River, ordered to take off their shoes,[222] shot in the back of the head and pushed into the river. By mid-May 1944, mass deportation began in earnest. Incredibly, within only ninety days, 70 percent of Hungarian Jewry was destroyed.

On the day that the deportation began, Hungary's undersecretary of state, Laszlo Endre, in a speech, declared: "The popes, as well as our own ancient and saintly kings, legislated draconian laws and imposed severe decrees upon this parasitic race. Thus, no one can complain that we are not acting in accordance with the spirit of Christianity when we enact draconian regulations against the Jews so as to protect our nation."

A Call to Prayer

In June 1944 as Jews were being rounded up and deported to Auschwitz-Birkenau, an article appeared in the *Arrow Cross* newspaper in the town of Veszprem announcing an upcoming thanksgiving prayer service. It read:

> With the help of Divine Providence our ancient city and province
> have been liberated from that Judaism which sullied our nation.

---

222   Shoes on the Danube Promenade, the Holocaust memorial on the bank of the Danube River in Budapest, honor Hungarian Jews killed by fascist *Arrow Cross* militiamen in Budapest during WWII. Jews were ordered to take off their shoes, and were shot at water's edge so that their bodies would fall into the river and be carried away. The memorial represents the shoes left behind on the bank.

In our thousand years, this is not the first time we have been freed from some scourge which had befallen us. However no previous event can compare in its importance to this event, for no previous foe threatening us, whether by force or by a political takeover, had ever succeeded in overcoming us to the extent that the Jews have succeeded, with the aid of their poisoned roots which penetrated our national body and took hold of it. We are following in the footsteps of our fathers in coming to express our thanks to our God who saves us whenever we are in distress. Come and gather for the thanksgiving service which will take place on June 25 at 11:30 AM at the Franciscan Church.

The Hungarian Jewish community was the largest community of European Jews to be deported and exterminated—late in the war with lightning speed. Destruction of this community, therefore, is one of the saddest chapters in Holocaust history. While the Wehrmacht was being routed in the East and the ultimate fate of Nazi Germany was being sealed by the successful Allied invasion at Normandy on June 6, 1944, when much of European Jewry had already been destroyed, when world leaders had undisputed knowledge of what was happening in the death camps, *and* while prayers were being offered in German Catholic Churches for German victory in an unjust war, 450,000 Hungarian Jews lost their lives in an operation that kept the Auschwitz-Birkenau crematoria burning night and day. On January 27, 1945, Auschwitz-Birkenau was liberated by Soviet troops, but, of course, liberation came too late for the Jews of Hungary, a most unfortunate and totally preventable unintended consequence.

Assigned as first secretary to the Swedish legation in Hungary, Raoul Wallenberg[223] arrived in Budapest on July 9, 1944. Despite lack of experience in diplomacy and clandestine operations, Wallenberg led one of the most extensive and successful rescue efforts for Jews during the Holocaust. His work with the War Refugee Board and the World Jewish Congress prevented deportation of tens of thousands of Hungarian Jews. For his heroic efforts, Wallenberg was recognized as a

---

223   On January 17, 1945, just six months after he began his mission in Hungary, Wallenberg, a person of conscience and true hero of the Holocaust, was captured by Russian soldiers and was never heard from again.

Righteous Gentile by Yad Vashem, the Holocaust Martyrs' and Heroes' Remembrance Authority in Jerusalem.

During the final months of the war, with the Wehrmacht in retreat on all fronts, Monsignor Angelo Rotta, nuncio in Budapest, also recognized as a Righteous Gentile by Yad Vashem, joined a group of diplomats, among them Angel Sanz Briz and Giorgio Perlasca of the Spanish embassy and Fredich Bom of the International Red Cross, in trying to save the remaining Jews in Budapest. Monsignor Rotta requested that the pope urge Hungarian bishops, who had not publicly opposed the killing, to join in the effort to stop deportations. Pius XII responded by writing letters to the bishops and to the Hungarian Regent, requesting them to demand that deportations cease. The effort bore fruit; the bishops finally issued a public protest, and the deportations did, indeed, stop. Unfortunately, however, by then most of Hungary's Jews were already dead.

Previously, in late 1942, Pius XII advised Hungarian bishops that speaking out against the carnage in the East would be politically advantageous. It should be noted that Pius's efforts to save Jews increased as it became more likely that the Allies would win the war. Fifty-two years later, in 1994, the bishops of Hungary issued a statement acknowledging their complicity for the Holocaust. It read: "(Catholics) who through fear, cowardice, or opportunism, failed to raise their voices against the mass humiliation, deportation, and murder of their Jewish neighbors must also be held responsible, and before God we now ask forgiveness for this failure."

Croatia

In April 1941, after Germany invaded, occupied, and partitioned Yugoslavia, another Versailles Treaty-created state, the Nazis permitted the local fascist organization, the Ustasa, to create the "Independent" State of Croatia. Croatia was the province of Yugoslavia with the largest proportion of Roman Catholics. Orthodox Catholic Serbs and Muslims resided primarily in the provinces of Serbia, Bosnia, and Slovenia, which dominated the rest of the divided country. Almost immediately, the Ustasa regime, under the leadership of dictator Ante Pavelic, unleashed a brutal reign of terror[224] in which hundreds of thousands of Orthodox Catholic Serbs, Jews, Muslims, and Gypsies were murdered. Serbs were considered to be the primary threat in Croatia; Jews were the secondary threat. The regime established concentration/death camps, the largest of which was the Jasenovac complex, southeast of Zagreb. Other camps were located at Danica, Loborgrad, Jadovno, Gradiska, and Djakovo. Despite being a secondary threat, more than 80 percent of Yugoslavia's Jews were murdered. As happened elsewhere in Occupied Eastern Europe, members of local nationalist militias and auxiliaries participated in the slaughter of targeted minorities. The Italian army, despite Italy's alliance with Germany, however, helped rescue thousands of Croatian Jews, refusing to comply with the Ustasa plan to deport them from Italian-held regions of Croatia.

Members of the clergy of the Croatian Catholic Church from priests to a cardinal were complicit in the mass murder occurring on Croatian soil, not only of Jews, but also of Orthodox Catholic Serbs, Muslims, and Gypsies (Sinti and Roma). From 1941 to 1945, Ante Pavelic's puppet regime carried out some of the more horrific crimes of the Holocaust, killing over 800,000 people—750,000 Serbs, 60,000 Jews, and 26,000 Gypsies. In these crimes, Croatia's fascist regime was supported by Cardinal Alojzije Stepinac, archbishop of Zagreb. Cardinal Stepinac, primate of Croatia, was an advocate for the elimination of Jews and Orthodox Catholic Serbs from Croatian society. A staunch nationalist and anti-Bolshevist, Stepinac asserted, among other things, that Jews were pornographers and that their doctors were the country's primary abortionists.

Priest Commandant

Many victims of the Pavelic regime were killed in the Jasenovac complex, where over two hundred thousand people died, mainly Orthodox Catholic

---

224   John Cornwell describes Ante Pavelic's "reign of terror": "(It was) an act of 'ethnic cleansing' before that hideous term came into vogue, it was an attempt to create a 'pure' Catholic Croatia by enforced conversions, deportations, and mass exterminations. So dreadful were the acts of torture and murder that even hardened German troops registered their horror. Even by comparison with the recent bloodshed (the 1992–95 Bosnian War) in Yugoslavia at the time of writing (1999), Pavelic's onslaught against the Orthodox Serbs remains one of the most appalling civilian massacres known to history" (Cornwell, *Hitler's Pope*, 249).

Serbs. Several fundamentalist priests were involved in the killing, notably Father Miroslav Filipovic, a Franciscan, and one of the commandants of Jasenovac, who was hanged for war crimes (wearing his clerical robes) after the war. Some 240,000 people were "rebaptized" into Roman Catholicism in "the Catholic Kingdom of Croatia" as part of the Pavelic regime's policy to "kill a third, deport a third, convert a third" of the Serbs, Jews, and Gypsies in Bosnia and Croatia.

John Cornwell charged that from the beginning of Pavelic's regime, the Vatican was fully aware of what was happening in Croatia. Nonetheless, in May 1941, according to Cornwell, Pius XII greeted Pavelic during a devotional audience at St. Peter's in Rome. At that time, the Vatican granted de facto recognition of the Pavelic regime, calling it a "bastion against communism," despite the fact that the Vatican still had diplomatic ties with the country of Yugoslavia.[225] Cornwell further charged that from the start of the Ustasa regime, Pavelic was known to be a puppet of Hitler and Mussolini, who, like them, promulgated anti-Semitic laws, but unlike them, favored forced conversions of Serbs from Eastern Orthodox to Roman Catholicism.

At war's end, the succeeding communist regime of Josip Broz Tito placed Cardinal Stepinac on trial for war crimes, namely, collaboration with the Nazis, collaboration with the Pavelic regime, allowing chaplains in the Ustasa army to act as religious agitators, forceful conversions of Orthodox Catholic Serbs, and high treason against the Yugoslav government.

After a trial in Zagreb, Stepinac was convicted and sentenced to seventeen years in prison. Prosecution witnesses testified, among other things, that a group of priests armed with pistols sought to convert or kill Serbs. One witness testified that up to 650 Serbs were stabbed or beaten to death while they were seeking sanctuary in a church. Specifically, Stepinac was convicted of collaboration with and glorifying the Pavelic regime in the Catholic press, pastoral letters, and speeches. The trial was condemned by the Holy See as "political theater." Pius XII excommunicated everyone involved in the court proceedings, including

---

225   The Holy See also officially recognized the German-speaking Wartheland segment of divided and Occupied Poland claimed by Germany, despite the fact that the Vatican still had official ties to the country of Poland. This, as noted previously, demoralized Poles, who considered the recognition to be betrayal of Polish sovereignty.

jury members, and termed the process *"un tristissimo processo"* (the "saddest trial"). Neither Father Filipovic nor Cardinal Stepinac was excommunicated. To this day worldwide, many traditionalist Catholics consider Cardinal Stepinac a hero for his resistance to communism and consider his trial, conviction, and imprisonment to have been unjust. Stepinac died under house arrest in 1960.

Michael Phayer, author of *The Catholic Church and the Holocaust, 1930–1965,* commenting on the Stepinac trial, wrote: "The charge that Stepinac supported the Pavelic regime was, of course, true, as everyone knew ... if Stepinac had responded to the charges against him, his defense would have inevitably unraveled, exposing the Vatican's support of the genocidal Pavelic."

Slovakia

Like Yugoslavia and Hungary, Czechoslovakia was a political entity created at the end of WWI, a so-called Versailles state. It included the Czech provinces of Bohemia, Moravia, and Slovakia. Despite its multinational population and tense relations with neighboring countries, all of which coveted its territory, Czechoslovakia remained a functioning parliamentary democracy until 1938. On September 29, 1938, Hitler, Mussolini, Neville Chamberlain of Britain, and Edouard Daladier of France signed the Munich Pact, which permitted Nazi Germany to annex the German-speaking Sudetenland, part of Czechoslovakia. The pact was another unsuccessful attempt by Britain and France to appease Hitler. Six months later, on March 15, 1939, Germany, in violation of the Munich Pact, invaded and occupied the Czech provinces of Bohemia and Moravia. A partitioned Czechoslovakia was then swallowed up by the Greater Third Reich.

Fascist Priest Heads Slovakia

Slovakia became an independent state headed by a fascist Roman Catholic priest, Father Jozef Tiso, whose followers established, as in Croatia under Ante Pavelic and in Hungary under Ferenc Szálasi, a one-party dictatorship, strongly aligned and supported by the separatist/nationalist Slovakian Roman Catholic hierarchy, and closely allied with Nazi Germany. The ruling party was the Slovak People's Party. Father Tiso's Slovakia, like Ante Pavelic's Croatia and Ferenc Szálasi's Hungary, participated in the Holocaust, with Jews targeted as enemies of the state. Anti-Jewish laws were passed patterned after the Nuremburg Laws. As in other Occupied European countries, transport to death camps became state policy, but, in addition, Tiso's regime agreed to pay five hundred reichsmarks to the Third Reich for every Jew deported.

Tiso continued his anti-Jewish policy despite several protests from the Vatican. The apostolic legate to Bratislava protested personally to Tiso, appealing to his "feelings as a priest of the Catholic faith." That a priest headed the government and that priests held leadership positions in it, no doubt, encouraged the local faithful to believe that the Slovak Catholic Church had given its imprimatur to eliminationist anti-Semitism. Father Tiso, however, did attempt to protect some Jewish converts to Catholicism by issuing approximately eleven hundred exemptions from deportation, mainly, however, to wealthy Jews.

For his involvement in the Holocaust, Father Jozef Tiso, fascist dictator of Slovakia, was hanged as a war criminal after the war. Tiso had claimed that it was "a Christian act to expel Jews so that Slovakia could free itself of 'its pests.'" Monsignor Domenico Tardini, an undersecretary in the Vatican's Secretariat of State, aware of the situation in Slovakia, in an internal Vatican memo dated April 7, 1943, warned that if the Vatican failed to disassociate itself from the mass murder taking place in Slovakia, it might not be able to avoid being blamed for it at the war's end.

First reports of the murder of Jews in Slovakia reached the Vatican by late 1941. In March 1942, Pius XII was asked to intervene to stop deportations, but he declined. The Allies entreated the pope to condemn publicly atrocities taking place in Slovakia. The Vatican did finally issue a protest statement, but limited itself to cautionary language that generally decried the horrors of the war. Daniel Jonah Goldhagen terms Slovakia and Croatia the "most striking cases of Catholic bishops and priests lending a hand to mass murder." Goldhagen wrote:

A priest was the country's president. An avowedly Catholic party governed the country, seeking to mold it according to Catholic principles. Many priests served in the country's legislature, which voted, as did all its legislator priests, to deport the country's Jews to their deaths. The Slovakian clergy, like other clergy, were under the discipline of the Pope. He had absolute authority over them. He could have commanded them to desist from acting in ways that violated the Church's doctrine and practices. Yet he did not command them not to deport their country's Jews to their deaths.

Father Tiso was not excommunicated. John Morley, author of *Vatican Diplomacy and the Jews During the Holocaust, 1939–1943*, lamenting Tiso's nonexcommunication, wrote: "Vatican diplomacy ... was content to limit itself to the narrow confines of strictly Catholic interests, and an opportunity for a great moral and humanitarian gesture was lost."

Lithuania

The Holocaust in Occupied Lithuania resulted in the near total destruction of Lithuanian Jews living in Nazi-controlled territories. Out of approximately 210,000 Jews, an estimated 196,000 were murdered before war's end. Only 6 percent survived.

The Soviet Union invaded and annexed Lithuania in 1940. The German invasion of the Soviet Union on June 22, 1941, came after a year of brutal Soviet occupation that culminated in mass relocations of Lithuanian nationals across the Baltics only a week before the German invasion. The Germans were, therefore, welcomed as liberators and received support from Lithuania's irregular militia against retreating Soviet forces. Many Lithuanians believed Germany would allow the reestablishment of the country's independence. To curry favor with the Germans, many of the locals joined in the killing of Jews.

Soon after the German invasion, the SS *Einsatzgruppen* entered Lithuania and immediately began murdering entire Jewish communities. Most Lithuanian Jews perished during the first months of the occupation before the end of 1941. About eighty thousand Jews were killed by October, and about 175,000 by the end of 1941. The majority of Jews in Lithuania were not required to live in ghettos or sent to death camps, which at the time were in the preliminary stages of operation. Instead, as part of the Holocaust by Bullets, they were shot in pits near their residences, the most infamous instances of mass murder taking place in Ninth Fort near Kaunas and the Ponary Forest near Vilna.

As did Poland, Lithuania in 1939 had a predominately Roman Catholic population. A significant aspect of the Holocaust there was that the Nazi occupation regime fanned local anti-Semitism by blaming the Soviet annexation of Lithuania, a year earlier, on the Jews. Another significant aspect was the large extent to which the occupation regime's plan to murder Jews relied on local auxiliaries. In June 1941, a rogue unit of insurgents headed by Algirdas Klimaitis instigated pogroms in Kaunas (Kovno)—over one thousand Jews were killed in the first one. Nazi commanders filed reports noting that the "zeal of the Lithuanian police battalions surpassed their own." The most notorious Lithuanian unit was a squad from the Vilnius area, which killed tens of thousands of Jews, Poles, and others.

Of the twenty-six local police battalions formed from the Lithuanian Security Police, ten were involved in systematic extermination of Jews. The Special SD and Germany Security Police Squad in Vilnius killed tens of thousands of Jews and ethnic Poles in Paneriai and other places. In Minsk, the Second Battalion shot about nine thousand Soviet prisoners of war; in Slutsk it massacred five thousand Jews. In March 1942, in Poland, the Second Lithuanian Battalion carried out guard duty in the Majdanek extermination camp. In July 1942, the Second Battalion participated in the deportation of Jews from the Warsaw ghetto. In August–October 1942, Lithuanian police battalions were in Ukraine: the Third in Molodechno, the Fourth in Donetsk, the Seventh in Vinnitsa, the Eleventh in Korostek, the Sixteenth in Dnepropetrovsk, the 254th in Poltava, and the 255th in Mogilev (Belarus). One of the battalions was also used to put down the Warsaw Ghetto Uprising in 1943.

As in other occupied countries of Eastern Europe, not all Lithuanians supported the Nazis. Out of a population of approximately three million (80 percent ethnic Lithuanians), only a few thousand were actual perpetrators, while many hundreds risked their lives to rescue Jews. Over seven hundred Lithuanians have been recognized as Righteous Gentiles by Yad Vashem. One of them was Dr. Petras Baublys, head of an orphanage in Kovno, who gave shelter to Jewish children in his orphanage until permanent places of refuge could be found for them; another was Ona Simaite, a librarian in Vilna, who regularly traveled into the city's Jewish ghetto, supposedly in search of unreturned library books. In actuality she was taking food and other provisions to residents of the ghetto, as well as helping the resistance. Captured in 1944, she refused to surrender any information to her Nazi captors despite enduring torture.

Soviet soldiers, parachuting into Eastern Poland and Western Russia, commanded units of Jewish volunteers. A Lithuanian Jewish brigade operated in the dense forests near Vilna. In Belorussia, the Bielski brothers led a Jewish combat group roaming the Naliboki Forest. The heroic exploits of the Bielski brothers is portrayed in director Edward Zwick's film *Defiance*. Chiune "Sempo" Sugihara, a Japanese national and the Japanese consul in Kovno, was a hero of the Holocaust who rescued several thousand Jews stranded in Lithuania after they fled Occupied Poland. Defying his government, he granted transit visas to Japan for at least thirty-five hundred Jews. The Japanese government cited Sugihara for insubordination and stripped him of his diplomatic post. He was also recognized as a Righteous Gentile.

Italy after Mussolini

The situation for Jews in Italy took a dramatic turn for the worse in July 1943, when the Allies invaded Sicily and bombed Rome; then Italy's fascist government fell, and Mussolini was arrested.[226] Pietro Badoglio became prime minister of Italy and began to negotiate an immediate cease-fire with the Allies. Enraged, Hitler used force to bring Italy back into the Axis fold. Despite the increasingly desperate situation on the Eastern Front, he sent troops to occupy northern and central Italy. On September 11, 1943, Rome came under German occupation: Marshal Albert Kesselring declared martial law. Soon thereafter, SS troops (22 percent Catholic), along with the most zealous of Mussolini's supporters (overwhelmingly Catholic), began rounding up Jews in Rome, Milan, Genoa, Florence, Trieste, and other northern cities.

According to documentary evidence, in October 1943, the pope was advised that deportation of Italian Jews was imminent. Publicly, he remained silent. Privately, his defenders claim, Pius instructed his diocesan clergy to provide refuge for Jews—even though he was aware of a Nazi plot to kill or kidnap him. Four hundred seventy-seven Jews

---

226 On September 12, 1943, Mussolini was rescued from prison in a daring raid by a unit of the German Special Forces. He and his mistress, Claretta Petacci, were eventually shot and left hanging by their feet at an ESSO gas station on April 24, 1945. Six days later, on April 30, 1945, ten days after his birthday, Hitler committed suicide.

were sheltered within Vatican City; another 4,238 were sheltered in Roman monasteries and convents.[227]

Powerful voices outside the Vatican were raised to stop the planned deportation from Italy. Several of those voices were German—Ernst von Weizsacker, ambassador to the Holy See, and Kesselring among them. A third objector was Albrecht von Kessel, German consul to Rome. All three were convinced that if deportation was allowed to proceed, a popular uprising against the occupation was likely, particularly if Pius protested publicly. But no protest came from the pope. Weizsacker wrote to a colleague in Berlin:

> Although pressed on all sides, the Pope did not allow himself to be drawn into any demonstration of reproof at the deportation of the Jews of Rome. The only sign of disapproval was a veiled allusion in *"L'Osservatore Romano,"* in which only a restricted number of people could recognize a reference to the Jewish question.

On October 16, 1943, the Nazis, despite receipt of a large ransom in gold paid by the Jewish community of Rome, rounded up over a thousand Jews and amassed them in a piazza within the Jewish ghetto, established by Pope Paul IV in the sixteenth century. The piazza was located within walking distance of the papal apartments in St. Peter's Square. Ironically, the piazza contained one of Rome's many churches, *Santa Maria del Pianto* ("Mother of Sorrows"). Many of the Jews rounded up, including women, children, and infants,[228] were leaving evening Yom Kippur services. The convoy of trucks transporting them to the railway terminal took a route along the Tiber that passed St.

227   Forty thousand Italian Jews (80 percent of the total) survived the Holocaust because ordinary Italians, including lower-level government officials, members of the Italian military, and church officials passively resisted the Nazi occupiers by, among other things, sheltering Jews, obstructing deportation, or helping Jews escape to unoccupied southern Italy. Pius's defenders contend that the pope should be credited for Italy's relatively high Jewish survival rate. Rabbi David G. Dalin, one of Pius's defenders, argued that Pius XII, for his efforts to save Jewish lives, deserves to be recognized as a Righteous Gentile by the Israeli government at Yad Vashem.

228   In January 2001, a special plaque was mounted in the piazza dedicated to the infants who lost their lives. It reads: *E Non Cominciarono Neppure A Vivere* ("They never even had a chance to live").

Peter's Square. Shortly after arriving at the terminal, they were deported to Auschwitz-Birkenau, where 811 of them were gassed upon arrival; only sixteen survived.[229]

On October 28, 1943, Ambassador von Weizsacker, in a telegram to his superiors in Berlin, wrote: "The Pope has not yet let himself be persuaded to make an official condemnation of the deportation of the Roman Jews ... Since it is currently thought that the Germans will take no further steps against the Jews in Rome, the question of our relations with the Vatican may be considered closed."

As in other European countries, there were clergy in Italy who attempted to rescue Jews from deportation. When approached by Jewish assistance groups to help coordinate rescue efforts, for example, Cardinals Pietro Boetto of Genoa, Ildefonso Schuster of Milan, Maurilio Fossati of Turin, and Elia Dalla Costa of Florence instructed the clergy and religious of their archdioceses to cooperate fully. In Florence, Cardinal Dalla Costa mobilized his archdiocese for Jewish rescue; at least twenty-one monasteries, convents, and parish churches were put in service for rescue operations. Monsignor Giuseppe Nicolini implemented a rescue program in his diocese of Assisi, on his own initiative, without being asked for help. Susan Zuccotti,[230] author of *Under His Very Windows*, credited Bishop Antonio Santino of Trieste and Capodistria with demonstrating "courage, initiative, and undeniable sympathy for Jews." Zuccotti cited an incident when Bishop Santino delivered a passionate homily in the presence of German Nazis and Italian fascists, castigating them for the suffering they were causing to "people from whose womb came (the Savior) as a man and in whose midst he lived and died."

Yad Vashem, the Holocaust Martyrs' and Heroes' Remembrance Authority in Jerusalem, has honored 281 Italians as Righteous Gentiles for their roles in saving Jewish lives, including Don Arrigo Beccari, a

---

229   About eight thousand Jews were deported from Italy to death camps during the Nazi occupation; most perished.

230   Dr. Susan Sessions Zuccotti is an American historian specializing in Holocaust studies. She holds a PhD in modern European history from Columbia University. She has won a National Jewish Book Award for Holocaust Studies and the *Premio Acqui Storia—Primo Lavoro* for *Italians and the Holocaust* (1987). She also received a National Jewish Book Award for Jewish-Christian Relations and the Sybil Halpern Milton Memorial Prize of the German Studies Association in 2002 for *Under His Very Windows* (2000).

teacher at the Catholic seminary in the village of Nonantola, who helped 120 Jews escape to Switzerland; Cardinal Pietro Boetto's secretary, Don Francesco Repetto; Fathers Rufino Nicacci and Aldo Brunacci of Assisi, who, together with Monsignor Giuseppe Nicolini, arranged for hundreds to be provided false credentials, to be hidden in private homes, and to be smuggled out of Italy; and Father Giovanni Simione and Father Angelo Della Torre, who cooperated in saving the lives of twelve Jewish women and their children.

Another Italian honored as a Righteous Gentile is Dr. Giovanni Passante, who, when inviting a Jewish family to hide in his family's home, said: "I ask you to stay with us for my sake, not yours. If you leave, I will forever be ashamed to be numbered among the human race."

According to Susan Zuccotti, claims by Pius's defenders such as Pinchas Lapide that the pope encouraged Italy's rescue efforts of Jews are "unsubstantiated and without foundation" and, in fact, "contradicted by credible evidence." She wrote: "Pius XII personally seems to have made no contacts and no appeal to Italians for the Jews. Likewise, he seems never to have appealed personally to any German officials. At the very least, he might have asked that Italian Jews be allowed to remain in internment on Italian soil. He did not do so."[231]

In act 3 of *The Deputy*, as Roman Jews are being rounded up for deportation, the fictionalized Father Riccardo, who later dies a martyr's death at Auschwitz-Birkenau, declares: "Doing nothing is as bad as taking part … God can forgive a hangman for such work, but not a priest, not the Pope!"

After the war, Pius continued as pope for another thirteen years, during which time he uttered no word of apology or regret and offered no requiem Mass of Remembrance for any Jew who perished in the Holocaust. Jacques Maritain, a prominent French Catholic philosopher, who became an exponent of emerging Christian Democracy in postwar Europe and assisted in drafting the United Nations' "Universal Declaration of Human Rights," tried unsuccessfully to convince Pius to speak out about the Holocaust and anti-Semitism. Maritain resigned

---

231 Pius' defenders, as noted previously, contend that Pius should be credited with instructing or, at least, inspiring rescuers of Jews in Italy and German Occupied Europe (Zuccotti, *Under His Very Windows*, 294).

his post as French ambassador to the Holy See in 1948, citing Pius's inaction on the issue of German guilt.

Papal Power

Among Pius's powers as pope were: access to the mass media, including the Catholic press and Vatican Radio, and to a worldwide audience; influence over an extensive international education system ranging from elementary schools to universities; access to the information gathering and communication capability of a worldwide diplomatic corps; the power of excommunication and interdiction; and placing books on the Index Librorum Prohibitorum.[232]

From his bully pulpit, he could have urged Catholics and all people of conscience to passively resist Nazi racist policies, as sixty years earlier, Pius IX urged German Catholics to passively resist antichurch legislation during *Kulturkampf* in newly unified Germany. He could have forbidden priests to serve as Reich race attestation agents by refusing to allow access to church records for the purpose of differentiating Jews from Catholics.[233] He could have publicly condemned Nazi extremism, thereby providing the faithful with indisputable facts needed to make an informed moral judgment on how to respond. And, like the Hebrew prophets,[234] he could have exhorted the faithful, in the name of God, to pursue justice for God's chosen people.[235]

---

232   Neither Pius XI nor Pius XII placed *Mein Kampf* on the *Index Librorum Prohibitorum. Mein Kampf,* first published in 1925, in which Hitler set forth his eliminationist/racist and territorial expansionist agenda, has been banned in Germany since 1945.

233   "There is no longer Jew or Greek, there is no longer slave or free, there is no longer male and female; for all are one in Christ Jesus" (Romans 4:28).

234   A prophet is God's spokesperson, a person chosen by God to speak on God's behalf to convey a message and to teach the faithful. Prophets were role models of holiness, scholarship and closeness to God. They set the ethical standard for the entire community. The Hebrew word for prophet, *navi* (*Nun-Bet-Yod-Alef*), comes from the term *niv sefatayim,* meaning "fruit of the lips," which emphasizes the prophet's role as a speaker.

235   *Tzedek, Tzedek Tirdof* ("Justice, justice, you shall pursue"), Deuteronomy 16:20.

Pius XII neither excommunicated nor threatened to excommunicate Adolf Hitler,[236] or any other Nazi or Nazi collaborator, including Joseph Goebbels, Heinrich Himmler, Reinhard Heydrich, Rudolf Hoess, Dr. Josef Mengele, Father Jozef Tiso of Slovakia, or Father Miroslav Filipovic of Croatia (both priests were executed for war crimes). However, he did excommunicate several German Catholics who advocated cremation as an alternative to burial. Additionally, after the war, he excommunicated any Italian who joined the Italian Communist Party or voted for its candidates. He also excommunicated all Catholic supporters of communism wherever located. And in postwar Croatia, after the trial of Cardinal Aloysius Stepinac, who was convicted of war crimes, he excommunicated everyone who participated in the court proceedings, but not Cardinal Stepinac.

Failure of Conscience

Clearly, anti-Judaism contributed to the culpability, complicity, and indifference[237] of so many, many Europeans during the Holocaust. Centuries of anti-Judaism had conditioned them to view Jews as "objects" outside the circle of Christian concern, excluded from Jesus's Gospel of Love. This conditioning anesthetized Christian conscience to injustice against Jews and dulled Christian capacity to feel empathy for them. A Marxist might characterize this phenomenon as yet another example of religion functioning like an opiate of the people. Lord Acton might characterize it as another example of absolute power corrupting absolutely. And the atheist writer Christopher Hitchens might cite it as another instance of religion poisoning everything. An ethically desensitized collective conscience caused

236 Pius defender Rabbi David G. Dalin contends that excommunicating Hitler would have been a purely symbolic gesture that "would likely have resulted in more persecution, not less." Yet, Pope John Paul II, using purely symbolic gestures, helped bring down the Soviet Union in 1989.

237 Letter of complaint to Reich authorities from Mrs. Eleonore Gusenbauer of Ried, a village in Austria near Mauthausen, September 1941:
"Inmates of the Mauthausen concentration camp are constantly being shot at the Vienna Ditch work site. Those who are badly struck still live for some time and lie next to the dead for hours and in some cases for half a day. My property is situated on an elevation close to the Vienna Ditch and therefore one often becomes the unwilling witness of such misdeeds. I am sickly in any case and such sights make such demands on my nerves, that I will not be able to bear it much longer. I request that it be arranged that such inhuman deeds will cease or else be conducted out of sight."

too many Europeans in the 1930s and '40s, including church leaders, to succumb to Nazi anti-Semitism, at least in its early milder form, with some even willing to become perpetrators in its final virulent form. For close to two thousand years, Jews had been objectified and dehumanized, making it easier for twentieth century Christians, so inclined, to murder them, individually or as a group.

Gordon C. Zahn, author of *German Catholics and Hitler's Wars*, as noted previously, charged that priests, intentionally or unintentionally, functioned as cheerleaders for the Nazi war effort, encouraging Wehrmacht combatants to fight and, even when the war was lost, to fight on. He also charged that the German Catholic Church not only implicitly sanctioned the war, but also failed to teach or model ethical behavior—a primary function of religion. Zahn wrote:

> The German Catholic who looked to his religious superiors for spiritual guidance and direction regarding service in Hitler's wars received virtually the same answers he would have received from the Nazi ruler himself ... To the extent that the Church accommodates itself to a secular regime, it becomes, in effect, an agent of that regime, supplementing the secular controls with those of the spiritual order.

In deciding how to respond to the Nazis, sadly, many, many Christians placed duty to obey secular authority ahead of their duty to obey conscience. Jesus taught: "Render to Caesar what belongs to Caesar and to God what belongs to God."[238] Far too many, however, ignored the distinction and rendered all to the Nazi Caesar. Making matters worse, most church leaders, Catholic and Protestant alike, the so-called "shepherds of the flock," failed, by word and example, to feed the flock (i.e., they failed to guide the flock in conscience formation).

Unquestionably, widespread failure of conscience was a major contributing cause of the Holocaust. On the issue of conscience, Vatican Council II in 1965 decreed:

> Deep within our conscience we find a law which we have not laid upon ourselves, but which we must obey. Its voice, ever

---

238   Matthew 22:21.

calling us to love and to do what is good and to avoid evil, sounds in our heart at the right moment … For we have in our hearts a law inscribed by God … Our conscience is our most secret core and our sanctuary. There we are alone with God whose voice echoes in our depths. "Pastoral Constitution on the Church in the Modern World" (*Gaudium et Spes*) and

It is through our conscience that we see and recognize the demands of the divine law. We are bound to follow our conscience faithfully in all our activity so that we may come to God, who is our last end. "Declaration on Religious Liberty" (*Dignitatis Humanae*)

Traditionalist interpreters of Vatican Council II insist almost exclusively on the continuity of the council with Catholic tradition. They dispute liberal/progressive interpretations that the council broke from the past and changed business as usual. The traditionalists, however, are hard-pressed to explain why council pronouncements on conscience, if only restating what had been church tradition, were not followed by church leaders before and during the Nazi era.[239] Or why popes who possessed papal infallibility on issues of morality failed so miserably to model and teach ethical conduct toward Jews.

---

239   See John W. O'Malley, SJ, *Vatican II: Did Anything Happen?* (2008) and *What Happened at Vatican II* (2010) for more information on the differences between traditionalist and progressive views on the impact of Vatican Council II and the dispute regarding continuity and change.

CHAPTER 9

Christian Righteousness

THERE WERE, OF COURSE, MEMBERS of the clergy throughout Europe whose words and deeds reflected Christian conscience. And some of them were martyred for their faith. One example was Father Max Josef Metzger, a WWI German army chaplain and founder of Peace Alliance of German Catholics. For publicly protesting against the Nazis, Father Metzger was arrested by the Gestapo, condemned for high treason, and executed in April 1944. Father Alfred Delp, a member of the Kreisau Circle resistance group, and Blessed Father Karl Leisner were two other examples. Father Delp was executed in Berlin; Leisner died at Dachau.

During the twelve years of the Third Reich, twenty-six hundred Roman Catholic priests were confined to the Priester-Block (priests' barracks) at Dachau. [240] At least 149 priests died at Auschwitz-Birkenau. A total of more than two thousand Polish Catholic clergy, including Father Maximillian Kolbe, canonized a saint in 1981, and five bishops, died at the hands of the Nazis between 1939 and 1945. Another example of a church leader motivated by conscience was Father Bernhard Lichtenberg.

---

240   Dachau, which opened shortly after Hitler became chancellor in 1933, served as a prototype for other Nazi concentration camps such as Buchenwald in Germany and Mauthausen in Occupied Austria. Between 1933 and 1945 more than 3.5 million Germans were confined, mostly for political reasons, in camps or prison. Just about every German community had residents taken away, often never to be seen again. Newspapers continuously reported of the "removal of enemies of the Reich to concentration camps."

Father Bernhard Lichtenberg

In contrast to most Catholic and Protestant clergy, Father Bernhard Lichtenberg was morally outraged by the treatment of Jews in Nazi Germany and responded according to Gospel values. In August 1938, Father Lichtenberg was put in charge of the Relief Office of the Berlin Episcopate, a group that helped Jewish converts emigrate from the Third Reich. After *Kristallnacht*, while most of the leadership of the German churches, including the dissident Protestant Confessing Church, kept silent, Father Lichtenberg protested publicly. He said: "We know what happened yesterday, we do not know what lies in store for us tomorrow. But we have experienced what has happened today: Outside burns the (Jewish) temple, a holy place of worship." From that fateful day in November 1938 until his arrest on October 23, 1941, Father Lichtenberg prayed daily and publicly from his pulpit for Jews and other victims of the Nazis.

When war broke out in September 1939, Father Lichtenberg wrote a letter to the official responsible for air raid shelters in Berlin protesting against racial segregation in the shelters. Predictably, his actions brought him in conflict with Reich authorities. Two students who heard him pray publicly for Jews and concentration camp detainees denounced him to the Gestapo, which in a search of Lichtenberg's home in October 1941, found a pulpit proclamation scheduled to be read the following Sunday. The proclamation, in response to a leaflet circulated by the Propaganda Ministry warning German citizens not to help Jews, declared:

> An anonymous slanderous sheet against the Jews is being distributed to Berlin houses. This leaflet states that every German who supports Jews with an ostensibly false sentimentality, be it only through friendly kindness, commits treason against his people. Let us not be misled by this un-Christian way of thinking. Rather follow the strict command of Jesus Christ: "You shall love your neighbor as you love yourself."

Prepared to suffer for his defiance of unjust state authority, Father Lichtenberg said:

> This [defiance] is because I reject with my innermost the evacuation of the Jews with all its side effects, because it is directed against the most important commandment of Christianity …

And I recognize the Jew too as my neighbor, who possesses an immortal soul, shaped after the likeness of God. However, since I cannot prevent this governmental measure, I have made up my mind to accompany the deported Jews and Christian Jews into exile, in order to give them spiritual aid. I wish to use this opportunity to ask the Gestapo to give me this opportunity.

In May 1942, the Berlin District Court sentenced Father Lichtenberg to a two-year term of imprisonment for insidious activity and abuse of the pulpit. Asked if he had anything to add, Lichtenberg replied: "I submit that no harm results to the state by citizens who pray for the Jews." The presiding judge summed up Lichtenberg's crime:

> On 29 August 1941, the defendant held evensong ... before a large congregation. He closed the service with a prayer in which he said, among other things: "Let us now pray for the Jews and for the wretched prisoners in the concentration camps" ... He states that he has included the Jews in his prayers ever since the synagogues were first set on fire and Jewish businesses closed.

Lichtenberg served two years in prison and died en route to Dachau on November 5, 1943. Many thousands of the laity also paid with their lives for opposing the Nazi regime, including the mostly Catholic members of the Munich nonviolent resistance group "White Rose," two of them brother and sister Hans and Sophie Scholl, who, after being caught distributing antiwar leaflets on the University of Munich campus in 1943, were convicted of high treason and executed by guillotine. Another lay martyr of Nazism was Franz Jägerstätter.

Franz Jägerstätter

In 1936, Franz Jägerstätter wrote to his godchild: "I can say from my own experience how painful life often is when one lives as a halfway Christian; it is more like vegetating than living ... Since the death of Christ, almost every century has seen the persecution of Christians; there have always been heroes and martyrs who gave their lives—often in horrible ways—for Christ and their faith. If we hope to reach our goal some day, then we, too, must become heroes of the faith." When the plebiscite to approve Germany's annexation of Austria was held on April 10, 1938, Jägerstätter was the only person in his town of Sankt Radegund to vote no. Although not involved with any political party, Jägerstätter was openly anti-Nazi and publicly declared he would not fight for the Third Reich. He joined the Third Order of Saint Francis in 1940 and worked as a sacristan at his local parish church. In 1940, at age thirty-three, he was conscripted into the Wehrmacht and completed basic training. Returning home in 1941 under a military exemption as a farmer, he began to examine the morality of the war and discussed the matter with his bishop. Jägerstätter emerged from the discussion saddened that the bishop seemed afraid to confront the issue.

After numerous delays, Jägerstätter was called to active duty in February 1943. Maintaining his position against fighting, upon reporting for military service on March 1, he declared himself to be a conscientious objector. His offer to serve as a paramedic was rejected. A priest from his village visited him in jail and tried unsuccessfully to convince him to serve. Accused of *Wehrkrafzersetzung* ("undermining military morale"), after a military trial he was sentenced to death and executed at Brandenburg-Gorden Prison in August 1943. His last words as he was led to the guillotine were: "I am completely bound in inner union with the Lord." The prison chaplain who ministered to him that day later remarked, "I can say with certainty that this simple man is the only saint I have met in my lifetime." Franz Jägerstätter is, unquestionably, an inspiration to people of all faith traditions. His witness demonstrated that a Christian with a well-formed conscience could indeed make a difficult and principled choice during a moral crisis of unprecedented proportion, even when that choice meant forfeiting his life—in the tradition of Jesus of Nazareth.

Before his death, Jägerstätter was criticized for failing in his duty as a German citizen, especially by fellow Catholics who served in the Wehrmacht. The town council of Sankt Radegund at first refused to allow his name to be included on the town's war memorial, and a pension for his widow was not approved until 1950. Jägerstätter's story was not well known until 1964, when Gordon Zahn published Jägerstätter's biography, entitled *In Solitary Witness: The Life and Death of Franz Jägerstätter.*

In June 2007, Pope Benedict XVI issued an apostolic exhortation declaring Jägerstätter a martyr. In October 2007, Jägerstätter became the second Nazi-era resister to be beatified by Benedict XVI; two years earlier Benedict beatified Cardinal Clemens August von Galen. Ironically, Jägerstätter was martyred on the one-year anniversary of St. Edith Stein's martyrdom at Auschwitz-Birkenau.

The *Newsweek* reviewer of *In Solitary Witness* wrote: "In death as in the months of his imprisonment, Jägerstätter was a solitary witness ... Zahn wonders pointedly whether a church which asks too little of its members will have the courage in the future to demand enough." And Thomas Merton, in his review of Zahn's biography, wrote: "The real question raised by Jägerstätter's story is that of the Church's own mission of protest and prophecy in the gravest spiritual crisis man has ever known."

Jägerstätter's inspirational story of conscience was indeed remarkable, but, unfortunately, such stories were the exception rather than the rule. Regrettably, there were many, many more stories of people mindlessly obeying unjust authority; of bystanders feigning ignorance of what was occurring. Guilt certainly falls on the perpetrators of the Holocaust, but a measure of guilt also falls on the doers of duty and on the bystanders. Cain, in the book of Genesis, asks this provocative question, "Am I my brother's keeper?" God's resounding answer in the affirmative is unequivocal. Abraham Joshua Heschel, the leading Jewish theologian of the twentieth century, wrote: "We must continue to remind ourselves that ... all are involved in what some are doing. Some are guilty, (but) all are responsible."

Rescue and Resistance

Notwithstanding the docility/passivity of most European Christians and the active participation of others, clearly, there were in Germany and in every Nazi-occupied or allied European country, people—clergy, religious, and lay—who behaved humanely, even heroically. These righteous people bore witness that compassion and decency still existed in what had become hell on earth. Despite considerable peril, these good people provided rays of light in the darkness of profound depravity. Among other things, they joined resistance movements; sheltered children and adults in their homes, convents, and schools; concealed and provided for individuals or entire families; established underground passage routes to neutral countries; provided false baptismal certificates and travel documents; shared their meager provisions; and refrained from denouncing their Jewish neighbors to Reich authorities.

In the face of unimaginable horror, people of conscience modeled respect for human life and empathic behavior. Making the moral choice,[241] they engaged in acts of kindness, large and small, reaching out to suffering people surely among "the least of (Jesus's) brethren." Clergy, religious, and laypeople were among the over 23,788 people who risked their lives to rescue Jews,[242] recognized as Righteous Gentiles by the Israeli government at Yad Vashem (through 2010). Most assuredly, these exemplary people deserve to be remembered and celebrated. Among the over fifty-nine hundred Righteous Gentiles from Poland were:

Irena Sendler, a social worker who smuggled many hundreds of Jewish infants and children out of the Warsaw ghetto. Eventually discovered, both her legs and arms were fractured during a vicious beating by the Gestapo. After the war, having kept a record of the rescued children, she attempted to reunite them with their families, but most of the parents had perished. Sendler then worked to have orphaned children placed for adoption with foster families. Asked why she did what she did, Sendler responded: "My mother taught me that what matters is whether people are honest or dishonest, not what religion they belong to."

Marie Szul, a member of Zegota,[243] who after receiving her recognition from Yad Vashem said: "I was scared to death, like everyone else. But I made up my mind then and there: If I can help, I will … my mother always taught me that God made everyone the same; He does not care if they are Jews or not, because everyone has the right to live."

Wladyslaw Bartoszewski, a founder of Zegota, worked to provide false documents to Jews living outside the Warsaw ghetto. In the fall of

---

241   "Let us not forget that there is a moment when the moral choice is made. Often because of one story or one book or one person, we are able to make a different choice, a choice for humanity, for life. And so we must know these good people who helped Jews during the Holocaust. We must learn from them, and in gratitude and hope, we must remember them" (Elie Wiesel).

242   "Whoever saves a single life is as if one saves the entire world."

243   Zegota, a group of Catholic activists, was the only organization formed in Nazi-Occupied Europe for the specific purpose of Jewish rescue. Members of Zegota placed over two thousand children in homes, convents, and orphanages in the Warsaw area. Only 10 percent of Polish Jews survived the Holocaust, and although Polish Catholics were persecuted as well, Poland ranked first among forty countries with almost one-third of the total of all those honored as Righteous Gentiles.

1942, he helped found Council for Aid to Jews, an organization that saved many from the gas chambers.

Anna Borkowska, a Polish nun in a Dominican convent outside Vilnius, Lithuania, who hid children and resistance fighters in her convent, even smuggling weapons into the ghetto. Polish nuns were especially active in the rescue of Jewish children in Poland, sheltering them in their convents and schools.

Dr. Jan Karski, the intermediary between Polish resistance groups and the Polish government in exile, who secretly entered the Warsaw ghetto to observe conditions there. Asked to describe what he witnessed, he reported to world leaders, including President Roosevelt.

Wladyslaw Kowalski, a retired colonel in the Polish army, who helped some fifty Jews in the Warsaw region, moving them to places of refuge with friends and remaining with some of them in an underground shelter, until the Soviets liberated Poland in January 1945.

Dr. Jan Zabinski, a zoologist and head of the parks department in Warsaw, who sheltered Jews in empty animal cages, described in *The Zookeeper's Daughter*, by Lori Space Day.

Leopold Socha, a Polish sewer worker in the formerly Polish city of Lvov (now Lviv, Ukraine) used his knowledge of the city's sewer system to shelter a group of Jews. After the war, when Socha was accidently killed in a vehicular accident, some townspeople viewed his death as God's punishment for saving Jews. Director Agnieszka Holland's film *In Darkness* dramatized the exploits of Socha and "Socha's Jews."

Archbishop Adam Szeptycki of Lvov who, like other bishops in Occupied Europe, encouraged priests of his diocese to provide false baptismal and marriage certificates to protect Jews in hiding.

Rescue efforts ranged from isolated actions of individuals to coordinated efforts of organized networks like Zegota which resulted, for example, in the survival of approximately one hundred thousand hidden children. The Allies' stated priority to win the war before attempting rescue operations, together with widespread indifference and lack of access to victims, however, hampered major rescue operations. Courageous people sheltering Jews faced formidable obstacles, including summary execution if discovered. Rescue activities were influenced not only by the extent of Nazi control of a geographic area, but by the level of hostility or sympathy for Jews within local populations. The degree of hostility toward Jews, especially in Eastern Europe, was a particularly daunting obstacle. Regrettably, not all rescuers acted from moral or humanistic conviction. Some provided aid only in exchange for compensation.

Jewish survival rates varied greatly in the countries of Western and Eastern Europe, ranging from 95 percent survival in Denmark to 12 percent Poland. Irving Greenberg, a member of the U S Holocaust Memorial Council, explains the variation in Jewish survival rates as follows:

> Clearly the difference [in survival rate] lay not in Jewish behavior, neither passive nor armed resistance. Armed resistance was a decision how to die, not how to live … The single critical difference was the behavior of bystanders. *The more bystanders there were who resisted, the greater the chance that Jews would survive.* (emphasis mine)

Dr. Nechama Tec, a Holocaust survivor, has written extensively on the characteristics of rescuers and resisters. She identified three common characteristics: (1) having a clear sense of right and wrong, (2) not being afraid to stand or act alone, and (3) having no need to follow the lead of others. Although thousands of Christians during the Holocaust acted humanely, even heroically, toward Jews, tragically, the vast majority did neither. Too seldom did Christians respond to suffering with compassion—a clear violation of Jesus's Gospel of Love.[244] This is a painful truth, and a most unfortunate and unintended consequence, but one that must be acknowledged because, as St. Pope Gregory the Great[245] (590–604) said centuries ago: "Though scandal be taken at a truth, it is better to permit the scandal than to abandon the truth."

---

244   "Christianity in Germany bears a greater responsibility before God than the National Socialists, the SS, and the Gestapo. We ought to have recognized the Lord Jesus in the brother who suffered and was persecuted despite him being a communist or Jew" (Pastor Martin Niemoeller).

245   St. Pope Gregory the Great, a doctor of the Church, famous for reforming the Catholic liturgy of his day, was the first pope to come from a monastic background. Protestant reformer John Calvin so admired Pope Gregory that in Calvin's seminal work, *Institutes*, he declared that Gregory was the last good pope.

Denmark

The rescue of Danish Jews is a unique story that deserves to be especially highlighted and celebrated. Most of Denmark's eight thousand Jews were saved by being ferried by Christian friends and neighbors in boats to neutral Sweden. Their rescue resulted from a combination of factors, including the circumstances of Denmark's occupation; the Danes' contempt for Nazis; the effectiveness of Danish resistance; the refusal of local security forces to cooperate with the occupiers; and the conscience-based resistance of Lutheran laity and church leaders. It is true that foreknowledge of the impending invasion and existence of an easy escape route to Sweden contributed to the Danish rescue effort's success; nevertheless, the rescue was remarkable because it was carried out by an entire nation, for which reason Yad Vashem awarded the title Righteous Among the Nations to the entire Danish population.

Holocaust scholar Leon Stein's assessment of the Danish Lutheran Church's response to the Nazi threat is most positive: "In Denmark the overwhelming majority of Lutheran laymen and pastors and the official institutional church opposed the Nazi persecution of the Jews and, when Denmark was occupied by the Nazis, joined the Danish resistance and rallied to help save the Jews of that country."

The Danish Lutheran Church and the Jehovah's Witnesses set a high ethical standard against which the response of other institutional churches to the Holocaust can be judged.

CHAPTER 10

Pius XII Controversy

PIUS XII'S ROLE BEFORE AND during the Holocaust, both as Pius XI's secretary of state and as wartime pope, as noted previously, is the subject of ongoing controversy.[246] The controversy started at war's end when the existence of

246   In 2009, a caption with Pius XII's photo at the Yad Vashem Holocaust Memorial Museum in Jerusalem caused controversy within the Vatican. It reads:

"In 1933, when he was Secretary of the Vatican State, he was active in obtaining a Concordat with the German regime to preserve the Church's rights in Germany, even if this meant recognizing the Nazi racist regime. When he was elected Pope in 1939, he shelved a letter (the "Hidden Encyclical") against racism and anti-Semitism that his predecessor (Pius XI) had prepared. Even when reports about the murder of Jews reached the Vatican, the Pope did not protest either verbally or in writing. In December 1942, he abstained from signing the Allied declaration condemning the extermination of the Jews. When Jews were deported from Rome to Auschwitz, the Pope did not intervene. The Pope maintained his neutral position throughout the war, with the exception of appeals to the rulers of Hungary and Slovakia towards its end. His silence and the absence of guidelines obliged Churchmen throughout Europe to decide on their own how to react."

The Vatican formally protested the caption's historical accuracy. On his May 2009 visit to Jerusalem, Pope Benedict XVI refused to visit the main museum building of the Yad Vashem complex where the caption and photo are located. In June 2012, the caption was revised, according to a Yad Vashem spokeswoman as a result of new research based, in part, on the opening of the archive of Pius XI. It now includes the following language:

"The Pope's critics claim that his decision to abstain from condemning the murder of the Jews by Nazi Germany constitutes a moral failure: the lack of clear guidance left room for many to collaborate with Nazi Germany, reassured by the thought this did not contradict the Church's moral teaching" It goes on to mention the pope's defenders, who "maintain that this neutrality prevented harsher measures against the Vatican and the Church's institutions throughout Europe, thus enabling a considerable number of secret rescue activities to take place at different levels of the Church."

ratlines came to light. It intensified in the early 1960s when German playwright Rolf Hochhuth's play *The Deputy* premiered in Berlin, London, and New York. And it continues today with attempts, primarily from members of the conservative Vatican Curia, including Pope Benedict XVI himself, to have Pius XII canonized a saint, despite opposition from Jewish groups and others who urge that no action be taken, at least until more information is available.

Abraham Foxman, US director of the Anti-Defamation League, has urged Pope Benedict to suspend indefinitely the canonization process until secret World War II Vatican archives are declassified and fully examined "so that the full record of Pius' actions during the Holocaust may finally be known." Regarding canonization, Rabbi Albert H. Friedlander, author of *Out of the Whirlwind: A Reader of Holocaust Literature,* asked this provocative question:

> Who is a saint in the time of evil? ... The question is not whether the Pope was evil, but: was he a saint? I must ask the Church to re-assess its conscience. Does not 'sainthood' indicate a superhuman effort? And if the Church wants to be a teaching testimony to everyone, should it not take extra care, even if it leaves the establishment of those days less than perfect?"

Father Peter Gumpel, SJ, relator (f.k.a. devil's advocate) in the cause of Pius XII's canonization, on the other hand, asserted: "The cause of the beatification and canonization of Pope Pius XII, who is rightly venerated by millions of Catholics, will not be stopped or delayed by the unjustifiable and calumnious attacks against this great and saintly man."

In one of his most forceful defenses to date, Pope Benedict in 2007 declared that Pius XII did all he could do—and more than most—to stop the Holocaust. "Wherever possible, he spared no effort in intervening in (the Jews') favor either directly or through instructions given to other individuals or to institutions of the Catholic Church. Pius' wartime interventions were 'made secretly and silently' precisely because, given the concrete situation of that difficult historical moment, only in this way was it possible to avoid the worst and save the greatest number of Jews."

In 2008, while celebrating a Mass commemorating the fiftieth anniversary of Pius's death, Pope Benedict declared: "In light of the concrete situations of that complex historical moment, he (Pius) sensed that this was the only way to avoid the worst and save the greatest possible number of Jews." Benedict then indicated that he prayed the process of beatification can proceed happily. In December 2009, Benedict confirmed the "heroic virtues" of Pius, opening the door to beatification, once a miracle is attributed to the late pope.

On February 16, 2010, nineteen Catholic scholars of theology and history wrote a letter to Pope Benedict asking him to slow down the process of the sainthood cause of Pius XII. Saying that much more research needed to be done on the papacy of the mid-twentieth-century pope, the scholars wrote that "history needs distance and perspective" before definitive conclusions can be reached on Pius's role during WWII and the Holocaust. Leading the effort were Rev. Dr. John Pawlikowski, OSM, professor of ethics at Catholic Theological Union in Chicago, and Rev. Dr. Kevin P. Spicer, CSC, Kenneally associate professor of history at Stonehill College in Easton, Massachusetts.[247] In an e-mail to Catholic News Service, Father Pawlikowski told CNS the scholars were not opposed to Pope Pius's canonization. "We sent this letter because

---

247   Other signatories of the letter were: Rev. Dr. James Bernauer, SJ, Kraft professor of philosophy, Boston College, director, Center for Christian-Jewish Learning; Dr. Suzanne Brown-Fleming, independent scholar; Dr. John Connelly, associate professor of history, University of California, Berkeley; Dr. Frank J. Coppa, professor of history, St. John's University, associate editor, New Catholic Encyclopedia, currently working on biography of Pius XII; Dr. Donald J. Dietrich, professor of theology, Boston College; Dr. Audrey Doetzel, NDS, associate director, Center for Christian-Jewish Learning, Boston College; Dr. Lauren N. Faulkner, assistant professor of history, University of Notre Dame; Dr. Eugene J. Fisher, retired associate director, Secretariat for Ecumenical and Interreligious Relations, US Conference of Catholic Bishops; P. Elias H. Fullenbach, OP, Dominikanerkloster Dusseldorf, Institut fur Kirchengeschichte der Universitat Bonn; Dr. Beth A. Griech-Polelle, PhD, associate professor of history, Bowling Green State University; Dr. Robert A. Krieg, professor of theology, University of Notre Dame; Dr. Martin Menke, associate professor of history, Rivier College; Dr. Paul O'Shea, senior religious education coordinator, St. Patrick's College, Strathfield, NSW, Australia; Dr. Michael E. O'Sullivan, assistant professor of history, Marist College; Dr. Michael Phayer, professor emeritus of history, Marquette University; Dr. Carol Rittner, RSM, distinguished professor of Holocaust and genocide studies and the Dr. Marsha Raitcoff Grossmann professor of Holocaust Studies, Richard Stockton College of New Jersey; Dr. Jose Sanchez, professor emeritus of history, St. Louis University.

we feel that too often the issue of Pius XII is portrayed as one of Jewish concern," Father Pawlikowski continued: "We wanted to make it clear that some Catholics who have worked on Holocaust issues have serious concerns about advancing the cause of Pius XII at this time." In the letter, the nineteen scholars asserted:

> For centuries the Christian churches, including the Roman Catholic Church, have propagated both religious anti-Judaism and religious anti-Semitism, however unintentionally or in ignorance. 'Nostra Aetate,' however, ensured that Catholics' views of Jews would be definitively changed.... Mistrust and apprehension still exist, [however]. For many Jews and Catholics, Pius XII takes on a role much larger than his historical papacy. In essence, Pius XII has become a symbol of centuries-old Christian anti-Judaism and anti-Semitism which, for example, the late Rev. Edward H. Flannery has documented and spelled out in his work *The Anguish of the Jews: Twenty-Three Centuries of Anti-Semitism*. It is challenging to separate Pope Pius XII from this legacy. Proceeding with the cause of Pope Pius XII, without an exhaustive study of his actions during the Holocaust, might harm Jewish-Catholic relations in a way that cannot be overcome in the foreseeable future ...

The International Catholic-Jewish Historical Commission, comprised of three Jewish and three Catholic scholars, was appointed in 1999 by the Vatican's Commission for Religious Relations with the Jews. In October 2000, the commission finished its review of Vatican archival material released to that date and submitted preliminary findings to the commission's president, Cardinal Edward Cassidy. The report, entitled "The Vatican and the Holocaust," indicated, *inter alia*, that several of the documents examined refute the Vatican's claim that it did everything possible to facilitate emigration of Jews out of Europe. For example, internal memoranda confirm, according to the report, that the Vatican opposed Jewish emigration to Palestine (i.e., "The Holy See has never approved of the project of making Palestine a Jewish home ... (because) Palestine is by now holier for Catholics than for Jews"). Moreover, the Holy See did not officially recognize the

State of Israel, founded in 1948, until 1994, close to fifty years later.[248] Ironically, the Holy See was first to recognize Nazi Germany in July 1933, within months of its founding.

His critics offer various explanations for Pius's feckless response to the Holocaust—his own anti-Semitism, preoccupation with protecting and preserving the institutional church, fear of Nazi reprisals, fear of causing schism within the German Catholic and other national churches, fear of his own kidnapping or assassination,[249] fear for the destruction of Rome, fixation with diplomacy, belief that private interventions would be more productive than public ones, belief that Nazism was the lesser of two evils, and desire to broker the peace treaty ending WWII. Such considerations, coupled with the Church's long tradition of anti-Judaism, anti-Modernity and papal inerrancy/infallibility, constrained Pius from acting prophetically—as the vicar of Christ. When the world desperately needed a prophet, his critics claim, Pius played the politician. They charge that, as the most visible and influential religious/spiritual leader in the world, as the preeminent "shepherd of the flock,"[250] from whom exceptional witness was expected, his performance during a moral crisis of extraordinary proportion was patently inadequate.

In the later stages of the war, Pius did appeal to representatives of several Latin American governments to accept emergency passports obtained by several thousand Jews. Through his efforts, thirteen Latin American countries decided to honor these documents, despite Nazi threats to deport passport holders. The Holy See also answered a plea to save six thousand Jewish children in Bulgaria by helping them flee to Palestine. Unquestionably, Pius engaged in various actions that bore good fruit, which raises the legitimate question of what more he might have done. Pius should be given credit for all that he did to save Jews but not given a pass for what he failed to do.

---

248   The primary reason the Holy See opposed creation of a Jewish state in Palestine was fear of reprisals from Muslims against Catholics living in the Middle East.

249   "The blood of martyrs is the life-giving seed of the Church" (Tertullian).

250   "It is true that each must finally answer personally for the condition of his own conscience. It is also true that when the flock drifts far astray and wanders into mortal danger, the 'shepherds' are uniquely guilty" (Franklin H. Littell).

Pius's Defenders

In Pius's defense, on the other hand, the Holy See counters that a "black legend" has developed since Hochhuth's play premiered, one which falsely maligns Pius XII, is without historical foundation, and is the product of a communist conspiracy to discredit the Church. His defenders, among them Rabbi David G. Dalin;[251] Pierre Blet, SJ; Sister Margherita Marchione; Ralph McInerny; Pinchas Lapide; Ronald J. Rychlak; Jose M. Sanchez; and Joseph Lichten, argue that Pius's behind the scenes diplomacy (realpolitik) saved hundreds of thousands of Jewish lives, preventing even greater catastrophe. Pius's failures, whatever they might have been, in their view, were those of a holy man with human shortcomings compelled to act in particularly tragic and dangerous circumstances. His defenders credit him both for general resistance to Nazi persecution of Jews in Italy and elsewhere, as well as for specific actions by clergy and religious who engaged in rescue and resistance. It should be noted that the Vatican sheltered about 470 Jews behind its walls during German occupation of Rome in 1943, while another forty-two hundred were protected in Roman monasteries and convents, including Castel Gondolfo, the papal summer residence. And, it is also accurate that, after the war, Rome's chief rabbi and various members of Italy's Jewish community praised Pius for his support during the Holocaust.

One of Pius's defenders, Rabbi David G. Dalin, suggests, as noted previously, that Pius should be honored as a Righteous Gentile for his (Pius's) role in saving "more Jews than Oskar Schindler" and because of the praise of Jewish leaders. Pius' admirers, according to Rabbi Dalin, include Chief Rabbi Yitzhak Halevy Herzog of the Palestinian Mandate and Israel, Israeli Prime Ministers Golda Meir and Moshe Sharett, and Israel's first president, Chaim Weizmann. Susan Zuccotti, however, argues that Jewish politicians who praised Pius's performance during the Holocaust actually had an ulterior motive, namely, as Jews dedicated to the creation of the State of Israel, they were attempting to urge Vatican diplomatic recognition of the Jewish state.

As proof that Pius spoke out against the Nazis, his defenders cite this *New York Times* editorial published on December 25, 1941: "The

---

251   Rabbi Dalin opined: "Anti-papal polemics of ex-seminarians like Garry Wills and John Cornwell, of ex-priests like James Carroll, and of other lapsed or angry liberal Catholics exploit the tragedy of the Jewish people during the Holocaust to foster their own political agenda of forcing changes on the Catholic Church." There is probably an element of truth in Rabbi Dalin's assertion.

voice of Pius XII is a lonely voice in the silence and darkness enveloping Europe this Christmas. He is about the only one who dares to raise his voice at all."

Another of his defenders, Sister Margherita Marchione, has written several books defending Pius's sanctity, advocating his canonization, urging he be named a Righteous Gentile, and pointing out that John Paul II, who proposed him for sainthood, consistently praised him. Sister Margherita writes:

> Pius XII strongly condemned the anti-Semitic persecutions, the oppression of invaded lands and the inhuman conduct of the Nazis. He urged the Christian restoration of family life and education, the reconstruction of society, the equality of nations, the suppression of hate propaganda and the formation of an international organization for disarmament and maintenance of peace. He was a champion of peace, freedom, human dignity, encouraging Catholics to look on Christians and Jews as their brothers and sisters, all children of a common Father …

A third defender, Father Pierre Blet, a Catholic scholar who spent fifteen years examining Vatican archival documents,[252] maintained that "(Pius's) public silence was the cover for a secret activity through Vatican embassies and bishoprics to try to stop the deportations." Father Blet admitted that Pius was fond of the German people but objected to the characterization that Pius was a Nazi sympathizer. Father Blet pointed out that Pius was forced to act within extremely difficult circumstances, which included a creditable threat of kidnapping and/or assassination. Father Blet and others also cite, in Pius's defense, an article appearing in the Israeli newspaper the *Jewish Post*, after the pope's death in November 1958, which read: "There was probably not a single ruler of our generation who did more to help the Jews in their hour of greatest tragedy, during the Nazi occupation of Europe, than the late Pope."

Joseph Lichten, in his book *A Question of Judgment*, labels any criticism of Pius's actions during WWII as "a stupefying paradox" in

---

252   It should be noted, however, that the Vatican has yet to open its wartime archives for public inspection.

that, "no one who reads the record of Pius XII's actions on behalf of Jews can subscribe to Hochhuth's accusation (in *The Deputy*)."

Elie Wiesel opined, on the other hand, that when all is said and done: "The principle that governs the biblical vision of society is, 'Thou shall not stand idly by when your fellow man is hurting, suffering, or being victimized.' It is because that injunction was ignored or violated that the catastrophe involving such multitudes occurred."

According to David Kertzer, one of Pius's critics, what is most important for understanding the Church's role in making the Holocaust possible is not discovering what Pius XII did or did not do. More important, said Kertzer, is bringing to light the role Pius's predecessors played over previous centuries in dehumanizing Jews and in encouraging Europeans to view them as evil and dangerous. Kertzer wrote:

> It is only in this context that we can understand why the special legislation (Nuremburg Laws) that in the 1930s served as a first step toward the Holocaust, making Jews second-class citizens, was greeted with indifference, if not pleasure, by large segments of the European population. Even for the more limited goal of making sense of Pius XII's behavior during the war, we need to understand this longer stretch of history. Only in its light can we understand why, as millions of Jews were being murdered, Pius XII could never bring himself to publicly utter the word "Jew."

Neither demon nor angel, Pius XII reigned as pope during one of the evilest times in human history. Not a free agent, he was molded and straitjacketed by close to two thousand years of church history, including traditions of anti-Judaism and papal absolutism. On occasion, he interceded to ameliorate the plight of Jews and was successful, which leads to legitimate speculation about what additional success he might have had, if he had done more. One can only imagine, for example, what might have been if, as vicar of Christ, he, or Pius XI, had threatened to excommunicate any Catholic who joined the Nazi Party or who cooperated with the Nazis. Or if he, or Pius XI, had excommunicated Hitler or any Catholic Nazi or Nazi collaborator and/or placed Nazi Germany under interdict. Or if, as a respected worldwide voice of conscience and the world's most influential religious/spiritual figure, he, or Pius XI, had publicly and explicitly condemned Nazi extremism. Or if, in the manner of Mahatma Gandhi or Martin Luther King Jr., he had urged passive resistance to blatantly unjust laws in Nazi Germany, fascist Italy, and elsewhere in Occupied Europe.

In March 1998, the bishops of Italy wrote an open letter to the Italian Jewish community, in which they acknowledged the "lack of prophetic action" on the part of the Church during the Holocaust, adding: "We recall these events with dismay and also with a profound and conscientious 'teshuvah.'"[253]

Law of Unintended Consequences

James Carroll, in *Constantine's Sword*, implicitly invoked the law of unintended consequences when he described the Church's dilemma regarding the Holocaust. Carroll contends, for example, that the Church did not fail to rise to the challenge posed by Hitler out of cowardice, anxiety over Bolshevism, or preoccupation with its own power and prerogatives. He cites Pius IX's response during *Kulturkampf* in Bismarck's Germany when the Church's institutional interests were threatened to dispel the notion of cowardice. No, according to Carroll, the cause of the Church's disappointing performance as a champion for justice rests squarely on its two thousand year history of anti-Judaism. He writes: "Nazism, by tapping into a deep, ever-fresh reservoir of Christian hatred of Jews, was able to make an accomplice of the Catholic Church in history's worst crime, even though, by then, it was the last thing the Church consciously wanted to be."

The law of unintended consequences posits that actions have effects that are both unanticipated and unintended. And, unfortunately, sometimes, as in the case in point, unintended consequences can turn out much worse than intended ones. This concept dates back to the eighteenth century and political economist Adam Smith, the Scottish Enlightenment, and Consequentialism (judging by results). However, it was American sociologist Robert K. Merton who popularized the concept in the twentieth century. In a seminal article published in 1936

---

253   *Teshuvah* in Hebrew means "return" and is the word used to describe the concept of repentance in Judaism. Jews believe that only by atoning for their sins can they restore balance to their relationship with God and with their fellow human beings.

entitled "The Unanticipated Consequences of Purposive Social Action," Merton identified five sources of unanticipated consequences:

1. *Ignorance:* It is not possible to anticipate everything, thereby leading to incomplete analysis.
2. *Error:* Incorrect analysis of a problem or following habits that worked in the past but may not apply to the current situation.
3. *Immediate interest:* A current and pressing interest may override long-term interests.
4. *Basic values:* Core values may require or prohibit certain actions even if the long-term result might be unfavorable; long-term consequences may eventually cause core values to change.
5. *Self-defeating prophecy:* Fear of some consequence drives people to find solutions before the problem occurs, thus the nonoccurrence of the problem is unanticipated.

The Holocaust, tragically, is a classic case of the law of unintended consequences in action. The Church certainly did not intend to become complicit in one of the worst crimes in human history, but core doctrines, in addition to anti-Judaism, including supercessionism, anti-Modernism, and papal absolutism, resulted in its complicity. Lack of intent to commit a crime mitigates the seriousness of a crime but does not exculpate the criminal from culpability or accountability for it. A drunk driver who causes the death of another in a vehicular accident, for example, is charged with criminally negligent homicide, not premeditated/intentional murder. Unfortunately, the law of unintended consequences also applies to the current worldwide priest sex abuse scandal.

Between 1950 and 2002, at least 4,392 priests sexually abused children in the United States, taking advantage of vulnerable school-age children in their pastoral care. Since then the US Church has paid well over $1 billion in expenses related to the scandal, while patterns of similar abuse by clerics have been exposed in several other countries. Bishops and Popes John Paul II and Benedict XVI have been accused of covering up the criminal activity of pedophile priests, compounding the seriousness and extent of the crimes. Surely there was no conscious intent to do so, but the Church's climate of secrecy, reluctance to cause or admit scandal, and what author Jason Berry terms its "structural mendacity, institutionalized lying," has once again resulted in complicity.[254]

On June 22, 2012, Monsignor William J. Lynn, of the Archdiocese of Philadelphia, a former aide and advisor of Cardinal Anthony J. Bevilacqua, now deceased, was found guilty of endangering children, becoming the first senior official of the US Church convicted of covering up sexual abuses by priests under his supervision. The twelve-member jury acquitted Monsignor Lynn of conspiracy and a second count of endangerment after a trial that prosecutors and victims' rights groups called a turning point in the abuse scandals that have shaken the Catholic Church worldwide. According to the *New York Times'* front page article covering the verdict, the trial sent a sobering message to church officials and others overseeing children around the country. It quoted Nicholas P. Cafardi, a professor of law at Duquesne University, a canon lawyer and frequent church advisor, who said: "I think that bishops and chancery officials understand that they will no longer get a pass on these types of crimes ... Priests who sexually abuse youngsters and the chancery officials who enabled it can expect criminal prosecution."

On September 6, 2012, Bishop Robert W. Finn of Kansas City-St. Joseph, Missouri, was found guilty in a county criminal court for failing to report suspected child abuse, becoming the first Catholic bishop to be convicted in a US court of shielding a priest who was a threat to children. The crime, a misdemeanor in Missouri, could have cost Finn a year in jail and a $1,000 fine. But after a brief nonjury trial, Jackson County, Missouri, Circuit Court Judge John Torrence gave the bishop a two-year suspended sentence of probation with nine conditions, including mandating direct reporting of future suspicions of child abuse to prosecutors.

---

254   See Jason Berry, *Render Unto Rome: The Secret Life of Money in the Catholic Church.*

CHAPTER II

Vatican Council II and Beyond

POPE PIUS XII DIED ON October 9, 1958, ending his nineteen-year reign. On October 28, Angelo Giuseppe Roncalli, the archbishop of Venice, was elected, to his great surprise, to be Pius's successor (the presumed frontrunner candidate was Giovanni Battista Montini, archbishop of Milan, who would become Pope Paul VI in June 1963). Roncalli had arrived in Rome for the election by the College of Cardinals with a return train ticket to Venice. Upon his election, Roncalli chose the name John XXIII, the first time in over five hundred years that the name John had been chosen, as previous popes had avoided its use since the time of the Antipope John XXIII during the Western Schism (1378–1417). After Pius XII's long pontificate, the cardinals chose a man who, because of his advanced age of seventy-seven, they presumed would be a short-term, "stop gap," or "caretaker" pope. The cardinals, however, would be proven wrong.

Far from being a mere "caretaker" pope, to the great excitement of most Catholics worldwide, Pope John called into session in 1962 an ecumenical council less than ninety years after Vatican Council I was interrupted by the Franco-Prussian War, never finishing its work. Cardinal Montini remarked to a friend that "this holy old boy doesn't realize what a hornet's nest he's stirring up." Cardinal Montini was right because from Vatican Council II would come changes that reshaped the Church and the face of Catholicism, changes associated with buzzwords such as: *aggiornamento* ("bringing up to date"), and *ressourcement* ("return to sources"), people of God, full participation of the laity, *communio* ("communion") of all the baptized, collegiality, dialogue, and ecumenism.

The bishops who attended Vatican Council II came from 116 different countries, whereas 40 percent of the bishops at Vatican I came from Italy. Many brought along with them a secretary or a theologian/ *peritus* or both. To this number must be added others who came to Rome because of official or semiofficial business related to the council, which included about a hundred observers from other churches, as well as representatives of the media. By the time it opened, the Vatican had issued about a thousand press cards to journalists. Probably close to ten thousand people were present in Rome at any given time while the council was in session because they had some kind of business relating to it.

Pope John set up ten commissions to compose documents on subjects that emerged from previous consultations. These commissions were headed by cardinals who, with one exception, were prefects of Vatican congregations that made up the Curia. A central Coordinating Commission was to oversee the work of the others. The commissions worked for two years to produce documents that they hoped the council would accept after discussion and amendment. The commission produced seventy documents, which were eventually whittled down to sixteen. Four sessions were required for the council to complete its business, each of which, held in the fall, lasted about ten weeks, 1962–65. On June 3, 1963, Pope John died of stomach cancer, and the council went forward under his successor, Paul VI.

On April 8, 1965, Vatican Council II published its sixteenth document, "Declaration on the Relationship of the Church and Non-Christian Religions" (*Nostra Aetate,* also known as "In Our Age"), in which, abandoning close to two millennia of religious intolerance, the Church finally committed itself to religious freedom. After the Council, Popes Paul VI, John Paul II, and Benedict XVI publically proclaimed religious liberty a fundamental human right—a proclamation that would have been inconceivable before 1965. Previously, in the "Decree on Religious Liberty" (*Dignitatis Humane,* also known as "Of the Dignity of the Human Person"), the council sanctioned the separation of church and state, the right to worship according to one's conscience, and the primacy of conscience over obedience to external authority.

These principles, however, met with resistance from the conservative fathers of the council and still do.[255]

Vatican Council II repudiated and reversed anti-Judaism, a change which could have been made by any pope during the papacy's nineteen-hundred-plus-year history. At last, this pernicious doctrine on Jews as Christ-killers and rejected children of God was ended. The council declared: "Mindful of her common patrimony with the Jews, and motivated by the gospel's spiritual love and by no political considerations, she deplores the hatred, persecutions and displays of anti-Semitism directed against the Jews at any time and from any source."

Specifically, *Nostra Aetate* declared:

- No collective guilt can be attributed to Jews, past or present, for the death of Jesus.
- God's covenant with the Jewish People is valid and not revoked.
- The Jews are not forsaken or condemned by God.
- Anti-Semitism is a sin and has no place in Christianity.

It should be noted further, however, that few issues sparked more controversy inside the council and outside in the media as the relationship of the Church to the Jews and to other non-Christian religions. Regarding non-Roman Catholic Christians, for example, how could the Church now receive as brothers and sisters those whom, until the council opened, it had regarded as heretics? The sticking point, in particular, for conservative fathers was the Church's relationship to the Jews (i.e., how responsible they were for the death of Jesus).[256] Cardinal Ernesto Ruffini, for example, had opposed the concept of tolerance of any non-Catholic faith. He argued that tolerance was a

---

255   In May 2012, the book *Le 'chiavi' di Benedetto XVI per interpretare il Vaticano II* (*The Keys of Benedict XVI for the Interpretation of Vatican II*), authored by Cardinal Walter Brandmüller (emeritus of the Pontifical Committee for Historical Sciences), Archbishop Agostino Marchetto, and Monsignor Nicola Bux was published by Cantagalli Press in Siena. At a presentation to the media in the studios of Vatican Radio in Rome, Cardinal Brandmüller referred to *Dignitatis Humane* and *Nostra Aetate* as "nonbinding" on the Church because of a lack of "binding doctrinal content."

256   See O'Malley, *Vatican Council II*, 9.

license for error, which, according to church doctrine, has no rights. And Cardinal Alfredo Ottaviani, prefect of the Congregation of the Holy Office (successor of the Holy Inquisition), stubbornly held to the position that in Catholic countries the state had an obligation to profess and favor the Catholic faith and to limit the practice of all other faiths. Vatican Council II renamed the Congregation of the Holy Office the Congregation for the Doctrine of the Faith.

John Courtney Murray

John Courtney Murray (1904–67), was an American Jesuit priest and theologian especially known for his efforts to reconcile Roman Catholicism and religious pluralism, particularly focusing on the relationship between religious freedom and the institutions of a democratically structured modern state. In his book, *We Hold These Truths: Catholic Reflections on the American Proposition*, Father Murray discussed the compatibility of Catholic doctrine with concepts espoused by America's Founding Fathers, including freedom of expression and religion. In discussing the relationship between church and state, he asserted that there existed a necessary distinction between morality and civil law; that the latter is limited in its capacity in cultivating moral character through criminal prohibitions, and that "it is not the function of civil law to prescribe everything that is morally right and to forbid everything that is morally wrong." Clearly, religion had a large role to play in helping the faithful define the difference between right and wrong.

During Vatican Council II, Father Murray played a key role in persuading the assembled bishops to adopt the council's groundbreaking "Declaration on Religious Liberty" (*Dignitatis Humane*), arguing that Catholic teaching on church/state relations was inadequate to the moral functioning of contemporary society. The Anglo-American West, he claimed, had developed a fuller truth about human dignity, namely the responsibility of all citizens to assume moral control over their own religious beliefs, taking back control formerly exerted by paternalistic states since at least the time of Constantine. For him this truth was an "intention of nature," or a new dictate of natural law philosophy. His claim that a *new* moral truth had emerged outside the Church, which claimed to be changeless, not surprisingly, led to conflict with Cardinal Ottaviani, prefect of the Holy Office, and the eventual Vatican demand, in 1954, that Murray cease writing on religious freedom and stop publication of his two latest articles on the issue. A proponent of change, Murray, nonetheless, questioned how the Church might arrive at new theological doctrines. If Catholics were to arrive at new truths about God, he argued, they would have to do so in conversation "on a footing of equality" with non-Catholics and even atheists. He suggested greater reforms, including a restructuring of the Church, which he saw as having overdeveloped its notion of authority and hierarchy at the expense of the bonds of love that more foundationally ought to define Christian living.

Despite the Holy Office's attempt to silence him, Father Murray was invited to participate at Vatican Council II as a peritus, becoming the American bishops' leading theologian, where he drafted the third and fourth versions of what eventually became the council's endorsement of religious freedom in *Dignitatis Humane*. After the council he continued writing on the issue, claiming that the arguments offered by the final version of *Dignitatis Humanae*, watered down at the insistence of conservative bishops,[257] were inadequate, though the affirmation of religious freedom was unequivocal. Father Murray's thoughts have been invoked by liberal Catholics to justify a "pro-choice" stance in the current debate taking place in the United States over abortion.

Watershed Event in Church History

Vatican Council II, like the Council of Trent and Vatican Council I, was undoubtedly a watershed event in church history, although traditionalist Catholics claim that little new ground was broken.[258] But unlike previous councils, Trent and Vatican I in particular, Vatican II was not called to deal with a particular crisis enveloping the Church. Rather, it was called to respond to "challenges facing the modern world." In the words of Blessed

---

257   Liberal bishops, especially Cardinal Gregory Meyer of Chicago, were disappointed with what seemed to be obstructive action by Paul VI and conservative bishops to weaken the language of *Dignitatis Humanae*. When subsequently asked whether he was impatient with the pope's obstructive action, Father Murray said no; rather, he was angry over the pope's action.

258   In an address to Roman curial officials on December 22, 2005, Pope Benedict XVI argued that Vatican Council II did not represent any kind of "rupture" with previous ecumenical councils of the Church. This was the case, he opined, because, in all of its essential details, the Church cannot change.

Pope John XXIII,[259] the Church needed *aggiornamento* ("updating" and "renewal"); it needed to enter into a more constructive engagement with the modern world. "It is not that the Gospel has changed," said Pope John, "it is that we have begun to understand it better ... and know that the moment has come to discern the signs of the times, to seize the opportunity and to look far ahead." Candidly, the Church needed to deal with the embarrassment of the many unintended consequences occasioned by, among other things, anti-Judaism, the papacy's siege mentality since Trent, Pius IX's and Pius X's war on Modernism and papal absolutism—all of which too often placed the Church on the wrong side of history. Attributing his idea to convene the council to "inspiration of the Holy Spirit," Pope John saw Vatican II as the solution for the problem preoccupying many critical-thinking Catholics, namely, how an ancient Church that prided itself on its tradition and unchangeable nature could survive in a world undergoing social, political, and cultural transformation of unprecedented magnitude.

Most Catholics and non-Catholics agreed that Vatican II accomplished a great deal of much-needed reform, but not without considerable opposition from conservative members of the Curia, spearheaded by Cardinal Ottaviani,[260] prefect of the Congregation of the Holy Office, who attempted to sabotage the council's work at every opportunity. In fact, Ottaviani and other members of the Curia, citing papal infallibility and other absolutist doctrines, argued against the need to convene a council at all. In their view, the Church, as a perfect society, repository of changeless truth, one true faith and only means to salvation, had no need to change. And this attitude continues within the Vatican to the present day. According to Father Mark S. Massa, SJ, in his book *The American Catholic Revolution: How the '60s Changed the Church Forever*, a small number of extreme traditionalist Catholics even view Vatican II as an anticouncil (i.e., they see the event of 1962–65 "as not being a real council of the Church at all, but rather an event

---

259   Known affectionately as "Good Pope John" and considered by many people as "most beloved pope in history," in September 2000, Pope John Paul II proposed Pope John XXIII for sainthood, at the same time he proposed Pope Pius XII.

260   Cardinal Ottaviani adopted as his motto the Latin phrase *Semper idem*, ("Always the same"). Like his predecessors, Ottaviani shared an outlook of moral certitude based on personal access to unchanging truth.

abetted by the Forces of Darkness against the Fortress Church of Pius IX and Pius X").[261]

Silencing Dissenting Theologians

Since the end of the council, the Vatican has attempted to silence theologians who dissented from traditionalist views of what happened there. For example, as prefect of the Congregation for the Doctrine of the Faith, Cardinal Joseph Ratzinger, now Benedict XVI, personally pronounced the excommunication of Sri Lankan priest Tissa Balasuriya, a seventy-two-year-old theologian. Father Balasuriya, the only theologian to have been excommunicated since Vatican Council II,[262] was accused of relativism (i.e., of placing the presuppositions of Christian revelation on the same level as those of other religions, in particular, Hinduism and Buddhism).[263] Balasuriya denied the charge, asserting that a participant in dialogue presumes the dialogue partner's right to his or her own point of view without prejudging it. Ratzinger disagreed, however, saying: "There can be no dialogue at the expense of truth." The future pope rejected pluralism—the notion that various religions offer, each in their own way, authentic avenues of access to God—and dismissed Vatican II's assertion that Christ's salvation was available to all, beyond religion, through the mysterious workings of God's grace.

Father Richard P. McBrien, author of *Catholicism, The Church: The Evolution of Catholicism,* and *Lives of the Popes,* asserts that Benedict's predecessor, Pope John Paul II, "betrayed the 'Spirit of Vatican II,'" by, among other things, censuring and/or disciplining liberal theologians like Fathers Tissa Balasuriya, Hans Küng, Jacques Pohier, Edward Schillebeeckx, Leonardo Boff, Charles E. Curran, and Matthew Fox. Clearly, Benedict XVI continues John Paul II's traditionalist legacy. Why were these theologians censured and/or disciplined?

Father Jacques Pohier, a French Dominican priest, was the first theologian to be disciplined by Pope John Paul II. In 1979, Pohier, the

261   Massa, *The American Catholic Revolution,* 158.

262   After agreeing to submit future writings to Rome for review before publication, Father Balasuriya's excommunication was revoked.

263   One of Buddha's insights was that to live a moral life was to live for others. In other words, it was not enough to experience religious insight. After enlightenment, Buddha said, a person must return to the marketplace and there practice compassion to all, doing anything possible to alleviate the misery of other people. Jesus, no doubt, would have agreed with this insight.

dean of the theology faculty at the Dominican theological school near Paris, lost his license to teach theology and was banned from celebrating Mass or participating in any liturgical gatherings. The Vatican objected to his views on Christ's resurrection. Pohier left the Dominicans in 1984.

Edward Schillebeeckx, a Belgian Dominican, was theologian of the Dutch bishops at Vatican Council II who endured several Vatican investigations. He was initially investigated in 1968 for questioning the virginity of Mary. The Dutch hierarchy, clergy, and laity rallied to his defense, and Father Karl Rahner, who himself would be investigated, convinced the Vatican of Schillebeeckx's orthodoxy. In 1979, a trial or "procedure" was convened to investigate his writings on Christology (theology of Christ). In the face of an international campaign of protest against the trial, the Congregation for the Doctrine of the Faith dropped the matter in 1980. He has since received several "notifications" from the congregation that his writings remain in conflict with church teaching.

Leonardo Boff, a leading proponent of liberation theology in Latin America, was silenced—ordered not to publish or speak publicly for a year, and assigned a personal censor to review his writings. Liberation theology is an attempt to interpret scripture through the plight of the poor. Father Boff was accused of having Marxist leanings.

Matthew Fox, a Dominican priest with a New Age bent, was silenced for a year and eventually expelled from the Dominican Order. Now a member of the Episcopal Church, Father Fox was an early and influential exponent of a movement that came to be known as Creation Spirituality.

In 2005, the Congregation for the Doctrine of the Faith, acting at the behest of Cardinal Ratzinger, effectively removed Father Thomas Reese, a political scientist and a Jesuit, from his post as the editor of *America*, a magazine published by the Jesuit Order. Father Reese had written on Church affairs for years, and continues to do so. His book *Inside the Vatican*, published before he became editor, is regarded as the authoritative modern account of the Holy See's operations.

On June 4, 2012, the Congregation for the Doctrine of the Faith sharply criticized another prominent theologian, Sister of Mercy, Margaret Farley, for her 2006 book *Just Love: A Framework for Christian*

Sexual Ethics. In its formal notification to Sister Farley, the Congregation said that her book, which aims to apply theories of justice to sexual ethics, "cannot be used as a valid expression of Catholic teaching, either in counseling and formation, or in ecumenical and interreligious dialogue" because its positions on masturbation, homosexual acts, homosexual unions, the indissolubility of marriage, and the problem of divorce and remarriage "contradicts," "is opposed to," or "does not conform to" church teaching.

The Role of Conscience

Vatican Council II reiterated church doctrine that conscience is the ultimate norm in making moral choices. It declared:

> Deep within our conscience we find a law which we have not laid upon ourselves, but which we must obey. Its voice, ever calling us to love and to do what is good and to avoid evil, sounds in our heart at the right moment ... For we have in our hearts a law inscribed by God ... Our conscience is our most secret core and our sanctuary. There we are alone with God whose voice echoes in our depths.[264]
>
> [and] ... "It is through our conscience that we see and recognize the demands of the divine law. We are bound to follow our conscience faithfully in all our activity so that we may come to God, who is our last end.[265]

According to Father John W. O'Malley, SJ,[266] while Catholics must take full and serious account of church teachings and guidance, they must ultimately be guided by the inner law of a well-formed conscience. Preachers, theologians, and saints have always taught in some form or other this primacy of conscience, but no council, according to him, had ever declared it explicitly. Father O'Malley summarizes his view of the

---

264 "Pastoral Constitution on the Church in the Modern World" (*Gaudium et Spes*).

265 "Declaration on Religious Liberty" (*Dignitatis Humanae*).

266 Father John W. O'Malley, SJ, outstanding scholar and priest, distinguished professor of church history at Weston Jesuit School of Theology in Cambridge, Massachusetts, is a renowned historian of the early modern Catholic Church, author of more than ninety articles and four books, and editor of six additional volumes.

Church's changes in style as evidenced by the council's vocabulary in its documents:

> From commands to invitations, from laws to ideals, from threats to persuasion, from coercion to conscience, from monologue to conversation, from ruling to serving, from withdrawn to integrated, from vertical and top-down to horizontal, from seclusion to inclusion, from hostility to friendship, from static to changing, from passive acceptance to active engagement, from prescriptive to principled, from defined to open-ended, from behavior-modification to conversion of heart, from the dictates of law to the dictates of conscience, from external conformity to the joyful pursuit of happiness.[267]

People of God Model of Church

The key to understanding Vatican Council II is best expressed in two phrases that characterized it, namely, the Church is *semper reformanda* ("always in need of reform") and the Church is *Populi Dei* ("People of God"). These phrases reflect a new self-understanding/model of church that began to emerge at the council, de-emphasizing the then existing institutional model of church as a monolithic, unchanging, dogmatic, and insular institution, in favor of a less doctrinaire, more pastoral, more ecumenical, and more egalitarian model. Leadership in the institutional model, as noted previously, was hierarchical in nature with the pope at the top, then in descending order—archbishops, bishops, priests, religious, deacons, and, at the bottom, the laity. Those at the top "possessed" the truth; those below "received" the truth; the laity's role was docile and compliant (i.e., to "pay, pray and obey"). Under the institutional model, church authority was absolute and not to be questioned; independent thought was discouraged and repressed. It should be noted that unquestioning obedience to evil authority and lack of self-generated initiative grounded in a well-formed conscience were among the causes of the Holocaust.

On the issue of authority, Noam Chomsky has written: "I think it only makes sense to seek out and identify structures of authority, hierarchy, and domination in every aspect of life, and to challenge them; unless a justification for them can be given, they are illegitimate, and should be dismantled, to increase the scope of human freedom."

267   O'Malley, *Vatican Council II*, 81.

One of the lessons of history is that religion can be a source of good or evil. Absolutist claims of religion, therefore, ought to be open to scrutiny, including claims that certain dicta be accepted "on faith." When it comes to issues of moral ambiguity, after all, religion ought to be part of the solution, not the problem. "God is greater than religion," wrote Rabbi Abraham Joshua Heschel. "Faith is greater than dogma." In other words, God should not be confused with religion. It is rank human presumptuousness and arrogance to claim that God, who is beyond human comprehension, is the exclusive property of any one faith tradition—to the exclusion of others.

Process Theology

In contrast to the institutional model of Church, the People of God model views the Church as an evolving process, not a static entity, a process that employs evolutionary and relational modes of thought to define itself. This model recognizes that popes and bishops do not have a monopoly on divine truth; they do not receive supernaturally infused knowledge at their episcopal ordination or installation. Rather, all the faithful have a role to play in the process of determining divine truth, including the laity. Docility and passivity, therefore, are discouraged. All the faithful, through the sacrament of baptism, are expected to participate fully in Christ's role of priest, prophet, and king, not just the ordained. In the People of God model, church leadership is diffuse, not concentrated at the top. *Sensum fidelium* ("sense of the faithful") is required to validate doctrine, not an infallible decree from a pope subject to human foibles. When members of the clergy, who are likewise subject to human foibles, stray from core Gospel values, they too should be held to account. The processive (progressive) nature of church is implicit in the expression *ecclesia semper reformanda*, namely, the Church will always be subject to renewal and reform because its members, from the pope to the laity, are human and sinful. The Church exists for the sake of God's kingdom but is not identical to God's kingdom. It is, therefore, not the manifestation of the kingdom on earth; it is, at best, an initial "budding forth" of the kingdom. It is not a perfect society, not a spotless bride of Christ, not the only means of salvation, or any other absolutist formulation.

Under the People of God model, the Church, apart from faith in Jesus, is essentially nothing at all. Dogmas, creeds, and doctrines, together with structures, hierarchies, and authorities, are merely ways by which the faithful articulate and organize their beliefs—constructs employed to express how the faith has been integrated into various moments of history.

The foregoing is an example of "process theology."[268] The People of God model is generally favored by Catholics who consider themselves liberal or progressive and is rejected by those who consider themselves orthodox, traditionalist, or conservative. The former believe, generally, that the Church should adapt itself to changing times and needs, while the latter believe the Church should adhere fully to the teaching authority of the pope, which, history amply demonstrates, is resistant to change. Progressives tend to concentrate on social justice issues such as poverty, homelessness, hunger, and lack of adequate health care;[269] traditionalists tend to concentrate on social issues such as abortion, birth control, human sexuality, and same-sex marriage.

Hans Küng

Hans Küng, a Swiss Catholic priest, theologian, prolific author, and a *peritus* (theological expert) at Vatican Council II, became the first major Roman Catholic theologian since the Old Catholic Church schism of 1870 to publicly reject the doctrine of papal infallibility. Father Küng also questioned doctrines on priestly celibacy, birth control, women in the priesthood, and other matters. As a consequence, on December 18, 1979, the Congregation for the Doctrine of the Faith on behalf of Pope John Paul II, citing "contempt for Church doctrine," stripped Father Küng of his canonical license to teach theology in Catholic schools and universities. However, he continued to teach as a tenured professor of ecumenical theology at the University of Tubingen until his retirement in 1996. Father Küng remained a persistent critic of papal infallibility, which

---

268   See, among others, Robert B. Mellert, *What Is Process Theology?*

269   Conservative Catholics in the United States today seem especially motivated by the issue of religious liberty, with their principal focus regarding a provision in President Barack Obama's landmark legislation on health care reform which allows the Department of Health and Human Services to mandate insurance coverage for certain procedures like contraception. The Church condemns contraception based on Paul VI's encyclical *Humane Vitae*, which reiterated its traditional doctrine that birth control is intrinsically evil. American liberal Catholics, on the other hand, are especially concerned about defending social justice programs, with the Affordable Care Act (derisively referred to as "Obamacare") representing the fulfillment of a generation-long struggle to enact universal health care.

he claimed is man-made (and, therefore, reversible) rather than instituted by God. In 2005, Küng published a critical article in Italy and Germany entitled, "The failures of Pope Wojtyla." In it he argued that what the world expected from Vatican Council II was a period of conversion, reform, and dialogue within the Church, but because Pope John Paul II favored restoration to the pre-Vatican II status quo ante, the pope was blocking reform and dialogue, reasserting the absolute dominion by the Holy See. Küng wrote:

> This Papacy has repeatedly declared its fidelity to Vatican II, in order to then betray it for reasons of political expediency. Council terms such as modernization, dialogue, and ecumenicalism have been replaced by emphasis on restoration, mastery, and obedience. The criteria for the nomination of Bishops is not at all in the spirit of the Gospel ... Pastoral politics has allowed the moral and intellectual level of the episcopate to slip to dangerous levels. A mediocre, rigid, and more conservative episcopate will be the lasting legacy of this papacy.

In the early 1990s, Father Küng initiated a project entitled *Weltethos* ("Global Ethic"), an attempt to describe what world religions have in common (rather than what separates them) and to draw up a minimal code of rules of behavior members of all faith traditions can accept. His vision of a global ethic was embodied in the document for which he wrote the initial draft, "Towards a Global Ethic: An Initial Declaration." This declaration was signed at the 1993 Parliament of the World's Religions by religious and spiritual leaders from around the world. Later, Küng's project culminated in the United Nations' "Dialogue among Civilizations," to which he was assigned as one of nineteen eminent persons.

Charles E. Curran

Father Charles E. Curran is a moral theologian who currently serves at Southern Methodist University as the Elizabeth Scurlock University professor of human values. Earning two doctorates in theology in Rome, he was ordained a priest of the Diocese of Rochester, New York, in 1958. As a young priest, he was a *peritus* at Vatican Council II. Appointed in 1965 to the theology faculty at Catholic University of America, Father

Curran was removed from his tenured faculty position there in 1967 for his views on birth control, but was reinstated after a five-day faculty-led strike. His reinstatement proved to be short-lived, however, because in 1968 he, along with a group of some six hundred theologians, authored a response to *Humane Vitae*, Pope Paul VI's encyclical affirming the Church's traditional ban on birth control. He continued to teach and write on doctrines concerning various moral issues throughout the 1970s and 1980s.

In 1986, Father Curran was again removed from the faculty of Catholic University as a dissident against the Church's moral teaching. That same year, the Vatican declared him no longer eligible to teach theology at any Catholic university or college, because clashes with Church authorities finally culminated in a decision by the Congregation for the Doctrine of the Faith, headed by then-Cardinal Joseph Ratzinger, that Curran was neither suitable nor eligible to be a professor of Catholic theology.[270] The areas of dispute included publishing articles that debated theological and ethical views regarding divorce, artificial contraception, masturbation, premarital intercourse, and homosexual acts.

"There is no doubt," Father Curran says, "that the strongest opposition to modern liberties and human rights during the eighteenth, nineteenth, and into the twentieth century came from the Roman Catholic Church." He argues that the Church vigorously opposed all forms of liberalism—political, social, economic, and most of all philosophical—because the rise of individualism could be interpreted as being separate or "sovereign from God," which threatened the existence of the Church. But heading into the mid-twentieth century, individualism, he contends, was not as threatening as totalitarianism, fascism, and communism. And under Pope John Paul II, who grew up in Poland under Communist rule, the Church underwent one of the biggest transformations in its history.

First recipient of the John Courtney Murray Award for Theology, Father Curran has served as president of the Catholic Theological Society of America, the Society of Christian Ethics, and the American Theological Society. In 2003, he received the Presidential Award of the College Theology Society for a lifetime of scholarly achievement in moral theology, and in 2005, Call to Action—a reform movement of twenty-five thousand Catholics—presented him with its leadership award. He

270   See Charles E. Curran, *Loyal Dissent, Memoir of a Catholic Theologian*.

continues to defend the possibility of legitimate dissent from teachings of the Catholic faith—not core or central to it—that are outside the realm of infallibility. Champion of progressive Catholics and scourge of traditionalist ones, he has worked in support of more academic freedom in Catholic higher education and for a structural change in the Church that would increase the role of the entire Catholic community—from local churches and parishes to all the baptized people of God. Father Curran remains a priest in good standing in the Diocese of Rochester, New York.

Preaching the homily during a funeral Mass in Rochester for his dear friend and fellow priest and scholar Monsignor William H. Shannon who died at age ninety-four in April 2012, Father Curran described Monsignor Shannon as "an extraordinary priest of our diocese … (whose) commitment to Biblical and liturgical renewal made him an enthusiastic supporter of the Vatican II reforms in the Church … The triumphalism and clericalism of the pre-Vatican Church was not for him." Father Curran continued: "Bill lamented the trajectory in our Church moving away from Vatican II. He was especially upset by the growing centralization in the Church that de-emphasized the role of the local church, the failure to recognize the role of the *sensus fidelium*, and the inferior role of women in the Church. But as a true pilgrim, he faithfully worked in every way to carry on the work of reform in the Church."

Society of St. Pius X

The Society of St. Pius X, hereinafter "SSPX," was founded in 1970 by French Archbishop Marcel Lefebvre (1905–91) in opposition to the reforms of the Second Vatican Council. SSPX is an international traditionalist Catholic organization that defines its mission as opposing innovation and modernity within the Church. Archbishop Lefebvre, who participated at Vatican II, heading one of its commissions, spent the last two decades of his life battling change within the Church. The traditionalist documents he and other conservative fathers drafted were rejected by the council. Later, Lefebvre would declare the devil and Antichrists inspired the council. For him opening up dialogue with Protestants, Muslims, and Jews was wrong because, as error has no right, it lent credibility to these other religions. Therefore, he rejected Vatican II's declaration of religious freedom, terming it a misguided effort to put Catholicism on an equal footing with other faiths.

In 1969, the year before SSPX's founding, Archbishop Lefebvre rejected the revised Vatican Council II recommended Mass rite in vernacular languages as a "bastard rite." For his defiance of authority, Pope Paul VI suspended Lefebvre from the priesthood in 1976. He, nonetheless, carried on undeterred, celebrating a Tridentine/Latin rite Mass before six thousand people in Lille, France, and saying, "Let us carry on the religion of our fathers." In 1978, Pope John Paul II, attempting reconciliation, restored Lefebvre to the priesthood. Ten years later, in 1988, Pope John Paul attempted to head off approaching schism by offering to name a priest of Lefebvre's choice as a bishop of the Church. But Lefebvre refused and, soon thereafter, on his own authority consecrated four priests as bishops without Vatican approval—Bernard Fellay, Bernard Tissier de Mallerais, Richard Williamson,[271] and Alfonso de Galarreta. This proved to be the last straw; Lefebvre and the four priests were excommunicated. Thus in 1988, Archbishop Lefebvre caused the first schism in the Church since the Old Catholics split in 1870 after Vatican Council I. In explaining his defiance of church authority, Lefebvre declared: "I prefer to be in the truth without the Pope than to walk a false path with him."

Politically, Lefebvre was known for his extreme right-wing views. He occasionally supported Jean-Marie Le Pen of France, leader of the right-wing National Front, and often expressed kind words for fascist dictator Francisco Franco of Spain and Chilean dictator Gen. Augusto Pinochet. An opponent of the French Revolution, Lefebvre supported restoration of the French monarchy. "Our future is the past," he was fond of saying.

Although its main focus is preservation of the Tridentine/Latin rite Mass as a form of worship, SSPX has promoted theological and conspiratorial anti-Semitism. In homilies, writings, websites, and publications, for example, its representatives have accused contemporary Jews of deicide, have endorsed the *Protocols of the Elders of Zion*, and have claimed that there is factual basis for the blood libel myth.

When Lefebvre died in March 1991, the four priests whom he consecrated as bishops continued to champion SSPX positions, along

---

271   Bishop Williamson is a Holocaust denier.

with the positions of like-minded organizations of traditionalist Catholics like Opus Dei,[272] founded in Spain in 1928 by Father Josemaria Escrivá,[273] who was canonized a saint by John Paul II in 2002. At his death, Lefebvre left behind about three hundred priests ordained by his order and a following, estimated at the time of the schism, of between fifty thousand and one hundred thousand. His followers have set up schools and seminaries in Germany, Latin America, Australia, and France, the country where he has the largest following. In the United States, SSPX claims about one hundred chapels and twenty-four schools. Its US monthly periodical, *The Angelus*, has about three thousand subscribers. The Reverend Franz Schmidberger, the German priest designated by Archbishop Lefebvre to succeed him as head of the order upon Lefebvre's death, said, "May God reward him (Lefebvre) for his life entirely devoted to defending the Catholic faith against heresy."

In 2007, Pope Benedict XVI issued a directive allowing the Latin Mass to be celebrated in certain circumstances, thereby narrowing the theological divide between SSPX and the Vatican. In January 2009, the Vatican lifted the excommunication of SSPX's four bishops and continues to seek reconciliation with the Society. It is noteworthy that the Vatican is far more interested in rehabilitating conservative theologians and clerics who stray from orthodoxy than liberal ones.

"We Remember"

"Anti-Semitism," wrote Pope John Paul II in 1994, "is a great sin against humanity." He made no mention, however, of anti-Judaism. The Holy See in 1998, thirty-three years after the publication of *Nostra Aetate*, acknowledged the causal link between church history and the Holocaust,

---

272 Opus Dei is portrayed in the novel *The Da Vinci Code*, by Dan Brown, and its 2006 film version of the same name. Opus Dei and its founder, St. Josemaria Escrivá, have aroused controversy, primarily revolving around allegations of secrecy, elitism, cultlike practices, and Escrivá's political involvement with right-wing causes, such as the dictatorships of Generals Francisco in Spain (1939–75) and Augusto Pinochet in Chile (1973–90).

273 In 1967 or '68, Father Escrivá allegedly said to his former personal assistant, Monsignor Vladimir Felzmann: "Vlad, Hitler couldn't have been such a bad person. He couldn't have killed six million. It couldn't have been more than four million … Hitler against the Jews, Hitler against the Slavs, this means Hitler against communism."

but attempted to exonerate the institutional Church from any culpability. In a document that took a decade to prepare, entitled "We Remember: A Reflection on the Shoah," the Holy See's Commission for Religious Relations with the Jews, on behalf of Pope John Paul II, wrote:

> In the Christian world—*I am not saying as part of the Church as such*—erroneous and unjust interpretations of the New Testament relative to the Jewish people and their presumed guilt circulated for too long, engendering sentiments of hostility toward this people. That contributed to a lulling of many consciences, so that, when Europe was swept by the wave of persecutions inspired by a *pagan anti-Semitism that in its essence was equally anti-Christian*, alongside those Christians who did everything to save those who were persecuted, even to the point of risking their own lives, the spiritual resistance of many was not what humanity expected of Christ's disciples. (emphasis mine)

The Church acknowledged that one of the parents of Nazi anti-Semitism was pagan anti-Semitism but failed to acknowledge that the other parent was Christian anti-Judaism. Together they spawned a "Rosemary's Baby."[274]

The Holy See in the same document also attempted to exonerate Pope Pius XII from complicity in the Holocaust. The Commission wrote:

> Those who did help to save Jewish lives as much as was in their power, even to the point of placing their own lives in danger, must not be forgotten. During and after the war, Jewish communities and Jewish leaders expressed their thanks for all that had been done for them, including what Pope Pius XII did personally or through his representatives to save hundreds of thousands of Jewish lives. Many Catholic bishops, priests,

---

274   *Rosemary's Baby* is a 1967 best-selling horror novel by Ira Levin about a satanic child, which sold over four million copies, making it the top best-selling horror novel of the 1960s. In 1968, the novel was turned into an acclaimed film adaptation directed by Roman Polanski.

religious and laity have been honored for this reason by the State of Israel …

Garry Wills, author of *Papal Sin*, charges that "We Remember" devoted more energy to exonerating the Church and excoriating Nazis for not following church doctrine than to sympathizing with victims of the Holocaust. "The effect is," Wills wrote, "of a sad person toiling up a hill all racked with emotion and ready to beat his breast, only to have him plump down on his knees, sigh heavily and point at some other fellow who caused all the trouble." The key distinction labored at through the text, according to Wills, is a pseudoscientific theory of race always condemned by the Church and anti-Judaism, which some Christians through weakness succumbed to at times, but not "the Church as such." The former is a matter of erroneous teaching, of which the Church is never guilty; the latter a matter of sentiment and weakness, sometimes using misinterpreted scriptural texts as cover for prejudices of a basically nonreligious variety.[275]

David Kertzer charges that the distinction made in "We Remember" between anti-Judaism (implied but not named), of which some unnamed and misinformed Christians were unfortunately guilty in the past, and anti-Semitism which led to the horrors of the Holocaust, will simply not survive historical scrutiny. "Every single element of modern anti-Semitism," wrote Kertzer, "was not only embraced by the Church but actively promulgated by official and unofficial Church organs." Kertzer asserts that the document's argument that Nazi anti-Semitism was the product of a new social and political form of anti-Judaism, foreign to the Church, and which mixed in new racial ideas that were at odds with church doctrine, was simply "not the product of a Church that wants to confront its history."[276]

On the issue of causality for the Holocaust, James Carroll, in *Constantine's Sword*, also disagrees with the Holy See's no culpability position, viewing the Church's role quite differently. Carroll, who termed anti-Judaism the "Church's primal sin," writes:

---

275   Wills, *Papal Sin*, 13–14.

276   Kertzer, *The Popes against the Jews*, 6–7.

Auschwitz, when seen in the links of causality, reveals that the hatred of Jews has been … a central action of Christian history, reaching to the core of Christian character … Because the hatred of Jews had been made holy, it became lethal … However modern Nazism was, it planted its roots in the soil of age-old Church attitudes and a nearly unbroken chain of Church-sponsored acts of Jew-hatred. However pagan Nazism was, it drew its sustenance from groundwater poisoned by the Church's most solemnly held ideology—its theology.

On the issue of church sinfulness, Carroll, in *Toward a New Catholic Church,* writes: "If transgressions occur, they are always the result of the aberrant behavior of individuals—perhaps including individual priests, bishops, or even a pope—but never of the institutional, theological, or dogmatic aspects of Catholicism."

Furthermore, as noted previously, James Carroll, Garry Wills, John Cornwell, David Kertzer, Daniel Jonah Goldhagen, and others dispute the Holy See's assertion that Pius XII has no complicity for the Holocaust. Regarding the issue of Christian culpability, John Shelby Spong, former Episcopal bishop of Newark, New Jersey, writes: "Until we (Christians) embrace the depth of the problem and identify what it is in the Christian faith itself that not only gave anti-Semitism its birth but also regularly sustains it, we will continue to violate the very people who gave us the Jesus we claim to serve."

The Holy See's reluctance to forthrightly acknowledge any church complicity in the Holocaust is troubling, particularly when viewed through the lens of the law of unintended consequences. Why? Because in this year of 2012, the fiftieth anniversary of the first session of Vatican Council II, it continues to backslide from pronouncements made in "Declaration on the Relationship of the Church and Non-Christian Religions" (*Nostra Aetate*), "Declaration on Religious Liberty" (*Dignitatis Humanae*), and "Pastoral Constitution on the Church in the Modern World" (*Gaudium et Spes*). If the past is indeed prologue, there may very well be unintended and perhaps calamitous consequences ahead.

Other Acknowledgments of Church Culpability

In a 1995 statement of regret, the bishops of the Netherlands acknowledged church causality in the Holocaust. The statement read:

> [There existed] ... a tradition of theological and ecclesiastical antiJudaism" and "the 'catechesis of vilification' (which) taught that Jewry after Christ's death was rejected as a people ... (the bishops of the Netherlands) reject this tradition of ecclesiastical antiJudaism and deeply regret its horrible results.

In September 1997, the bishops of France issued a document entitled "Declaration of Repentance," in which they acknowledged the Church's "culpable silence"[277] during the Holocaust. It read:

> Too many of the Church's pastors committed an offense, by their silence, against the Church itself and its mission. Today we confess that such a silence was a sin. In so doing, we recognize that the Church of France (shares) with the Christian people the responsibility for failing to lend their aid, from the very first moments, when protest and protection were still possible as well as necessary.
>
> We must recognize that indifference won the day over indignation in the face of the persecution of the Jews and that, in particular, silence was the rule in face of the multifarious laws enacted by the Vichy government, whereas speaking out in favor of the victims was the exception ... The end result is that the attempt to exterminate the Jewish people, instead of being perceived as a central question in human and spiritual terms, remained a secondary consideration. In the face of so great and utter a tragedy, too many of the Church's pastors committed an offense, by their silence, against the Church itself and its mission. Today we confess that such a silence was a sin ... We confess this sin. We beg God's pardon, and we call upon the Jewish people to hear our words of repentance.

---

277   "Silence gives consent" (Pope Boniface VIII).

Also in 1997, the bishops of Switzerland issued a similar statement in which they stated:

> For centuries Christians and ecclesiastical teachings were guilty of persecuting and marginalizing Jews, and we bishops 'shamefully declare' that the perpetrators and collaborators in the Holocaust used religious motivations. It is in reference to these past acts of churches for which we proclaim ourselves culpable and ask pardon of the descendants of the victims ...

In 2001 the US Conference of Catholic Bishops, in "Catholic Teaching on the Shoah: Implementing the Holy See's 'We Remember,'" wrote:

> Christian anti-Judaism did lay the groundwork for racial, genocidal anti-Semitism by stigmatizing not only Judaism but Jews themselves for opprobrium and contempt. So the Nazi theories tragically found fertile soil in which to plant the horror of an unprecedented attempt at genocide.

Reining in Wayward Nuns

In April 2012, the Vatican appointed an American bishop to rein in the largest and most influential group of Catholic nuns in the United States, saying that an investigation found that the group had "serious" doctrinal problems. The Vatican's assessment charged that members of this group, Leadership Conference of Women Religious, hereinafter "LCWR," with a membership of 1,500 representing 80 percent of Catholic sisters, had challenged church teaching on homosexuality and the male-only priesthood, and promoted "radical feminist themes incompatible with the Catholic faith." The sisters were also reprimanded for making statements that "disagree with or challenge the bishops, who are the church's authentic teachers of faith and morals."

News of the Vatican action took LCWR by complete surprise, said the group's communication director, Sister Annemarie Sanders, noting that LCWR leaders were in Rome for what they thought was a routine annual visit to the Vatican when they were informed/blindsided by the outcome of the investigation, which began four years earlier in 2008. "I'm stunned," said Sister Simone Campbell, executive director of

Network, a Catholic social justice lobby founded by women religious. Her group also was cited in the Vatican document, along with LCWR, for focusing its work too much on poverty and economic justice, while keeping "silent" on abortion and same-sex marriage. "I would imagine that it was our health care letter[278] that made them mad," Sister Campbell said. "We haven't violated any teaching; we have just been raising questions and interpreting politics."

The verdict on the nuns, who apparently were unaware of both the investigation and the trial, was rendered by the former head of the Congregation for the Doctrine of the Faith, American Cardinal William Levada, formerly the archbishop of San Francisco. He appointed Archbishop J. Peter Sartain of Seattle to lead the group's reformation process, assisted by Bishop Thomas J. Paprocki and Bishop Leonard

---

278   During the public debate in 2010 over the long overdue but controversial health care overhaul, American bishops came out in opposition to President Obama's Affordable Health Care Act, but dozens of sisters, many of whom belong to LCWR, signed a letter supporting it.

Blair, who was in charge of the secret investigation of LCWR.[279] Their eminences have been given up to five years to revise the group's statutes, approve every speaker at the group's public programs, and replace a handbook the group used to facilitate dialogue on matters that the Vatican deemed to be settled doctrine not open to question. They are also to review LCWR's links with Network and another organization, the Resource Center for Religious Life.

Later, during the summer of 2012, American nuns assembled in St. Louis, Missouri, to decide how to respond to the Vatican's scathing critique of their doctrinal orthodoxy. What prompted the Vatican's action, church scholars contend, is the power struggle that had been

---

279   Cardinal Bernard Law was archbishop of Boston in 2002 when the priest sex abuse scandal erupted in the United States. He was named in hundreds of lawsuits accusing him of failing to protect children from known child-molesting priests by reassigning them around his archdiocese, enabling them to continue their predatory conduct undetected for many more years.

Under questioning, the cardinal stated that, when a priest committed a sex crime, his practice was to seek the analysis of psychiatrists, clinicians, and therapists in residential treatment centers before deciding whether to return a priest accused of sexually abusing a child to the pulpit. Cardinal Law became the first high-level Church official to be accused of actively participating in the cover-up of child molestation and the first, and so far only, US bishop to resign over priests who sexually abused children.

After eighteen years leading America's fourth-largest archdiocese, Law resigned in 2002, having asked Pope John Paul II twice before receiving permission to step down prior to reaching the mandatory retirement age for bishops of seventy-five. After resigning his office, he left Boston for Rome where, critics say, the Vatican provided him refuge so he could avoid impending criminal prosecution in Massachusetts. Ten months later, Law's successor, Sean P. O'Malley, helped broker an $85 million settlement with more than 550 victims of sex abuse by priests.

Once in Rome, rather than being disciplined for his failure to protect children in his archdiocese or encouraged to retire to a monastery to end his life in quiet contemplation, Benedict XVI, in 2004, appointed Cardinal Law archpriest of the Basilica di Santa Maria Maggiore in Rome, one of the Vatican's most prestigious, and rewarded him with a position in the Curia's Congregation for Bishops, where he helped select men with conservative credentials to serve as bishops worldwide. He was also named titular cardinal priest of Santa Susanna, the American Catholic church in Rome. Ironically, Cardinal Law was allowed to implement the Vatican's effort to rein in the LCWR, which guides the majority of American nuns who taught many of the child victims of pedophile priests in the Archdiocese of Boston. On November 21, 2011, Benedict XVI accepted the eighty-year-old Law's resignation as head of Santa Maria Maggiore.

building for decades between nuns and the all-male church hierarchy. At issue are questions of obedience and autonomy, what it means to be a faithful Catholic, and different understandings of Vatican Council II. Sister Pat Farrell, president of LCWR, said in an interview that the Vatican seems to regard questioning as defiance, while the sisters see it as a form of faithfulness. "We have a differing perspective on obedience," Sister Farrell said. "Our understanding is that we need to continue to respond to the signs of the times, and the new questions and issues that arise in the complexities of modern life are not something we see as a threat."

The LCWR flap is symptomatic of the polarization that increasingly exists between progressive Catholics still eager for change and reform within the Church in the "spirit of Vatican II," and traditionalist Catholics focused on what they view as doctrinal fundamentals of unchanging truth. The sisters have been caught up in the crosswinds of that polarization struggle. Most of them have dedicated their lives in service to the sick, the poor, children, and immigrants, by and large, refraining from theological disputes. But when some sisters after the Second Vatican Council began to question church prohibitions on women serving as priests, artificial birth control, or the acceptance of same-sex relationships,[280] their religious orders did not attempt to silence them. In fact, their orders have continued to insist on the right of women religious to debate and challenge church teaching, which has angered the Vatican. Cardinal Levada said after meeting with Sister Farrell in June 2012, just before he retired, that they should regard his office's harsh judgment as "an invitation to obedience." "I admire religious men and women," Cardinal Levada said in an interview with the *National Catholic Reporter*, "but if they aren't people who believe and express the faith of the Church, the doctrines of the Church, then I think they're misrepresenting who they are and who they ought to be."

The disciplinary action against the nuns comes at a time when American bishops are struggling to reassert their authority with a wayward, critically thinking flock. "The Church must speak with one voice," Archbishop Carlo Maria Vigano, papal nuncio to the United States, said in an address in June 2012, to American bishops at their

---

280 Polls show that about 95 percent of Catholic women have used birth control at some point in their lives, and 52 percent support same-sex marriage, little different from the American public at large.

meeting in Atlanta. "We all know that the fundamental tactic of the enemy is to show a Church divided." He added that at this "difficult time," there is a special need for women and men in religious orders, and for Catholic universities, to "take on an attitude of deep communion" with their bishops.

Conclusion

Hitler's ascent to absolute power from total obscurity within a republic was by no means a foregone conclusion. Plenty of opportunities existed along the way to stop him, if more people of conscience had had the will to do so. He first published *Mein Kampf* in 1925, eight years before becoming chancellor in 1933 and seventeen years before his death camps reached full killing capacity in late 1942. Hitler clearly set forth his vision for the Greater Third Reich—a vision that included territorial expansion into Western and Eastern Europe and creation of a racially pure society dominated by an Aryan master race. He minced no words in calling for the elimination of Jews from Germany and all of Europe, referring to them as vermin, parasites, maggots, polluters, and destroyers of Aryan humanity and corrupters of society. His virulent brand of anti-Semitism was apparent for the world to see, although, admittedly, few envisioned he would come so close to success. Words, nonetheless, have consequences, intended and unintended, for good and evil. Tragically, many centuries of Church-sanctioned Jew hatred, violent rhetoric, institutionalized intolerance, forced baptisms, expulsions, scapegoating, myths, and libels, and charges of deicide and collective guilt transformed Jews into "the other," easy prey for what was to come in the 1930s and 1940s.

During the twelve years of what was intended to be a Thousand Year Reich, many millions of Christians went about their lives attending religious services, receiving the Eucharist, reciting creeds, praying the rosary, wearing crucifixes around their necks, and celebrating Christmas and Easter. Two popes reigned, bishops administered their dioceses, priests ran their parishes, military chaplains ministered to combatants, parents catechized children, pastoral letters were written, homilies were preached, confessions were heard, and spiritual counsel was given—while their Jewish neighbors were being systematically stripped of their dignity, their legal rights, and, ultimately, their lives.

Beginning in 1933, Jews were sent to prison and concentration camps. By 1940, they were forcibly rounded up and herded off, first to transit or concentration camps, then to ghettos, and finally to killing camps. By 1941, entire Jewish communities in Eastern Europe were massacred by SS mobile killing units and buried in trenches. By 1943, smokestacks were belching out thick black smoke, visible and smellable for miles around.

In Matthew's Gospel, Jesus proclaims: "Not everyone who says to me 'Lord, Lord,' will enter the kingdom of heaven, but only the one who does the will of my Father in heaven."[281] With these words, Jesus warned against self-deception, deluding ourselves into thinking we are doing God's will, when, in fact, we are doing quite the opposite. Time and time again in scripture, Jesus, who was born, lived, and died a Jew made it crystal clear that to be his disciple required more than lip service. It required action, ethical behavior grounded in love of God, and love of neighbor.[282] "Love one another as I have loved you"[283] means love unconditionally, without exclusion, the "least of my brothers and sisters" in particular,[284] like innocent victims of evil authority. Discipleship requires the pursuit of justice.[285]

Sadly, however, because Jews were deemed to be outside the circle of Christian concern,[286] too many Christians wrongly perceived that the Gospel of Love excluded Jews. That was a blasphemous concept because no one is outside God's circle of love. Indeed, Jesus, the very personification of love, was born to teach us how to be human, and how to live in community as brothers and sisters, made in the image and likeness of our common Creator. And the test of our humanity is how we treat the weakest and neediest among us, especially those beyond our comfort zone. Clearly, something went terribly wrong for Christianity

---

281 Matthew 7:21.

282 Luke 10:27.

283 John 15:12.

284 Matthew 31:40.

285 *Tzedek, Tzedek Tirdof* ("Justice, justice, you shall pursue") (Deuteronomy, 16:20).

286 NB, in his September 1933 letter to Reich authorities in defense of non-Aryan Catholics, Secretary of State Cardinal Pacelli was careful to acknowledge that the Holy See's concern was not with the fate of other non-Aryans. His letter began, "The Holy See (has) no intention of interfering in Germany's internal affairs. That is to say, the Holy See recognizes that the fate of non-Aryans is a matter *'outside the circle of Vatican concern ...'*" (emphasis mine)

during the Holocaust, for what was practiced by most of the faithful was certainly not what Jesus preached. And what resulted from the obvious disconnect between belief and practice was the worst human catastrophe in history. Jews ponder the Holocaust and rightly ask: Where was God? Christians must do the same, but also ask: Where were we Christians? And where was the Church? It was not only the perpetrators who were guilty, but also the accomplices and bystanders.

Religion is as religion does; all the rest is talk. This underlies Elie Wiesel's provocative indictment: "Christianity died at Auschwitz." Right action, orthopraxy, is more important than right belief, orthodoxy. The challenge for us post-Auschwitz, post-Vatican Council II critical-thinking Christians throughout the world, therefore, is to prove Wiesel's indictment wrong. One obvious reason to study the Holocaust is to learn history's lessons so as not to be condemned to repeat them. Another, perhaps less obvious reason, is to learn why Christians allowed the Holocaust to happen in the first place.

Bibliography

Armstrong, Karen. *The Great Transformation: The Beginning of Our Religious Traditions*. New York: Random House, 2007.

Bernstein, Philip P. *What the Jews Believe*. New York: Farrar, Straus and Company, 1950.

Berry, Jason. *Render Unto Rome: The Secret Life of Money in the Catholic Church*. New York: Crown, 2012.

Blech, Arthur. *The Causes of Anti-Semitism: A Critique of the Bible*. Amherst: Prometheus Books, 2006.

Bokenkotter, Thomas. *A Concise History of the Catholic Church*. New York: Image Books Doubleday, 1990.

Carroll, James. *Constantine's Sword: The Church and the Jews*. New York: Houghton Mifflin, 2001.

———. *Practicing Catholic*. New York: Houghton Mifflin, 2009.

———. *Toward a New Catholic Church*. New York: Houghton Mifflin, 2002.

Chadwick, Owen. *A History of the Popes 1830–1914*. New York: Oxford University Press USA, 2003.

Childers, Thomas. *A History of Hitler's Empire*. 2nd ed. Course Guidebook. Chantilly, VA: Teaching Company, 2001.

Chittister, Joan. *Called to Question: A Spiritual Memoir*. New York: Sheed and Ward, 2004.

Cornwell, John. *Hitler's Pope: The Secret History of Pius XII*. London: Penguin Group, 1999.

Crossan, John Dominic. *Who Killed Jesus: Exposing the Roots of Anti-Semitism in the Gospel Story of the Death of Jesus*. San Francisco: HarperCollins, 1996.

Curran, Charles E. *Loyal Dissent: Memoir of a Catholic Theologian*. Washington, DC: Georgetown University Press, 2006.

Dalin, David G. *The Myth of Hitler's Pope: How Pope Pius XII Rescued Jews from the Nazis*. Washington, DC: Regnery Publishing, 2005.

De Rosnay, Tatiana. *Sarah's Key*. New York: St. Martin's Press, 2007.

Dulles, Avery Robert. *Models of Church*. New York: Doubleday, 1974.

Eco, Umberto. *In the Name of the Rose*. Boston: Houghton Mifflin Harcourt, 1994.

Ehrman, Bart D. *Jesus: Apocalyptic Prophet of the New Millennium*. New York: Oxford University Press USA, 2001.

———. *Jesus Interrupted: Revealing the Hidden Contradictions in the Bible*. New York: HarperCollins, 2009.

———. *The Lost Gospel of Judas Iscariot*. New York: Oxford University Press USA, 2006.

———. *Lost Scriptures*. New York: Oxford University Press USA, 2003.

———. *Misquoting Jesus: The Story Behind Who Changed the Bible and Why*. San Francisco: HarperCollins, 2005.

————. *The New Testament, Parts 1 and 2.* Course Guidebook. Chantilly, VA: Teaching Company, 2000.

Flannery, Austin, general ed. *Vatican Council II: The Basic Sixteen Documents.* Northport, NY: Costello Publishing, 1996.

Friedlander, Henry. *The Origins of Nazi Genocide.* Chapel Hill: University of North Carolina Press, 1995.

Goldhagen, Daniel Jonah. *Hitler's Willing Executioners: Ordinary Germans and the Holocaust.* New York: Random House, 1997.

————. *A Moral Reckoning: The Role of the Catholic Church in the Holocaust and its Unfulfilled Duty of Repair.* New York: Random House, 2002.

Goldstein, Phyllis. *A Convenient Hatred: The History of Anti-Semitism.* Brookline, MA: Facing History and Ourselves Foundation, 2012.

Gutterman, Bella, and Avner Shalev, eds. *To Bear Witness: Holocaust Remembrance at Yad Vashem.* Jerusalem: Yad Vashem Press, 2008.

Hahnenberg, Edward P. *A Concise Guide to the Documents of Vatican II.* Cincinnati: St. Anthony Messenger Press, 2007.

Heschel, Abraham Joshua. *The Insecurity of Freedom.* Philadelphia: Jewish Publication Society, 1966.

Heschel, Susannah. *Moral Grandeur and Spiritual Audacity: Essays of Abraham Joshua Heschel.* New York: Farrar, Straus and Giroux, 1966.

Hitchens, Christopher. *God Is Not Great: How Religion Poisons Everything.* New York: Hachette Book Group, 2007.

Hochhuth, Rolf. *The Deputy.* Baltimore: Johns Hopkins Press, 1964.

Kertzer, David I. *The Kidnapping of Edgardo Mortara.* New York: Random House, 1998.

———. *The Popes against the Jews: The Vatican's Role in the Rise of Modern Anti-Semitism*. New York: Random House, 2002.

———. *Prisoner of the Vatican: The Popes, the Kings, and Garibaldi's Rebels in the Struggle to Rule Modern Italy*. New York: Houghton Mifflin, 2004.

Kornberg, Jacques. *Hitler and the Vatican: Inside the Secret Archives That Reveal the New Story of the Nazis and the Church*. New York: Free Press, 2004.

Küng, Hans. *Theology for the Third Millennium: An Ecumenical View*. New York: Doubleday, 1988.

Lapide, Pinchas E. *Three Popes and the Jews*. New York: Dial Press, 1956.

Lewy, Guenter. *The Catholic Church and Nazi Germany*. Boston: Da Capo Press, 2000.

Littell, Franklin H. *The Crucifixion of the Jews: The Failure of Christians to Understand the Jewish Experience*. Macon, GA: Mercer University Press, 1975.

Longerich, Peter. *Heinrich Himmler*. New York: Oxford University Press USA, 2011.

Marchione, Margherita. *Pope Pius XII: Architect for Peace*. Mahwah, NJ: Paulist Press, 2000.

Massa, Mark. *The American Catholic Revolution: How the 60's Changed the Church Forever*. New York: Oxford University Press USA, 2010.

McBrien, Richard P. *The Church: The Evolution of Catholicism*. San Francisco: HarperCollins, 2008.

———. *Lives of the Popes*. San Francisco: HarperCollins, 1997.

McInerny, Ralph. *The Defamation of Pius XII*. South Bend, IN: St. Augustine's Press, 2001.

Mellert, Robert B. *What Is Process Theology?* Mahwah, NJ: Paulist Press, 1975.

Merton, Robert K. "The Unanticipated Consequences of Purposive Social Action." *American Sociological Review,* Vol. 1, Issue 6, December 1936.

Moehlman, Conrad Henry. *The Christian-Jewish Tragedy.* Rochester, NY: Printing House of Leo Hart, 1933.

Murphy, Cullen. *God's Jury: The Inquisition and the Making of the Modern World.* New York: Houghton Mifflin Harcourt, 2012.

Murray, John Courtney. *We Hold These Truths: Catholic Reflections on the American Proposition.* Evanston, IL: Sheed & Ward, 2005.

Niewyk, Donald. "Solving the 'Jewish Problem'; Continuity and Change in German Anti-Semitism, 1871–1945." *Leo Baeck Institute Yearbook* 35, 335–70.

Noble, Thomas F. X. *Popes and the Papacy: A History.* Course Guidebook. Chantilly, VA: The Teaching Company, 2006.

Norwich, John Julius. *Absolute Monarchs: A History of the Papacy.* New York: Random House, 2011.

O'Malley, John W. *What Happened at Vatican II.* Cambridge: Harvard University Press, 2010.

O'Malley, John W., Joseph A. Komonchak, Stephen Schloesser, and Neil J. Ormerod. *Vatican II: Did Anything Happen?* Edited by David G. Schultenover. New York: Continuum, 2008.

Orringer, Julie. *The Invisible Bridge.* New York: Alfred Knopf, 2010.

Phayer, Michael. *The Catholic Church and the Holocaust, 1930–1965.* Indianapolis: Indiana University Press, 2000.

Perry, Marvin, and Frederick M. Schweitzer, eds. *Anti-Semitic Myths: A Historical and Contemporary Anthology*. Indianapolis: Indiana University Press, 2005.

Rittner, Carol, and John K. Roth, eds. *"Good News" after Auschwitz?* Atlanta: Mercer University Press, 2001.

Rittner, Carol, Stephen D. Smith, and Irena Steinfeldt. *The Holocaust and the Christian World*. New York: Continuum International, 2000.

Rush, Ormond. *Still Interpreting Vatican II*. Mahwah, NJ: Paulist Press, 2004.

Russell, Mary Doria. *A Thread of Grace*. New York: Ballantine Books, 2005.

Rychlak, Ronald J. *Hitler, the War, and the Pope*. Huntington, IN: Our Sunday Visitor, 2000.

Sanchez, Jose M. *Pius XII and the Holocaust: Understanding the Controversy*. Washington, DC: Catholic University of America Press, 2002.

Spicer, Kevin P. *Hitler's Priests: Catholic Clergy and National Socialism*. DeKalb, IL: Northern Illinois Press, 2008.

Spong, John Shelby. *Re-claiming the Bible for a Non-Religious World*. New York: HarperOne, 2011.

————. *Rescuing the Bible from Fundamentalism: A Bishop Rethinks the Meaning of Scripture*. New York: HarperCollins, 1991.

————. *The Sins of Scripture*. San Francisco: HarperCollins, 2005.

Steinfeldt, Irena, et al. *How Was It Humanly Possible? A Study of Perpetrators and Bystanders during the Holocaust*. Jerusalem: Yad Vashem, 2002.

Sullivan, Maureen. *The Road to Vatican II: Key Changes in Theology*. New York: Paulist Press, 2007.

Treece, Henry. *The Crusades*. New York: Random House, 2004.

Weber, Louis. *The Holocaust Chronicle: A History in Words and Pictures*. Lincolnwood, IL: Publications International, 2000.

Wiesel, Elie. *Night*. New York: Farrar, Straus and Giroux, 1985.

Wills, Garry. *Papal Sin, Structures of Deceit*. New York: Doubleday, 2000.

————. *Why I Am a Catholic*. New York: Houghton Mifflin, 2002.

Wilson, Barrie. *How Jesus Became Christian*. New York: St. Martin's Press, 2008.

Zahn, Gordon C. *German Catholics and Hitler's Wars: A Study in Social Control*. South Bend: Notre Dame University Press, 1989.

————. *In Solitary Witness: The Life and Death of Franz Jagerstatter*. Springfield, IL: Templegate, 1986.

Zuccotti, Susan. *Under His Very Window: The Vatican and the Holocaust in Italy*. New Haven: Yale University Press, 2000.

Made in the USA
Lexington, KY
04 August 2013